TAKE IT OFF
KISS Truly Unmasked
Greg Prato

Take It Off
KISS Truly Unmasked

A Jawbone book
First edition 2019
Published in the UK and the USA by
Jawbone Press
Office G1
141–157 Acre Lane
London SW2 5UA
England
www.jawbonepress.com

ISBN 978-1-911036-57-9

Jacket design Paul Palmer-Edwards,
www.paulpalmer-edwards.com

Printed by Everbest Printing Investment Ltd.

1 2 3 4 5 23 22 21 20 19

★ CONTENTS ★

FOREWORD
BY CHRIS JERICHO

In the fall of 1984, I turned on the television to watch my weekly dose of rock videos. I can't remember if the show I was watching was *Friday Night Videos* on NBC, or maybe the local Winnipeg show *Citivision*, but what I do remember was a video that started with this really cool-looking guy with long curly hair and a devil-may-care smirk on his face, yodeling while his hands were on fire.

Then the song kicked in, and what followed over the next three minutes was this guy and his band seemingly having the time of their lives. He was dancing onstage, making out with women, sucking on his finger, singing harmonies with the drummer … and then, for the grand finale, he jumped through a FLAMING HOOP OF FIRE. I had never seen anybody in a band do anything like that before, and I was instantly hooked. The guy was of course Paul Stanley, and the band was of course KISS.

The next day, I went to the store and bought my first KISS album, *Animalize*, and my lifelong obsession with KISS began. Now, of course I had heard of KISS and knew who they were, but I wasn't really into the whole makeup thing, as I felt it was an outdated remnant of the 70s. However, I had no idea that they had taken their makeup off, so I was totally surprised when I saw them, sans greasepaint, looking cool and contemporary in that video. I wanted to *be* those guys!

Paul once said that it didn't matter what floor of the KISS elevator you got on as a fan, as long as you got on. Well, non-makeup 80s KISS is and always will be *my* floor. Paul, Gene, Bruce, and both Erics are my classic KISS lineup, and I don't care who disagrees.

Now obviously over the last thirty-five years, I've gone back through their catalogue and completely embraced all of KISS's work from the 70s and the 90s, all the way up to the present day. But there's just something about those albums they released from 1983 to 1997 that resonates with me more than their other music. Maybe it's because I grew up with those records as they were released, maybe it's because I'm a nonconformist, or maybe it's because I admire and respect the balls it took for KISS to unmask and totally reinvent themselves. It's something I've done many times in my own career.

Now, they've always done that musically—by using elements of disco, pop, glam, grunge, and thrash in their songs, depending on the era. But to me, their willingness to change their entire image and embrace what was going on in the early and mid-80s makes KISS mk. II almost as popular and relevant as the original version. Name another band that transitioned from the 70s to the 80s as successfully as KISS did? Sure, there are a few—like ZZ Top and Rush—but KISS not only transitioned into the 80s but they were tailor-made for the excess and debauchery of the times, and they obviously had more fun with it than those other bands. Believe me, *Rush Exposed* or *ZZ Top X-Treme Close Up* never would've cut it!

When KISS put the makeup back on for the reunion in 1996, I have to admit I was a little disappointed. I thought then (and still do) that the Stanley/Simmons/Kulick/Singer lineup was their tightest and best. But I understood the reason they did it, and why they felt the need to reinvent themselves once more. It's what they have always done.

And now we are here in 2019, and KISS are about to embark on the End Of The Road tour. I'm sure they will play the bulk of their hits from the 70s ... but I always get just a little more excited when they launch into an 80s classic, like 'Lick It Up' or 'Hide Your Heart.' And I'm even more stoked at the prospect of them adding 'Heaven's On Fire' back into the set! It's their best-written song of the 80s, with one of the best choruses in rock history.

But the main reason why I'm so happy when they play a song from the non-makeup days is because they are few and far between in the modern setlists. And that's another reason why I love that era: those songs can only be heard on our devices and streams. They will never be played into the ground live, so they always remain fresh ... they are like lost artifacts found only in Abner Devereaux's laboratory.

In closing, both Paul and Gene have said that when they are ready to hang up the platform boots, KISS will continue on without them, and I have no doubt that it will. I just hope that when they find a replacement Starchild and Demon for the 70s-era KISS, they find alternates for a non-makeup KISS lineup, as well! After all, the world needs more neon-pink cloaks and Body Glove costumes in these troubled times, doncha think?

CHRIS JERICHO, FOZZY, JANUARY 20, 2019

INTRODUCTION
BY GREG PRATO

I must confess, after becoming a major KISS fanatic at the ripe old age of five (thanks to a friend who let me view his KISS trading cards at our school bus stop), there was a period of time during the early 80s when I took a KISS sabbatical.

I could deal with the grief I took for even uttering the words 'I like KISS' when friends and acquaintances discussed music (and, to this day, I've never seen a rock band get such an instantly vehemently negative reply from the majority of others—usually 'KISS SUCKS!'). I could even deal with the fact that KISS were now mostly allotted to the covers of *16 Magazine*, *Teen Beat*, and *Tiger Beat*, rather than *Circus*, *Creem*, or *Hit Parader*. But what I could no longer stomach was that when you stacked their last few albums (*Dynasty*, *Unmasked*, and *Music From The Elder*) up against their hard-rockin' output from '74–78 (OK, OK, *besides* Peter Criss's flaccid solo album), there was simply no comparison. Musically, it appeared as though KISS had completely lost the plot, and were beyond the point of no return.

And while a viewing of the killer 'I Love It Loud' video did pique my interest, it was not enough for me to pick up the *Creatures Of The Night* album at the time of its initial October '82 release. But during the summer of '83, and after a 'musical realignment' when I began soaking up the peaceful and serene sounds of AC/DC, Ozzy, and Maiden, I decided to re-inspect my old, well-worn KISS vinyl. A pleasant surprise was in store for my earholes—*Destroyer*, *Rock And Roll Over*, and *Alive II* fit in splendidly with my then-current playlist of *Highway To Hell*, *Speak Of The Devil*, and *Piece Of Mind*.

Even so, thinking back on this precise point in KISStory, it sometimes gets lost how it was undoubtedly the lowest point of the band's entire career. Their last few albums had not come close to the platinum-certified heights of their aforementioned 70s classics, while it appeared as though their once-massive fan base had dwindled and turned their attention elsewhere—including to up-and-coming metal bands (some of whom were more than happy to pick up the slack in the makeup 'n' metal department), plus more easier-to-digest MTV acts.

Today, however, *Creatures* is rightfully considered a glorious return to form, and one of KISS's best studio efforts. But it underperformed on the charts upon its release, peaking at only #45 on the *Billboard* 200. And when KISS promoted the album with a US tour (their first in three years), they were consistently playing to half-empty venues, and performed a meager fifty-six concerts. It was a far cry from the days of headlining Anaheim Stadium and multiple nights at Madison Square Garden. It didn't take a genius to recognize that KISS had to do something drastic—*and quick*.

So, when it was announced that KISS were planning on finally unmasking and preparing a new album for release, I was certainly interested. I unfortunately missed the official unmasking of the band on MTV (back in the pre-internet era, it was often difficult to find out about these things in a timely manner), but I did make a point of remaining in my seat one day when an MTV VJ announced that the music video for the song 'Lick It Up' would be coming up in a jiffy.

Admittedly, if you were to view the video today, you would probably think it a bit foolish (it's a mini-movie with visuals à la *Escape From New York*), but in its proper time and place, it was one heck of a cool video clip and song— especially to someone like me, who was just about to enter teenagerdom. Soon after, not only did I secure a copy of *Lick It Up* but I also went back and purchased *Creatures Of The Night*. By the time of *Animalize*—and with the prompting of a chum who was an even bigger KISS fanatic than yours truly—I was ready to proclaim KISS as my new favorite rock band (sorry, AC/DC). I remained faithful to KISS throughout the 80s, turning an entire bedroom wall into a photo shrine to the band, and began a crusade of introducing as many of my fellow friends to their music.

And while they did not quite become the cultural phenomenon that they were in the 70s, there was no denying that KISS did successfully re-establish themselves as one of the most popular hard-rock/heavy-metal bands around for the remainder of the 80s. Gene Simmons and Paul Stanley's mugs were consistently back on the covers of rock mags, each new album was a guaranteed gold or platinum seller, they were one of the select *Headbangers Ball* bands whose music videos also enjoyed rotation on MTV during non-vampire hours, and they once again returned to headlining arenas. And, as a bonus, it was during the non-makeup era that KISS finally conquered Europe, and especially Britain, where they nearly hit the top of the charts in 1987 with the single/album combo, 'Crazy Crazy Nights' and *Crazy Nights*.

On a personal note, by the early 90s, my musical tastes had broadened beyond listening to 100 percent headbanging music. By the time of the grunge/ alt-rock revolution of '91, I had fully embraced the change, and KISS took a backseat once again. However, I experienced a second 'rediscovery' of KISS later in the decade when the original lineup reunited, and I was once again reminded how great KISS's 70s output was. Eventually, I began revisiting the non-makeup era, too, and while admittedly it was not as consistently stellar as the 70s, there is no denying that every album has at least a few solid tracks, and that if they could be stripped of their 80s pop-metal sheen and replaced with rawer 70s-style production, certain tunes would measure up well against their earlier classics. I also firmly believe that if you take KISS's hits of the 80s and compare them to the Mötley Crües, Ratts, and Poisons of the day, they stack up just as well—and, in many cases, have held up *better* than the aforementioned chart-topping competition.

Nowadays, KISS are—rightfully—widely considered to be one of the greatest and most influential rock acts of all-time. And I feel that the non-makeup era is certainly a contributing factor. In the 70s, they were consistently panned by music critics, and by the end of the decade they were considered nothing more than a 'kiddie band,' due to the oversaturation of merchandise aimed at young children (who served as a major portion of their audience by 1979). It was during the non-makeup era that KISS did away with all the merch and put the focus entirely back on the music. Interestingly, as a result, critics seemed to take the band much more seriously circa 'Lick It Up,' 'Heaven's On Fire,' and 'Tears Are Falling'—more so than when they were first offering up such classic arena-rock anthems as 'Rock And Roll All Nite,' 'Detroit Rock City,' and 'Love Gun.'

At the time of this book's publication, KISS are as popular as ever, rocking arenas and stadiums worldwide as part of their End Of The Road World Tour. And while they are going out in makeup and costumes, the non-makeup era remains incredibly popular. Turn on the popular Sirius channel *Hair Nation* and you are certain to hear a KISS tune from this period before long. On the 2019 compilation *KISSWORLD: The Best of KISS*, six non-makeup-era tracks are included (with 'Crazy Crazy Nights' kicking things off). On the 2018 KISS Kruise, Bruce Kulick performed a full set of material from the non-makeup era, which was considered one of the top highlights of the entire cruise. And, as I write, four of the most-played KISS tracks on Spotify are from the non-makeup era ('Heaven's On Fire,' 'Lick It Up,' 'Crazy Crazy Nights,' and 'Forever,' in case you're curious).

When I revisited the non-makeup KISS era with my 2011 book *The Eric Carr Story*, I found out via readers that this period still meant a lot to them. However, most recent KISS books still tend to home in on the makeup era, and when the non-makeup era *is* discussed, it is mostly via Gene and Paul's views and memories. So, how about a book that serves as the perfect companion to the non-makeup years, featuring analysis from either renowned admirers or contributors, plus reviews, interviews, lists, and photos?

It ain't a crime to be good to yourself,

GREG PRATO, SUMMER 2019
PS Questions? Comments? Feel free to email me: gregprato@yahoo.com.

LICK IT UP

Released September 18, 1983. Produced by Michael James Jackson, Gene Simmons, and Paul Stanley. US #24, UK #7. US certification: platinum.

SIDE ONE

Exciter (Paul Stanley/Vinnie Vincent)

Not For The Innocent (Gene Simmons/Vincent)

Lick It Up (Stanley/Vincent)

Young And Wasted (Simmons/Vincent)

Gimme More (Stanley/Vincent)

SIDE TWO

All Hell's Breakin' Loose (Eric Carr/Simmons/Stanley/Vincent)

A Million To One (Stanley/Vincent)

Fits Like A Glove (Simmons)

Dance All Over Your Face (Simmons)

And On The 8th Day (Simmons/Vincent)

SINGLES

Lick It Up / Dance All Over Your Face (US #66, UK #31)

All Hell's Breakin' Loose / Young And Wasted (US/UK did not chart)

★

Seemingly throughout KISS's career from 1974 to 1983, a recurring question in interviews and articles was, 'When will KISS take off their makeup, and be photographed *au naturel?*' Well, this inquiry was finally answered in September 1983, with the release of their eleventh studio album, *Lick It Up*, which featured the band sans makeup on the cover. But while the same production team that had assembled its predecessor, the monumental return to form *Creatures Of The Night*—Michael James Jackson, Gene Simmons, and Paul Stanley—were back together for another go-round, *Lick It Up* was neither as thunderously heavy nor as front-to-back flawless. However, it was still one heck of a record—and, in my humble opinion, stands as KISS's best non-makeup-era release.

Like *Creatures*, *Lick It Up* finds KISS continuing to update their sound and move with the times in hard-rock music. This is most obviously detected in the guitar work of Vinnie Vincent, who was much more of a shredder when compared to the more bluesy/melodic style of his predecessor, Ace Frehley. And besides his guitar skills, Vincent made his presence felt throughout the album in the songwriting department, co-penning eight of the album's ten tracks. *Lick It Up* is also the first KISS album for which he was properly credited for his six-string contributions and photographed for the cover.

Also of note: *Lick It Up* was the first ever KISS studio album to solely feature songwriting contributions by the four band members and no outside songwriters (their self-titled debut from 1974 initially also contained no outside contributions, until a cover of 'Kissin' Time' was added to subsequent pressings).

What makes *Lick It Up* one of the strongest KISS records of this era is the fact that, even though Gene Simmons was no longer sporting his demonic makeup and costume, he was still—for the time being—singing and writing from this persona. It's not unreasonable to close your peepers and picture him growling 'Not For The Innocent,' 'Young And Wasted,' or 'Fits Like A Glove,' for example, in his *Creatures* garb. But that said, the listener will also find some of Mr. Simmons's most ill-advised lyrics here, on the blatantly misogynistic 'Dance All Over Your Face' (a direction he would continue to pursue on such future compositions as 'Burn Bitch Burn').

One disappointment concerning *Lick It Up* is that the colossal John Bonham–esque drum sound that put Eric Carr front-and-center on *Creatures* has been noticeably dialed down here—probably a conscious attempt to keep pace with the sonics of the new crop of hard-rock chart toppers (something KISS would be guilty of more and more on later 80s-era recordings).

It's probably Paul Stanley who gets the 'MVP award' for this album. Case in point: besides co-producing the album, he is also in peak form vocally (especially on the largely-forgotten 'Gimme More'). Additionally, he co-penned the album's best-known track—the anthemic title song—plus such additional standouts as 'All Hell's Breakin' Loose' (an early rap-rock experiment, which for some reason KISS never get any credit for), the album-opening ass-kicker 'Exciter,' and especially the shoulda-been-a-single 'A Million To One.'

The unmasking ploy certainly worked—after largely ignoring the band previously, MTV backed them this time around by airing a 'KISS unmasking' segment, hosted by VJ J.J. Jackson, and spinning the 'Lick It Up' clip frequently upon the album's release. And while the supporting tour didn't exactly pack 'em in like their stadium/arena jaunts circa 1976–77, it certainly helped solidify the idea that KISS were making America a priority again, after playing just one full performance on US soil during 1980–81, as the tour in support of *Lick It Up* included ninety-four dates.

Thanks to the combination of dropping the makeup (leaving a new crop of bands like Mötley Crüe, W.A.S.P., and Mercyful Fate to gladly fill the void), another strong album, the success of the 'Lick It Up' single and video, and extensive touring, *Lick It Up* was the first KISS album since 1980's *Unmasked* to obtain gold certification in the USA. KISS were certainly coming back—no question. But could they continue their ascent back to the top of the hard-rock/ heavy-metal heap? Their next release would offer a resounding *roar* as an answer.

KNOW THE SCORE: EDDIE TRUNK

The host of *Eddie Trunk Live* and *Trunk Nation* on Sirius Radio, and co-host of *That Metal Show*, weighs in on the start of the non-makeup era … and the end of Vinnie Vincent's time with the band.

Where was KISS's career at, just before *Lick It Up* came out?

Their career in America was at rock bottom. They were probably at the lowest point they had been—in terms of popularity. The irony of that is the album they were coming off of, *Creatures Of The Night*, was a great return for them. It's widely considered to be one of the three best KISS studio records. But they had done so much damage before—to their history and their reputation—that they were playing to two thousand people in ten-thousand-seat arenas. It was just a bad, bad situation. They weren't really being taken seriously as a band, and they were considered old news and washed up. They had a really difficult time prior to *Lick It Up*, in terms of getting anything going with any sort of career in America. Even though, musically, what they did at that time [*Creatures*] was real good, they just couldn't get the audience and couldn't get people interested—or caring about what they were doing.

How would you describe being a KISS fan in the early 80s? It seemed like KISS were testing their fans' patience ...
I'm sure a lot of people felt that way, but I was such a hardcore KISS fan that I was down with anything they were doing. I was OK with the experimentation. The disco stuff [on *Dynasty*] was a little off-putting, but I actually liked *Unmasked* as a pop record, and I liked some elements of *The Elder*, and I loved the studio tracks that were on *Killers*. I liked some of the turns the band was taking. And, of course, *Creatures* was an amazing record. So, I was still going to shows—when they did play—and I was still totally on board.

But it was tough to be a KISS fan—there was no question about that. You were a bold person and a brave person if around that time you proudly identified yourself as a KISS fan—which I did. There weren't a lot of people that felt that way, and you would be mocked and ridiculed for even liking them. But from my perspective—in terms of what they were doing musically—I kind of liked all the different changes and different stuff they were going for.

I was very happy when *Creatures* came out. The first sign that things were turning was the four studio songs on *Killers*. I thought that was a big sign to fans: like, *OK, maybe they're starting to get back on track*. And then, when *Creatures* came out, it was like, *Yeah, this was what we were hoping for*.

What were your thoughts when you first heard KISS were going to be taking off the makeup?
I kind of had mixed feelings about it. I think that something had to change

at that time, and I think I understood it and I was OK with it. I was always way, way, way more into KISS because of the records and the songs and the music, more so than I was anything else. Of course, the image and the show and all that is great, but for me, I was always about the records and the music they were making. So, as a fan, I was kind of like, *I get this, I see the need to do this*—because they were struggling so bad. They needed to send up a flare—they needed to do *anything* that would help get attention and people talking about the band again.

I think it's really hard for people who didn't live in that era, or are not my age, to understand just truly how down-and-out that band was. I mean, now it's viewed as like … pop culture, and people celebrate the band and get a kick out of them, and like them, and they're on TV shows, and people talk about them and what have you.

Unless you lived it, you can't imagine what an utter joke they were regarded as at that time. *Everywhere.* Except for the very hardcore fans—which I was one of. So I understood the need at that point for them to do something drastic—and I was OK with it.

What did you see first—the unmasking on MTV, the 'Lick It Up' music video, or the *Lick It Up* album cover?

Well … I have a very unique perspective on this, because I saw the album cover *long before* anyone else. And it was a mistake. What happened was, I was working in a record store at that time, and, prior to the record coming out, PolyGram accidentally shipped us a box of *Lick It Up* albums—about a month before they were supposed to be on the shelves. And we had that record about three weeks before release date. Before *anything* happened with that—before the video, before the unmasking.

I'll never forget: we opened the box, and we were stunned, because we saw the cover and we were just shocked—we couldn't believe we had it, and we couldn't believe we had it before anyone else. So it was a really, really weird, quirky thing to have had happen. And somebody at the warehouse at PolyGram … I think we ordered a box of, like, a John Cougar Mellencamp record, and they just put the wrong records in and shipped the wrong box of records. So I saw it and heard it before anyone, and that was my introduction to it.

14

What did you think of the album?

I liked it. I didn't think it was as good as *Creatures*, but I did like it. And it continued the thread of *Creatures*—it continued the heaviness of *Creatures*. Most people know *Lick It Up* because of the title track—which is not necessarily a heavy song—but it's a surprisingly heavy record by KISS's standards. I don't think people really think of it like that. But when you listen to 'Not For The Innocent,' 'Fits Like A Glove,' 'Gimme More,' 'Exciter,' and some of that stuff, it definitely continues the *Creatures* vibe of a much heavier, harder-rocking band. And that's what they needed to re-establish at that time. One of the things I loved so much about *Creatures* was the drum sound—which was just *massive*. I remember being a little disappointed that the drums didn't sound exactly the same. But it still was a good-sounding record, and I liked it.

Vinnie Vincent seemed to play a major role in the album, as he co-wrote many of the songs, and was properly credited for the first time on a KISS album.

Creatures was a weird thing, because, with *Creatures*, we were told Ace was still in the band ... when he wasn't. And he was still featured on the album cover, so, I think a lot of people went into that thinking, *OK. Ace is coming back. Ace is still a part of this.* We later found out he wasn't, and we were pretty much being lied to. People who were really hardcore fans knew that Vincent Cusano was Vinnie Vincent, and that Vinnie was a part of *Creatures*—even though he wasn't credited as a band member or whatever. So, when *Lick It Up* came out, I think people had seen Vinnie play on the tour for *Creatures*, and then at that point it was sort of like the affirmation of, *OK. He is the guy now, and he's in the band.*

I don't know how many people looked closely at the songwriting, or really realized at that time how big a role he played on that record, and how he co-wrote so many things ... because again, same thing with *Creatures*, he was a big part of it but not credited as such. And then, with *Lick It Up*, he's being really presented as 'the new guy,' and being credited. He had a big hand in the resurgence of KISS—especially in the writing department. But it was tough—anyone will tell you it was tough to see KISS without Ace.

Like, with *Creatures*, a lot of people knew, *Hey, that doesn't sound like Ace on the record. Ace doesn't have any lead vocals on that record. Ace doesn't have any writing credits on that record. Is Ace really a part of this?* But even if you were in denial, you still kind of took comfort in, *Well, he's on the album cover. There was a press release saying he's coming back.* And then *Lick It Up* was, *OK. This is another change in the band, and this is really a major, major change.*

It was tough, but at that time, KISS were in such a place that they needed to do anything and everything they could to get back on track. And obviously, with Ace, the wheels were coming off on him at the time, and Vinnie brought a lot to the table. But if you were a hardcore KISS fan like I was, you were just rooting for them to do *anything* that they had to do to get on MTV, to get on the radio, and to have a chance at being taken seriously as a band again. So, if that's what it took, fine.

Do you agree that *Lick It Up* helped re-establish KISS?

Absolutely. The fact that they got radio and video airplay for the song 'Lick It Up' … *Lick It Up* was a hugely important record. And here's one of the reasons why I remember this very clearly, too—in *Billboard* magazine, when that record went gold, there was an ad that just showed the album cover with half of the record coming out and painted gold, and it just said, 'KISS … *Lick It Up* … gold.' You know, a few years earlier, *anything* KISS put out would have shipped platinum. In a way, it showed how far KISS had fallen—that it was a big deal that they had a gold record again—but it also showed how much KISS were on somewhat of a reinvention and comeback, because they had a gold record.

This was a statement, saying, *hey, look what's happened here. We're on our way back.* I thought it was really interesting and really telling, and kind of important. It was a full-page ad—I pulled it out and had it on my wall as a kid—announcing [to] everybody who thought this band was dead and over [that they were] back, looking different, reinvented, and now, just sold half a million records. I remember that was a really important statement, that signaled to us fans, *OK, maybe we've turned a corner as far as popularity*, and it signaled to the industry that this band that you thought was over and done … *might not be.*

You saw KISS perform during a two-night stand at Radio City Music Hall on the *Lick It Up* tour. There is a rumor that there was a confrontation between Paul and Vinnie over the length of a guitar solo during one of the shows.

Oh, it wasn't a rumor—*I watched firsthand what happened.* That unfolded onstage more than one night on that tour! The *Lick It Up* tour was very difficult for KISS, because they really did not know how to dress, behave, or act at that time—out of makeup and costume. I think, by their own admission, they would tell you that they struggled with that—especially Gene. Because Gene just didn't know what he was supposed to do. It was like … he's not the demon anymore, but he's kind of still acting like the demon, without the makeup. *Is he still going to breathe fire? Is he still going to drool blood? Does that make sense anymore because he's not the demon? Or is he still the demon?* There was a real identity crisis going on there with Gene.

Even the way Gene moved onstage, he just didn't know what to do there for a while, I think. Paul was always very flamboyant and running around anyway, so he kind of did OK with it. Vinnie—no one really knew much about Vinnie, and what he was supposed to be. He had not really had a big established persona before, so that wasn't a big deal. And Eric sat behind the drums, and he was still only a couple of records into the band at that point, so he seemed to be fine. But Gene struggled *a lot* with what they were supposed to do.

Again, I think people were just happy knowing that they were on the upswing, people were attending the shows, and despite that we weren't really sure what to make of the image and the show going forward, it was still encouraging to see that things were turning.

What exactly did you witness between Vinnie and Paul at Radio City?

Vinnie would take these solo breaks where Paul would be talking to the crowd, and then Vinnie would kind of answer him by doing a quick guitar run. I don't remember what song it was—it might have been 'Fits Like A Glove,' which was something that was in the set *constantly* back then. And there are parts where there's stops in the song, and Vinnie would do this guitar-break thing, and there would be this call-and-response with the audience, where Vinnie would go to the front of the stage and do a little guitar run, and Paul would answer it with a vocal thing.

I was very close to the front of the stage at that time, and I saw with my own eyes that there were times where Vinnie would overplay, and Paul would want him to stop, and Paul would walk away from the microphone, take a few steps so no one could hear him, look at Vinnie and point, and go, 'Watch! You watch! Watch!' Meaning, like, his cue to stop, because he wouldn't stop. He would point to him, and say, 'Stop! Stop!' You could see there was a point where he was trying to shield it from the crowd, but he really would actually reprimand him onstage, because Vinnie was overplaying, or taking the spot too long. I saw a lot of that.

The tensions I think were pretty obvious, if you were a fan. And the irony of all that is that KISS ... you've got to remember what was happening too, at that time. KISS *so wanted* the sign of the times—the shredders of the world. They never had that before—Ace was not that kind of guitar player. So, they went out and got a shredder ... but reprimanded him and threw him out for shredding and going too crazy! And then they replaced him with a guy who shredded *even more* on record, with Mark St. John. It was really a bit of a contradiction. Although I think they just looked at it as Vinnie was trying to upstage them a little bit, and didn't serve the song that he was doing and the way he was playing.

And, just recently, Vinnie kind of agreed with that. Vinnie said although at the time he was trying to send a message and obviously become well-known and establish himself and all that, and wanted to quickly become a guitar hero, he has said that, in retrospect, those guys were right: they had the experience, and they knew what their band needed the most, and he should have listened. But at that time, he was younger, and he just wanted to do anything he could to get attention.

Do you remember being disappointed when you heard Vinnie was leaving?

I don't know if I acknowledged enough at that time how important Vinnie was in the writing department, to be really upset about it. I didn't feel—as an old-school KISS fan—that he was the right fit. So I was kind of OK with it, because my problem with him was not what he did on songs from *Creatures* or *Lick It Up*, but I didn't like the way he played the old stuff. And I think he took too many liberties with that, and he turned it into his own thing, in the way that he delivered those solos. And the solos with Ace … no matter how you feel about Ace as a guitar player, the beauty of those solos is they were songs within songs, and four little notes mean more than a thousand notes, the way Ace played.

I think that's where, for KISS fans, the problem was with Vinnie—when KISS would play Ace songs from the 70s, Vinnie did *not* reproduce those solos. He did not stay with those solos. He went for his own thing. And, sometimes, it was really jarring. You'd be like, *Wow … that's not even close to what the solo is supposed to be.* And anybody that's a big KISS fan knows that those solos are so impactful, you actually *sing* those solos. You look forward to them. They're a big part of the whole song. But in that regard, I was kind of happy he was going, because I'm like, *Maybe they're going to bring a guy in that would be able to do his thing with the new material, but also will faithfully reproduce the old stuff.*

KNOW THE SCORE: KEITH ROTH

The host of *Ozzy's Boneyard* and *Hair Nation* on Sirius Radio, and the *Electric Ballroom* radio show adds his thoughts on *Lick It Up*.

What do you recall about the *Lick It Up* era?

I kind of lost interest in KISS after *Unmasked*, and, with *Creatures*, it was one of those late nights that I came home and flipped on MTV, and I saw the video for 'I Love It Loud' and thought it was a great song. Then, at the record store, I saw the album cover, and I thought that was such a great album cover. So I said, I'm going to check it out, and I was really happy, because I thought they got a little heavier from what was going on at the time. The songs were infectious and it definitely sparked my interest again with KISS.

By the time *Lick It Up* came out, they had that whole big MTV thing— when they made the announcement. I remember the one thing that really annoyed me about it was Vinnie Vincent saying, like, 'Now I can't walk the streets.' *The guy was in the band for 30 seconds … and he's acting like he's been there since '73!* But 'Lick It Up' was a great song, and one song I really dug off of it was 'All Hell's Breakin' Loose,' because it kind of had a 60s/revolution theme to it. It had that Detroit/creating a revolution/sing-along thing. That one really brought me back to music as a kid—especially with what was going on in the 80s at that point, where everything was very sappy and cheesy. It had a different message from things I heard at that time.

And 'Exciter' was heavy—at that point, the New Wave Of British Heavy Metal stuff was happening, and they seemed more focused on that album. The album was very infectious, catchy, sing-along … it was very easy to digest. They also seemed a lot cooler. Like, *Unmasked* and *The Elder*—later on in life I rediscovered them, and I appreciated them many years after it came out, but *Lick It Up* was easily digestible. It was almost like an oldies act that people remembered from their youth—but they were probably only in their late twenties, early thirties by that point.

Were you disappointed that they didn't continue with the *Creatures*-style production—specifically Eric Carr's Bonham-esque drum sound?
Yep, no doubt. I think if *Creatures Of The Night* had been the follow-up to *Dynasty*, KISS would have sailed right on. That would have been the perfect follow-up. I thought the production—and *Creatures* overall—was a better record than *Lick It Up*. The drums, you *really* got to hear Eric Carr for the first time—even though he played on *The Elder*—with the Bonham sound. He definitely brought a whole new element into that, and it was disappointing that it wasn't continued on *Lick It Up*.

On *Lick It Up*, it appears that Gene—for the most part—was still writing inspired and focused tunes, such as 'Not For The Innocent,' 'Young And Wasted,' and 'Fits Like A Glove.' It also seemed like he was still singing from the Demon persona, which diminished more and more as the 80s went on.
It's funny, the three that you mentioned are also my favorites, too. 'Fits Like A Glove,' with different lyrics, that could have been a Cheap Trick song! There's no doubt Gene was focused, and some of the best songs on the record were written by him. 'Not For The Innocent' was a great song. But 'Fits Like A Glove' is just one of those songs … it's infectious. It's undeniable. Especially the pre-chorus—if you like The Sweet or Slade, you can feel a little influence of that on him. Gene's got good taste in music, so you can say some of his influences came out on that one. But his songs were strong on there—no doubt.

It's funny that you mentioned Cheap Trick, because listening to 'Fits Like A Glove' and 'Young And Wasted' today, I think they have almost a punk-rock vibe to them.

No doubt. Gene probably ventured into Max's Kansas City a few years prior and was checking out bands. I think it's a combination of that, and they were probably still living in New York at that point. And some of the bands that he loved growing up—you can get a little taste of that. 'Fits Like A Glove' could have been on a Sweet record. It seems like they were focused. They had made that decision to take the makeup off, which was a big thing. I'm sure they were saying, 'It's do or die. We might be playing Yonkers Raceway after this.'

And Paul's vocals are especially great throughout *Lick It Up*.

His voice made it special. I'm a big fan of his voice. Paul Stanley is one of those guys that could sing the weather, and if he's on, it will always keep you interested. I always believed in my heart that if KISS never made it, Paul would have found a way to be successful. He's a great frontman—his style, he's a great singer/songwriter. He's a special guy. Somehow I felt he would have found his way, without KISS.

Looking back, is *Lick It Up* your favorite non-makeup KISS album?

I would probably say it's *Revenge*, and then *Lick It Up*. Those are the only two records from the non-makeup era that I actually own. You respect the fact that they just went for it, because they took a big chance, and it worked out. Then they started the 'unmasked army' after that, because I've talked to people—and some of them that are even much younger than me—that enjoy that period *even more* than the classic 70s period. *Creatures Of The Night* filled the cracks in the foundation, and *Lick It Up* started a second wave to infect the next generation. So, in that sense, they were very pivotal records.

You interviewed KISS when they appeared on Sirius's *Town Hall* in 2018, to discuss their *End Of The Road World Tour*.

Yeah, I've interviewed them a lot over the last year. And I've had a long relationship with Ace, too. I like Ace—I never got to see the side that those guys did. But they are really all great guys. They're all very different … in a crazy way, they're like the Ramones, four very different personalities. But they're all really cool. I like Gene. Gene is kind of like that goofy uncle—you know what he's going to say, and you take it with a grain of salt. But I think he's got a big heart—I really do. I think there's a very soft side to him that a lot of people don't get to see. And Paul's a rock star, but he's a cool guy. I enjoy talking to those guys—they're a lot of fun, and they make it easy. I feel like I have a good bond with all of them.

LICK IT UP: THE TOUR WITH CURT GOOCH

The co-author of *KISS Alive Forever: The Complete Touring History* looks back at the *Lick It Up* live era, which saw the return of the *Creatures* stage and KISS trying to find their footing as a non-makeup 'n' costumes live act.

For *Lick It Up*, KISS recycled their *Creatures Of The Night/10th Anniversary Tour* stage from the previous outing—probably for economic reasons, mainly. It was the 'tank' stage, and fans seemed to love that stage, even to this day. I wish they would actually recycle that. But the *Lick It Up* tour—believe it or not—when you look at the attendance figures, actually did *worse* than *Creatures*. The problem was there was still a bunch of fans that loved the makeup, and just had no desire to see the band out of makeup. And the fans that were going to come on board hadn't quite done so yet. Over the course of the tour, the numbers did get stronger. But there was a reason why they went to Europe first on that one.

On the *Lick It Up* tour, it was more or less a re-creation of the *Creatures* show, minus the makeup and costumes, and some of the theatrical effects—in particular, the blood-spitting was 86'd. There have been rumors that Gene spit blood at the first show in Lisbon [Portugal, at the Pavilhão de Cascais on October 11, 1983], but that is absolutely false, according to everybody I spoke with. Gene did continue to breathe fire. And the staging at certain venues may have been honed in a little bit—the side fills may not have been included, because they did do some theaters. But for the most part it really was just an exact replica of the *Creatures* stage—minus the makeup, costumes, and the blood-spitting.

Lick It Up followed the precedent they started with *Creatures*, where a lot of new material was put into the set. KISS did—and rightfully so—really believe in their album at that point. And that is certainly reflected in the setlist at that time. Starting with *Creatures* and going for several tours afterward—all the way up to *Crazy Nights*—every tour would see usually five or six songs in the setlist. With *Lick It Up*, there was certainly no exception—they added 'Exciter,' 'Gimme More,' 'Lick It Up,' 'Fits Like A Glove,' 'Young And Wasted,' and, later, 'All Hell's Breakin' Loose.' And I've got to tell you—I really think that was a strong tour, setlist-wise. I think that would have been a really good tour for a KISS fan from that period to attend. I know a guy whose first KISS show ever was *Lick It Up* in Houston, and he still raves about it to this day. So there was something about that period of time where they were kind of the underdogs, and there was a belief that they were going to be bigger and 'get on board now' type of thing. You could feel the momentum building as a KISS fan at that time.

So, *Lick It Up* was a strong album and a strong tour, but obviously they had some serious personnel problems going on behind the scenes, with Vinnie Vincent, who by all accounts has some sort of disease when it comes to success—he tends to self-harpoon himself on every conceivable opportunity. And there was no difference there. In fact, one interesting thing that a lot of people don't know is that after the *Lick It Up* tour ended, Vinnie actually went to Dallas and spent the day riding around in a limo, as 'Vinnie Vincent of KISS,' going to and making appearances at several guitar shops—doing little meet-and-greets at guitar stores. I'm pretty certain he knew he was already out of KISS at that point, but just didn't publicly announce it, and he went along for whatever money or payday he could get out of that.

It's well known that Vinnie Vincent would extend his guitar solos while onstage during the *Lick It Up* tour. And, as the tour progressed, this presumably became [more] of an issue. In his autobiography, Paul Stanley claims that this came to a head at a show in Long Beach, and that he actually had to cut Vinnie off in the middle of his solo. There's no doubt in my mind that after the last note of the last song in Evansville, Indiana [on March 17, 1984, at Roberts Stadium], Gene and Paul instantly knew that Vinnie was gone.

[Australian costume designer] Fleur Thiemeyer was brought in, starting with the 'Lick It Up' video. By leaving the makeup outfits behind, *Lick It Up* is where they really began their journey through 80s fashion. The results were mixed at best. One interesting critique is that during the *Lick It Up* tour—and in particular, you might even say the *Lick It Up* European tour—the band seemed to be wearing unnecessarily heavy stage makeup. To the point where it was almost like … *feminine*. Way too much rouge, way too much lipstick—to the point where you go, *what's going on here?* I think that definitely dissipated as the *Lick It Up* tour went on. But they had these unique and interesting outfits that were designed for them by a professional. This was the same person that designed Mötley Crüe's *Shout At The Devil* outfits, Van Halen's *1984* outfits, and Bon Jovi's *Slippery When Wet* outfits. All of this was coming from the same person. So KISS were right there with their peers. But, for some reason, KISS always seemed to be kind of following the trends during this period—or are at least accused of that—more so than leading the pack.

GIMME MORE: KISS UNMASK ON MTV

On September 18, 1983, KISS appeared for the first time without their makeup in an MTV segment with VJ J.J. Jackson—broadcast live. In this excerpt from one of my earlier books, *MTV Ruled The World: The Early Years Of Music Video*, some of rock's biggest names of the era look back on this important moment in KISSTORY.

ALAN HUNTER [MTV VJ] That was an amazing day, and J.J. was really excited. He was good friends with Paul Stanley. I thought it was pretty major. It was another example of how MTV was a platform for any kind of announcement that a band wanted to make. KISS decided to 'unveil,' and they chose MTV. Of course, there was no other choice. There was nothing else to do it on. They weren't going to do it on late night television or *The Today Show*.

J.J. was pretty pumped. I remember hanging on the edge, watching. I remember everybody from the office of MTV came down. Whenever something big happened, all the secretaries and everybody came down from the office. [*Laughs*] It was like, *What are you all doing down here?* 'We want to see KISS unveiled!' So the hubbub and the entourages and the publicists and the record company people—it was just packed. The pressure was on. And I remember we only really had one shot at it. It's not like a drawing—you couldn't screw it up. And I remember J.J. would get very sweaty under those circumstances. As much of a pro as he was, he'd get real tight and nervous.

MARK WEISS [rock photographer] I think I did take photos that day. J.J. was Geraldo [Rivera] discovering Al Capone's safe, uncovering it. But instead of Geraldo having nothing in there, J.J. had the prize of uncovering rock royalty for the first time. I know they did the whole hype-up, and then they did the unveiling. It was a good lead-up, but it was kind of anticlimactic.

JOE ELLIOTT [singer, Def Leppard] They obviously saw MTV or the medium of video as a great opportunity to do this *en masse*, rather than just do it at a press conference in New York, hoping it would sneak into all the broadsheets. It was a smart thing to do, actually—as it was in '96, to put it all back on again.

WARREN DeMARTINI [guitarist, Ratt] It was pretty shocking to see what those guys really looked like. You're just so used to the makeup. It really did conceal their real faces. It was just a total, unforgettable TV moment.

RIK EMMETT [singer/guitarist, Triumph] The Paul Stanleys, the Gene Simmonses, and these kind of folks, they are just performers. And at some point you have to say, *OK, forget all the artifice, the imagery, and all the histrionics of show business. Now I'll just show my talent. I'll show my ability. I'll write a song, and I'll present the song as best I can.* It gets down to that elemental kind of thing. And I do think television and big rock shows, they tend to take you away from that. But that core value, that never goes away. No matter what happens in the music business, it will always boil down to when you distill it to its pure essence. It's still going to be a songwriter who has written a song that is being performed by a good musician. *Period.* A lot of the bands that I've always respected are bands that always understood that.

NINA BLACKWOOD [MTV VJ] I thought it was great. In fact, that was the period I liked them the best. Because it was real, and I thought Bruce Kulick was a great guitar player. I just liked that approach. When they put it back on, it was like, *Oh come on*. It's like the band that just keeps going.

ERIC BLOOM [singer/guitarist, Blue Öyster Cult] Looking back, it didn't hurt. It certainly made a buzz. But then they put the makeup back on and retired ten times. In retrospect, they never made a mistake. I love the original version, with Ace and Peter, and the Bruce Kulick era was great. Early on, KISS opened for us, on New Year's Eve 1973. When I saw them that first night, they were an opening act jammed onto our show. It was us—we were the headliner—Iggy & The Stooges were the special guests, and Teenage Lust was the opening act. And KISS were *under* the opening act, as a favor to somebody. They came out, did their thing, and it was like a *holy shit* moment. They've stood the test of time.

CARMINE APPICE [drummer, Vanilla Fudge, Beck Bogert Appice, Rod Stewart] I don't remember if I saw that or not, but I knew those guys. I knew them without the makeup, so it wasn't that big a deal to me. I used to hang out with Paul Stanley. In LA, we would sort of be a team. We'd go see Angel in Long Beach and sit in the audience. I'd be mobbed, and nobody would know who Paul was. We'd go to Midas Mufflers to fix my Jaguar, and nobody would know who Paul was. A guy there asked, 'Hey … *are you guys in a band?*'

RUDY SARZO [bassist, Ozzy Osbourne, Quiet Riot, Whitesnake] It was a ballsy move, something that they felt they needed to make. What was really interesting about that, everybody in the industry thought, *Well, that's it. They cannot go back to wearing the makeup again*. Which actually was not it. The makeup is kind of like that Superman/Clark Kent alter-ego thing. Now, they can do both: with the makeup, or without the makeup.

MIKE RENO [singer, Loverboy] I thought it was not a very good move, just because they had created this *illusion*. I personally would have rather kept it that way. The illusion was created. It's kind of like finding out the magic you just watched was actually just a trick. I liked the illusion. I wouldn't have done an 'unmasked' situation, but that's just me. I just thought it was a very cool illusion. But it was almost as big as watching the Super Bowl when they came on TV. It was big. That's why they did it. It was probably a Gene Simmons idea.

GEDDY LEE [singer/bassist, Rush] No, I didn't see that. I already knew what they looked like. [*Laughs*] I didn't really think about it, and frankly, I haven't thought about. I don't think it was such a big deal.

LITA FORD [solo artist, singer/guitarist] I think it was too late. I think people just didn't really care. They just loved their music, and that was it. Wanting to see what they looked like without the makeup, I think that wore off. And when they did take their makeup off, people were like, *Eh … they should have done that a few years ago.*

PHIL COLLEN [guitarist, Def Leppard] I thought, *Oh man … don't do that!* That's what everyone really wanted, for them to be the characters that are KISS. But it's cool. That's what you do in a band, you constantly change … or you should. You try different things. It would be really boring if you've done the same thing over and over again. You have to mix it up a little bit.

BRUCE KULICK [guitarist, KISS, 1984–96] It was pretty interesting. I mean, I knew what the guys looked like, so it was more like, *How are they going to handle it? How are they going to present this?* And I thought it was really cool. The only odd thing to me was I was always going to keep my eye on the position that I wanted … *which was Vinnie Vincent.* He didn't look like he belonged.

PETE ANGELUS [video director whose credits include Van Halen's 'Hot For Teacher' and David Lee Roth's 'California Girls'] I might have thought, *This is interesting, because they have created such a substantial brand.* And now, this is almost like when the curtain comes down on *The Wizard Of Oz.* Now you're seeing the guy behind all the smoke and mirrors.

ANN WILSON [singer, Heart] I think everyone had the same kind of response to that. [*Laughs*] I think it was: 'Put the makeup back on.' Not because of them personally, but just because they were so much more interesting with the makeup on. They had come out with that as their 'cartoon.' Their whole thing was that. So for them to suddenly not be that, there were tons and tons of other bands that were just like them. That set them apart.

MIKE PELECH [MTV cameraman] When KISS decided to take their makeup off, I think Scott Fishman was directing, and he said, 'Now we know why they put their makeup on in the first place.' They were the four ugliest guys.

GERALD CASALE [bassist, Devo] I thought, *Jesus ... put it back on.*

02 ANIMALIZE

Released September 13, 1984. Produced by Paul Stanley.
US #19, UK #11. US certification: platinum.

SIDE ONE

I've Had Enough (Into The Fire) (Paul Stanley/Desmond Child)
Heaven's On Fire (Stanley/Child)
Burn Bitch Burn (Gene Simmons)
Get All You Can Take (Stanley/Mitch Weissman)
Lonely Is The Hunter (Simmons)

SIDE TWO

Under The Gun (Eric Carr/Stanley/Child)
Thrills In The Night (Stanley/Jean Beauvoir)
While The City Sleeps (Simmons/Weissman)
Murder In High Heels (Simmons/Weissman)

SINGLES / EPS

Heaven's On Fire / Lonely Is The Hunter (US #49)
Heaven's On Fire / Lonely Is The Hunter / All Hell's Breakin' Loose (UK #43)
Thrills In The Night / Burn Bitch Burn (US/UK did not chart)

★

In one of the greatest spoof music documentaries of all-time, *This Is Spinal Tap*, the band in question have never-ending difficulties retaining a drummer. In KISS's case during the 1980s, it was the lead guitar position that replicated Tap's dilemma. When Ace Frehley jumped ship after *Creatures* (an album on whose cover his face appears, but that he supposedly did not play on), Vinnie Vincent was given the nod … only to be handed his walking papers after the tour in support of *Lick It Up* concluded. Simmons says Vincent's exit was because he never signed a contract with the band; Vincent says because his salary was not enough to support his family. Either way, KISS were on the lookout for a new guitarist—and they felt like they specifically needed a shredder, to keep pace with the Eddie Van Halens of the world. And they certainly found a speedy guitarist in the form of Mark St. John (real name Mark Norton)—on the recommendation of guitar luthier Grover Jackson.

With Simmons focused on launching an acting career at the time (and filming his first ever motion picture, *Runaway*), Paul Stanley was largely in control of the all-important follow-up to *Lick It Up*. Michael James Jackson was in line to return to the producer's chair once more, but he bowed out early in the recording—supposedly because he felt like he was no longer needed—resulting in Stanley being named as the sole producer of a KISS album for the first time in the group's recording career.

As a whole, the resulting album, *Animalize*, was not as consistent, front-to-back, as the group's previous two releases. But amid some tunes that could be classified as filler, there are certainly several inspired rockers. And speaking of rockers, *Animalize* is one of the few KISS albums that does not include what could be neatly categorized as either a 'ballad' or 'power ballad' (although 'Thrills In The Night' comes close).

Unlike its predecessor, *Animalize* welcomed back outside songwriters to lend a hand—including the return of Desmond Child, who had previously struck songwriting gold with KISS as co-writer of the 1979 disco smash 'I Was Made For Lovin' You.' And while Child's background was initially in pop and dance sounds (as the leader of the band Desmond Child & Rouge), by the mid-80s he was ready for a hard-rock makeover, and would eventually become one of the go-to songwriters for hire within the rock world. His work on *Animalize*—including co-penning the album's instant KISS klassic, 'Heaven's

On Fire,' plus two of the album's heaviest tracks, 'I've Had Enough (Into The Fire)' and 'Under The Gun'—would also soon catch the attention of other artists (including penning smash hits for Aerosmith, Bon Jovi, Cher, Joan Jett, and Alice Cooper).

Also included is the aforementioned tune that shoulda/coulda become a hit, 'Thrills In The Night'—a mid-paced, highly melodic tune co-penned by Stanley and ex-Plasmatics bassist Jean Beauvoir. There are also several largely forgotten tunes that serve as pleasant surprises all these years later, largely due to their sturdy guitar riffs ('Get All You Can Take,' 'Lonely Is The Hunter,' and 'Murder In High Heels'). That said, *Animalize* contains a few tunes that are simply best *forgotten*—the throwaway 'While The City Sleeps,' and the *Spinal Tap*-worthy 'Burn Bitch Burn,' which contains the Shakespearian phrase, '*Ooh, baby, want to put my log in your fireplace.*'

But back to KISS's latest guitarist. According to various interviews with Simmons and Stanley over the years, it supposedly became apparent during the recording of *Animalize* that St. John would not cut the mustard. And the reasons were multiple—while he was indeed fleet-fingered on the fretboard, he supposedly had difficulty replicating his solos, lacked soul in his playing, and, perhaps most obviously, was not a songwriter. (Unlike his predecessors, who contributed songs from the get go, St. John did not receive a single songwriting credit on *Animalize*.) Simmons and Stanley ended up having to seek outside help in a few spots in the solo department, including enlisting a chap by the name of Bruce Kulick on the tunes 'Lonely Is The Hunter' and 'Murder In High Heels'—the outro to which contains one of the best *and longest* solos on the entire album.

The *Animalize* album cover is quite possibly tied with the *Hot In The Shade* and *Carnival Of Souls* covers as the dullest of the era. It is comprised simply of three animal furs, with a blank black area in the upper left corner, reserved for where the KISS logo and album title were displayed. In my humble opinion, a better graphic that could have been utilized can be found on the back of the *Animalize* tour book (and as part of the *Animalize Live Uncensored* VHS cover), showing a woman's long red nails ripping through white paper, with dripping blood marks added in for good measure.

Looking back on *Animalize* today, its two greatest historical significances are the inclusion of 'Heaven's On Fire' and its status as St. John's one-and-done album with KISS. As rehearsals began for the album's supporting tour, the story goes that St. John had developed a form of arthritis called Reiter's Syndrome, which caused his hands to swell and prevented him from playing guitar properly. As a result, Kulick was invited to fill in on the album's European tour, and then to continue into the US dates. (St. John also traveled with the band on tour, in case his condition improved—which resulted in him performing a grand total of two-and-a-half concerts.)

By the time a performance at Cobo Arena in Detroit (the same location that bits of *Alive!* were recorded at) was to be filmed for the aforementioned *Animalize Live Uncensored* video on December 8, 1984, Kulick had been named KISS's permanent guitarist, and St. John had been sent home. He would later be part of short-lived hair-metallists White Tiger, play in a band with original KISS drummer Peter Criss (who never issued any recordings), offer the solo release *Magic Bullet Theory*, and appear at KISS conventions/expos. Sadly, his story ended tragically—he died from a brain hemorrhage at the age of fifty-one, on April 5, 2007.

Sales-wise, *Animalize* was the success that KISS had been clamoring for years for—it was their first Top 20 and platinum-certified album in the US since 1979's *Dynasty*, and it solidified their status as a North American arena headliner once more. (The tour in support of *Lick It Up* had taken in a mixture of arenas and theaters, as a precautionary measure, in the wake of the woefully underwhelming ticket sales that plagued the *Creatures* tour.) Additionally, KISS were once again a hot commodity in the metal mags, with seemingly every issue of *Circus* and *Hit Parader* containing an article about the band (and, quite often, including a KISS member on its cover). As a result of the band clawing their way back toward the top of the metal mountain, the wise folks at PolyGram Records realized that the demand for all things KISS was on the rise, and would soon decide to dust off and re-release an earlier underappreciated album …

KNOW THE SCORE: MITCH WEISSMAN

The co-writer of 'Get All You Can Take,' 'While The City Sleeps,' and 'Murder In High Heels' on *Animalize*, plus 'Thief In The Night' from *Crazy Nights*, Mitch Weissman had played the role of Paul McCartney in the Broadway musical *Beatlemania* prior to entering the KISS orbit. Here, he discusses his memories of working with KISS professionally, and also the behind-the-scenes hijinks he shared with them personally.

How did you first cross paths with KISS?

Unbeknown to either Gene or me, back when I was a thirteen-year-old, attending somebody's bar mitzvah in my town of Great Neck, New York, there is a picture of me and a girl dancing in front of the band—which is on a concrete patio in the back of her house. The band is The Long Island Sounds, and the bass player is … Gene Simmons. He was fifteen and I was thirteen. I discovered it years later, when I used to write with him. I'd go into the closet with all the photos—I'd have keys to his apartment [when he was] on the road, and I'd be recording in his little walk-in closet with a Portastudio. I saw this photo of The Long Island Sounds, and I said, 'Holy shit!' I looked at this photo from the bar mitzvah, and there's Gene. I met them around '76—during rehearsals for *Beatlemania* at SIR in New York, KISS came in one day to watch us rehearse.

Then you appeared on Gene's solo album in 1978.

Like I said, they came to see us rehearse for four hours. Then they called us into the studio the next day, to play for us—I believe they were doing 'Detroit Rock City'—and Gene pops a bass string and Ace's amp starts smoking! I found out from Lydia Criss four days later, at a club in Manhattan, that the guys were so upset, because they really felt like they were playing for The Beatles … and then everything went wrong. And Paul and Gene confirmed that years later. That was in '76; then, in '77, when they played the Garden, we went there and hung out with them.

So, all of a sudden, we're doing *Beatlemania* in LA in '78, and we're about to go to Chicago. I get a phone call from the press officer at my management office, Leber-Krebs, saying, 'Gene Simmons wants to get ahold of you.' I call back, and I find out that they want me and Joe Pecorino [who played John Lennon in *Beatlemania*] to do harmony vocals for songs on his solo album. And of course Gene in the press back then said, 'I wanted to get the real John and Paul, but they were busy—so I got the next best thing.' Nice press indeed. So it was me, Joey, Gene, and Eric Troyer.

I was in LA, we got reacquainted, I walk into the studio, and there is [Cheap Trick's] Rick Nielsen finishing up his part, and [Aerosmith's] Joe Perry finishing up his part. Rick and I played ping-pong with this guitar picks, and Phoebe Snow was finishing up her thing. I was there a few different nights doing the vocals with Gene—it was a lot of fun.

How did you then come to co-write songs with KISS?

In 1981 or 1982, Peppy Castro from The Blues Magoos had a party at his townhouse downtown, and he invited all his friends over. We were up on the roof. At that party, I was reintroduced to Paul Stanley, who was there. We have a great time, Paul and I hit it off, and he said, 'Call me.' The next day I wake up, I look at the phone number, I look at my wife, and said, 'I can't call him.' She goes, 'Why not?' And I go, 'Because it's *PAUL STANLEY*!' Again, next year at the same party, I run into him, and he says, 'Why didn't you call me?' I told him the story I just told you, and he hits me and says, 'Don't do that again! Call me!' So we became friends, and then Gene was reintroduced into the mix. They didn't have a lot of friends between them. The only person that seemed to go out with them—together or separately—was me.

They knew I was a musician, so we started throwing around some ideas, even for *Creatures*, but nothing made it there. They called me from the studio on speakerphone, and they told me that they weren't using any of the songs on that record. They said later on, 'Do you remember what you said to us?' And I said, 'Yeah. I think it was something like, *OK. That's fine. Bummer. So, when you come back on Tuesday, where are we going to eat?*' There was silence. And then Gene said, 'Did you hear that? *We're not going to use any of your songs.*' I said, 'Yeah, I get it. That's fine. So … where are we going to eat next week?' They were flabbergasted that a friend of theirs that they had taken in to write with and was turned down, still remained their friend.

I also [co-wrote] a lot of songs [with them] that have never been released by them. There is a project in the works that I talked to Gene about—doing my versions of the songs they recorded, the outtakes, and the other stuff. A lot of people said they would do that record with me, and Gene said if I get all these people lined up, to let him know, because he may be interested and may want to release it.

So that's how that came about, back then—we were friends, we wrote, and we worked together. And they actually said to me, when *Animalize* came up, and all the songs I submitted—I got those three songs on it, and one song that didn't make it that ended up later on, on *Crazy Nights*. Which was funny, because Paul didn't even realize it was a Wendy O. Williams track—that's how much he was listening to what Gene was producing! But then he and Nevison found out that it was on that record [1984's *WOW*], and they were pissed. But it was a good track.

Did you attend the *Animalize* recording sessions?

I did get to the sessions, and I actually co-produced with Paul his vocal for 'Heaven's On Fire.' That 'yodeling' in the beginning was his way of doing vocal exercises, and the tape was running. He couldn't hear the click track, he yodeled, and Eric's drumbeat came in. We all just froze. It's not a splice—it wasn't even planned. He just sang, doing his warm-ups—it came in serendipity-like. He said to me, 'How was the vocal?' There was nobody there, except him, me, and the engineer—his girlfriend at the time, Cathy St. George, was out in the waiting room. He sang about two passes, and I said, 'That's it. You're done.' He was that good and that proficient singing this stuff. And I was there at Right Track when Michael James Jackson said to them, 'You don't need me anymore.' And then Paul pretty much took over—Gene was doing *Runaway*.

I remember Mark St. John coming in to record, and he was amazing. He's the guy who taught Allan Holdsworth how to play, and yet he couldn't figure out how to write a song. He was a technician—he was not a guy who could put some chords together and songs. I played rhythm guitar on 'Murder In High Heels,' 'While The City Sleeps,' and 'Get All You Can Take.' Paul was going through some issues with his family, and his parents were in the lounge, and he said, '*You play.*' It was a big compliment. Obviously, they overdubbed a lot of different guitars.

35

I will tell you a funny story: on 'Murder In High Heels,' that riff is mine. And when I recorded it, the bass line, because Gene was filming … I wrote the song, I wrote the riff, and I played the chorus wrong. Jean Beauvoir had to come in and correct it!

I was there for a lot of that stuff at Right Track. I watched Mark do overdubs. And on 'Get All You Can Take,' it's basically Paul comp'ing himself. Mark was not good at reproducing the same solo. There is a story about Jeff Beck—he would do a bunch of passes, each solo would be different, they would comp the solo, and then he would learn it later to play live. Mark St. John could not get it, so, on 'Get All You Can Take,' Paul actually plays lead. Mark did maybe one or two little sections, and then Paul overdubbed almost the entire guitar solo.

During the *Animalize* sessions, how were Gene and Paul getting along?
Gene went off to do *Runaway*. He got the part and it was great. He tried showing me in his apartment how menacing he was—because his first scene, he's at a hotdog stand, and says, 'Coffee … black.' So, he reads from the script, and goes, 'Coffee … please.' I go, 'Oh, *nice Jewish boy*.' It took a lot for him to act like 'the mean guy.' And for *Runaway*, he cut his hair off.

I think I took him to my wigmaker guy for *Beatlemania*, to get wigs. The tour after that, he's wearing a wig held on by the headband—until his hair would grow out. He said, 'Where do you guys get your wigs?' I took him down to the theater district, to Bob Kelly's—where they made $800 wigs— and watched them put plastic all over his head to make the mesh, and that's where he got his wig.

Any other memories about Mark St. John?
Mark was nice, very polite. Any sort of attitude that I've heard he had wasn't evident when I was there. He was quiet during the sessions. Paul did not run over him. Like I said, he tried to get him to play these solos. He genuinely was amazed at how we wrote songs. Because, as I said, the guy could play like crazy, but he had no sense of how to put a song together. He would ask me, 'How do you come up with that?' I remember when they went to do the first tour in Europe, his hand was not doing well. Paul had actually foreseen that, because

when we were at Right Track, doing stuff with Michael James Jackson, before he bowed out, Paul one day handed me the Queens phonebook, and said, 'I need you to find Bruce Kulick.' He had a sense of the fact that things were going to get weird. To finish up the solos, Bruce actually plays on *Animalize*— and Paul said, '*Find him.*'

So I open up the Queens phonebook, and thank God there weren't a billion Kulicks! I start dialing, and I was probably into my seventh or eighth leaving of telephone messages for Bruce, of me saying, 'Call me, because Paul Stanley is looking for you.' Bruce was going through his first divorce, and he was at his parents' house in solitude, just trying to get over everything. And, as he puts it, 'I'm not talking to anybody, and I hear Mitch's voice on the answering machine, and I said to myself, *well, this is a guy I don't mind talking to.*' He heard my voice and answered the call. So, that's how he got involved. I was working at a graphic design studio still, because I didn't want to spend all the money that I had saved. Plus I was a graphic designer anyway, so I went back to the guys that I worked with beforehand.

It was funny—I'd be in the bullpen at this art studio, and the phone would ring on the wall, and every kid in the place would go racing for it, because it would be, 'Mitch, Paul Stanley is on the phone,' 'Mitch, Gene Simmons is on the phone,' 'Mitch, John Waite is on the phone.' It was insane … but that was my life. And just because I had these guys as friends, I needed to work—they didn't do any charity for me. I wasn't a hanger-on that way. It was pretty heady stuff. I remember I wasn't doing a lot of sleeping, because I would work at the art studio all day, and then join them at night for the recording sessions. When you're happy, who the hell needs sleep?

How did the pay agreement work at the time, for your contributions?
I have all kinds of comments about Howard Marks and his managing, and when they dumped him. My relationship with him was very good, also. They spoiled me rotten, because the royalties would come in, and they'd hold them—they were administering for my stuff. I recall saying, 'Howard, I'm trying to figure out my budget until June. Can you tell me what I might receive by then?' And he says, 'Well, I've got about forty grand right now. Do you want it?' They used to pay me every time there was money there. I

wasn't even thinking about taking advantage, because I wouldn't spend all that money, but if I got into a jam or trying to figure out how I was going to live until this point, they'd say, 'OK, you can take this.'

I got checks a bunch of different times during the year, when it was there, as opposed to the normal procedure: *we hold it for six months and then pay you twice a year*. Which happened when they were out of the way, and then I was getting royalties from PolyGram. They were very nice to me on the phone, but if I needed something earlier, Gene would say, 'OK, just give him the money and take it out of my share, and take it back out when the royalties come in.' So PolyGram would advance me money on his say-so, because *they* were holding the money now, not any management company.

Besides songwriting, you were friends with both Gene *and* Paul at the time— which you said was uncommon.

They had their separate lives. I mean, I'm the guy who actually picked the *Lick It Up* album cover photo. I was at Paul's house, socializing. This was before he had the apartment on Madison Avenue—he had a little place where Tom Snyder lived, on 52nd Street, by the East River, that he was renting. I think Bob Kulick used to rent it, also. But in New York, they had this rule—if you had a primary residence, you can't have another one. The landlord found out later, when he had the place on Madison, and then we'd go hang out at the other one—watching TV and stuff like that.

So I come in one night, and the cover photos from the photo session for *Lick It Up* are there. And the big giant C-prints are strewn all over the living room—on tables and on the couch—and he's going over all the shots from the sessions. And Gene's on the phone, and I'm on the phone—I'm in the bathroom, on one of those big, giant, long curly cords. Paul's in the living room and I'm in the bathroom, and all of a sudden I yell, 'I've got it! I've got the cover!' Because Gene had copies of the same photos at his apartment. I come out and show Paul: 'Look at this photo. What is different about this photo, that tells you who the band is? I know this generic taking off the makeup … you want to look like a regular rock'n'roll band.' And Vinnie and Eric are standing on phonebooks, and Vinnie is wearing a wig, because his hair when it got wet would fall down on his face, and look like a drowned rat—as Paul said. And then Paul would hold his cheeks and pull them down, like a big basset hound.

So I say, 'What is different about this photo? What is the one piece of KISS paraphernalia you can never remove, but would give you a hint as to who the hell the band is? *The tongue!*' And I picked the cover. Gene told me, 'The photographer said, *OK, I have one more shot*, and I stuck my tongue out.' And *that* became the cover. Out of all the other photos, there's no tongue, there's no mugging, there's all this serious stuff/trying to be rock stars. And then … Gene sticks his tongue out.

How would you compare writing songs with Gene and writing songs with Paul?
The two of them have different styles. Gene is the sort of guy that, when a title pops into his head or a thought, he writes it in a book—it's like a book of titles. So, we were at my apartment on 74th Street with my first wife, and she's sitting in the other room. She actually over the years has come up with a couple of titles. This time, we were talking about doing songs, and a song that wound up on a Keel record, KISS actually recorded a basic version of, and Paul changed it. I was all pissed off about it, because he changed it into a Rolling Stone song—which he didn't use. But instead of being pissed, I said, 'You know what? I have another song here … *so who cares?*'

So Gene and I were talking about, and my wife said, 'Sooner said than done.' And we wrote it down, and it turned into Keel's 'Easier Said Than Done' [from their 1985 release *The Right To Rock*, which Gene produced]. Which I didn't like, because there was already a song called 'Easier Said Than Done' [a pop hit from 1963, by The Essex]—but you can't copyright titles. So it was originally 'Sooner Said Than Done,' and Gene didn't like it, because he thought it should be *no sooner said than done*. And then he just came up with 'Easier Said Than Done.' When you listen to Keel sing it, it doesn't roll off the tongue to me. But big deal—it's a great song, Keel recorded it, I was happy.

Gene would throw things out, to see what would stick on the wall. Titles. He had a whole book of lines or song ideas or something that goes through your head. And sometimes, they would manifest to me—I'd start writing music to it, and we'd figure out the choruses later on. So we would do these things—on the song lyric list to 'Easier Said Than Done,' there is a song called

'What You See Is What You Get,' and it's still never been used. There's a demo of it up on my page. I can't tell you how many KISS fans said, 'Why they hell didn't they record this?' Well, that's going to be on my upcoming album, the one that Gene and I were talking about [at the time of this book's release].

So he would write stuff and throw things out—that's how Gene would write. Just seeing if it stuck. Change it, whatever. The songs I wrote with him, usually the music was mine, and that lyrics sheet, when he looked at it, Gene said, 'I can't feel comfortable taking half the writer's share on this'—because we both have the same handwriting, so whatever gaps I had, he'd fill in with three or four words. I said, 'I'll tell you what. You know how you got the publishing on the first album, and I just got the writer's share? I'll do it this way—give me my writer's share and half the publishing, and I'm still making more money than the last time.' He said OK, but the song still didn't make it on the album. He was very reasonable with that sort of stuff.

Now, writing with Paul, 'Get All You Can Take,' I probably have the long legal pad that you see in lawyer's offices—the yellow-lined paper—when we did that song, it was literally 'Taxi' by Harry Chapin. Twelve verses, and I wrote them all, and then we just edited it down. But Paul was more introspective and 'thought process.' So we would do these lyrics, and I would edit them later. As I said before, he let me play on his albums on guitar, so he had faith in me for coming up with more ideas. 'Get All You Can Take' started off a song that I called 'Only Fools And Englishmen Go Out In The Midday Sun,' and it was a slower, AC/DC-sort-of-paced thing. Then he came to me, and said, 'Listen to *this*.' We were at SIR, the two of us—I'm on drums, he's on guitar—and he turned it into what we hear now. But the verses [were] very introspective.

I remember him telling me once—he, Billy Squier, and I were sitting together—'I don't understand how you can be yourself, and just let that stuff out there, and be so personal.' Because he had created this persona, and for him, it was hard to just be *Paul Stanley*. What KISS fans saw was that creation. But it started to come through when he started to write stuff like 'I Still Love You,' *Paul Stanley* started to emerge. But the other stuff was that character, or the KISS Paul Stanley. We would have these discussions about … how you do that. I said, 'Well, I haven't figured out who I am yet, so I write with everybody else, so I can be a chameleon.' Because I have so much stuff inside me, I love writing other stuff—all kinds of stuff. But with Paul, it was much more personal, digging into it. And I've got to tell you, there are some great verses that were never used. But that's why I said it was like 'Taxi'—it just went on and on and on. But we paired it down to three or four verses, so that was a nice process on his end.

What do you recall about co-writing 'Murder In High Heels' with Gene?
Gene would come over to my little second apartment on 74th Street and we would write there. Toni, my first wife, was a photographer, and she took pictures that ended up as the police photos of Luther in *Runaway*, when they show a quick scan of him from his file of arrest pictures. But he's still there, and I've got the demo of the song playing on the Portastudio, and he said, 'We need a lyric here.' And I just went, '*You know she could, she's a get rich bitch, you better get her while the getting's good.*' He said, 'Write that down!' Because we were just in the mood of writing like a guy like that. We would just sing and see what comes out, and a lot of times a line would come out completely.

When the song on *Monster* came out, 'Eat Your Heart Out,' he just used the title, but no lyrical idea of ours even showed up in this thing. So the title is what meant the most to him. The song still stands—and these are the things that I will record, that didn't make it anywhere. And like I said, that 'What You See Is What You Get' song is the one that got away, as far as the KISS guys are concerned. When Gene and I would do demos, we would have Drumdrops or prerecorded drum tracks. Gene—very wisely, from *Creatures* on—had Eric's drums run off separately for backing tracks, to write songs to. So the demo for 'What You See Is What You Get' is actually the 'Lick It Up' drum track, which I altered slightly. The fills all come in at weird places, but they actually sound amazing. And we would write to Eric's drums for other albums and other songs. There are a bunch of tracks like that.

You also appeared on an episode of MTV's *Heavy Metal Mania*—which Paul hosted—in 1985.
We were close, and Paul said, 'Would you want to come on this show? I'm going to have all these women at the apartment. It's going to be a fun gig—a sight gag.' That's how I came up with, *we're going to have beer, we're going*

to have pizza … and Paul McCartney! Or is it? And MTV put a disclaimer: 'PAUL McCARTNEY??!!! (This guy isn't fooling anyone!)' But we had a lot of fun doing it. There are fun outtakes, where we are talking on the couch, we start play fighting and fall over backward over the couch. I just ad-libbed that whole thing about, 'I've got them in crates.'

How is Paul in real life, compared to his KISS persona from back in the 80s?

If you listen to interviews with him in the past, where he seems a little bit more subdued, that's the Paul Stanley that I know. Plus he was also very funny. But he was not the guy in the videos—not the flamboyant guy. We were in New York City once, traveling, and we were in a Porsche, and we were doing a U-turn on 57th Street. I always felt secure with him, and I said, 'I want to thank you for driving really well when I was in the car.' And he said, 'Well, I have very precious cargo in this car.' And I go, 'Well, thank you.' And he goes. '*No, not you. Me.*' [*Laughs*]

In New York, Cafe Central was a place that was on Amsterdam Avenue and 75th. It eventually turned into a much bigger place. And a girl that I knew in high school, we reconnected, and she said, 'Let's go there for drinks.' And I'm noticing we're in this restaurant, and at that table is Al Pacino talking with Robert De Niro, and Robert Duvall. And then you've got Robin Williams at another table, and this guy and that guy at that table. So, by the time I started to go with Paul there, these guys all knew me! I walk in, and De Niro goes, 'Hi Mitch.' Paul goes, '*You know them, too?*'

Was there ever talk of writing with Gene and Paul again? And didn't you almost write with Bon Jovi around this time, on a recommendation from Paul?

Things took them in a different direction, and then I went somewhere else. Gene moved to Los Angeles, so the *come over and see what you got* thing didn't happen. I think my attention kind of waned on that front, too. Paul and I were still friendly at that point—I just think he was into something else at that point in time.

After *Animalize*, I get a phone call from Richie Sambora and Jon Bon Jovi on conference call: 'We'd like to write with you. Paul Stanley suggested writers for our next project, and your and Desmond Child's names came up.'

Desmond had songs on *Animalize*, and so did I. I remember when we went to pick up the gold and platinum albums, Paul said, 'Can we take them to your apartment?' I said sure, and Desmond picked us up to go to this showcase, and I got the albums, and took them back to my apartment—where those albums stayed in my house *forever*.

The way that ended was, I was going through a tough period with my marriage at the time. I realized this was not the right time to do it, so, thinking logically and practically, I had money coming in—thousands of dollars—I thought, *I can take some time off.* And they totally understood that, because they weren't the hugest guys yet, at that point in time. But they understood the personal thing of, *I like you guys, and I thank Paul for recommending me and I thank you guys for calling me, but I'm going to have to turn it down, because I need to spend some time on this marriage. We've been together for eight years, and I'm going to take some time off.*

The joke—the *cosmic* joke—is that at end of these eight or nine months, we called it quits, and Bon Jovi's album *Slippery When Wet* comes out, and sells how many millions of copies, and Desmond is all over the place—and turns into 'Sir Desmond.' [*Laughs*] *And I have nothing.* I laugh about it. I say, 'I turned it down for love, the love didn't work out.' Would I have had anything on that album? You don't know. But my ex-wife apologized to my years later—she was like, 'I guess you should have done that record, huh?'

Do you still see royalties from your songwriting with KISS?

Now, they're small as hell. With streaming, I got a couple of checks for three cents or four cents! But I saw those royalties for the longest time, and then they trickled down to a hundred bucks or two hundred bucks a year. Because none of my songs were *radio-play* songs—they were always *album* songs. So some of the stuff has come back again, because of streaming.

Are you still in contact with Gene and Paul?

Gene yes, Paul no. And, as I said, this record that I'm thinking about doing—recording the songs that we wrote but didn't go anywhere, of the KISS demos and the songwriter version of the songs that KISS recorded, Gene said, 'That's the one I'm interested in. When you have that lined up, *call me.*'

KNOW THE SCORE: RICHARD CHRISTY

The *Howard Stern Show* writer, and drummer with Charred Walls Of The Damned, Iced Earth, and Death talks about how *Animalize* was an important album for him growing up.

How did you discover KISS, and how did you get into the *Animalize* album?

I discovered KISS when I was just five years old. My aunt Theresa gave me *Alive!* and Peter Criss's solo album on vinyl—for my fifth birthday. I was just always drawn to Gene Simmons, because I saw a picture of him in some magazine, spitting out blood, and I was really into horror movies—even as a really little kid. So, right away, I wanted to know more about KISS. And I had a really cool aunt, who knew about music, and I think my parents told her that I liked KISS and I thought Gene Simmons was scary, so she got these albums for my birthday, and I loved it right away.

I had one of those old record players that was a little box that you open up, covered in blue jean material. I'd play *Alive!* pretty much every day—all day—when I was a kid. Then in 1984, when I was ten, I had just started playing drums in the school band—because I was starting fifth grade, and that was the first year that they offered music at school. So I picked drums, because I had heard Van Halen's 'Hot For Teacher,' was blown away, and decided that I had to learn how to do that. Unfortunately, I still don't know how the hell to play the drum intro to 'Hot For Teacher'—it's *still* a work in progress. But I heard 'Heaven's On Fire' on the radio, and just the drumbeat and the chorus and the catchiness of it, I immediately loved it, and went out and bought the cassette. I think that was the third cassette that I ever bought—right behind Quiet Riot's *Metal Health* and Twisted Sister's *Stay Hungry*.

What were your initial thoughts on *Animalize*?

I thought it was really heavy. For KISS, that's a pretty heavy album—the way it starts out, and Eric Carr's double bass [drum] work throughout the album is really good. It had some pretty fast songs for KISS. And 'Heaven's On Fire' is probably the most mainstream song, but there are a lot of other really heavy songs on that album, and I really like that about that album. And when I heard it, at that point I was ten years old, and had yet to discover thrash metal, so hearing *Animalize* was kind of a bridge for me—to go from regular music into heavier stuff.

Eric Carr's drumming on *Animalize* is excellent. He was so tasty, too—like the chorus on 'Heaven's On Fire,' he does this little tom thing, and it's just *so* cool. The second drumbeat I ever learned was 'Heaven's On Fire'—right after I learned the intro to Slade's 'Cum On Feel The Noize,' which is one of the easier drumbeats. So Eric Carr is definitely a huge influence on me—I always thought he was a real tasteful drummer. He let the song shine, but he also had moments where he would show what he could do. It was just incredible. And he was so cool-looking, too—he had the biggest-looking drum sets in the world. Being a ten-year-old kid and seeing Eric Carr on MTV, that was a dream drum kit to play. He probably had a twenty-piece drum kit in every video they did, and live! I just thought that he was *so* cool, that he was really solid, and just an amazing drummer.

Did you practice to *Animalize* on drums?
Oh yeah, absolutely. At the time, I didn't have a double bass pedal, so I was kind of limited. But that's what made me want to play double bass—hearing Alex Van Halen and Eric Carr, and then I heard 'Fast As A Shark' by Accept right around then. I was like, *Wow. I've got to save up money to buy another bass drum.* So, Eric Carr really inspired me to want to play double bass. And I think some of his drum kits, he even has *four or five* bass drums—which was mind-blowing.

But yeah, I used to put that cassette on. Even before I had my own drum set, my buddy had a drum set, and I was always super-jealous he had this nice Tama drum set. I'd go over to his house and sit in his room while he was watching TV, and I'd play 'Heaven's On Fire' over and over again, because I was able to figure that one out. And of course, I loved that song, because it was such a catchy song.

On *Animalize*, Paul Stanley wrote several songs with Desmond Child—'I've Had Enough,' 'Heaven's On Fire,' and 'Under The Gun' …
Well, if you're writing with Desmond Child, you know it's going to be good! That guy is incredible. Anytime anybody would work with him … like Alice

Cooper worked with him on the *Trash* album—the song 'Poison,' which I loved right away. If you listen to a lot of 80s metal, you can tell Desmond Child's style. He has this cool, real catchy style—that's also pretty heavy. I was always excited whenever anybody would work with him. Even as young as I was, I recognized the name, and I was like, *Oh, this will be good! Desmond Child's name is on it.*

What's interesting is, Desmond Child is best known for his 'pop-metal' writing with Bon Jovi, but he also co-wrote some of the heaviest songs on *Animalize*. Yeah, totally. And I remember really liking 'Burn Bitch Burn,' because I was a little kid, and hearing a dirty word in a song right away made me like it! I remember that and 'Dick In The Dirt' by Sammy Hagar were two of my favorite songs, that I was playing for my friends. I'm like, *Can you believe they're saying this?* But definitely, the lyrics on *Animalize* haven't aged well with the time—they are very un-politically correct. But they are still fun to listen to.

As a kid, hearing that stuff, I thought I was getting away with something—hearing lyrics like that. I was so young when I heard those songs, I just thought they were funny, because they were so dirty. I was too young to get the sexual message out of them. I didn't really know the meaning of them—I just thought they were funny.

A funny little story about when I was in sex-ed. class in high school, and this song isn't on *Animalize*, but the song 'Uh! All Night,' my sex-education teacher said, 'Bring in a song about sex and we will dissect and discuss the lyrics.' So I brought in 'Uh! All Night.' The teacher just shook her head and couldn't believe it. She goes, 'You know it's not physically possible to actually *uh all night*, right?' And I was like, 'Well … *I bet KISS can do it.*' So we argued about whether Gene Simmons could last all night or not. A lot of KISS lyrics, you can't really take them at face value. You can't really take them too seriously.

Let's discuss some of your favorite songs on *Animalize*.
The first song is really heavy: 'I've Had Enough (Into The Fire).' It's got kind of a cool double bass beat, and it's a really heavy way to start the album. It's

got a great chorus, cool riffs, and I remember as soon as I heard it, I said, 'Oh … this is going to be a cool album! This is going to be *heavy*.' I liked it right away.

Since you're an Eric Carr fan, what did you think of the song 'Under The Gun,' which he co-wrote?

I love that one, too. I remember back in the cassette days, they'd usually put a really good song for the first song of the second side. And I remember sometimes, I'd fast-forward to the second side, so I could hear that song, because I loved it. It was really heavy. And it's a cool title too, 'Under The Gun.' And there was 'Under The Blade' [by Twisted Sister]—I think there's been a few 'Under The *Somethings*.'

'Under The Gun' is a cool title and has a cool chorus—but it's heavy, too. I really like that KISS went through their disco phase and were just kind of 'rock'n'roll' in the 70s, but then, in the 80s, they got heavier. I think they saw what was going on around them, and kind of adapted to that. I think their heaviest was when they did 'Unholy' in the early 90s. I love when they surprise people and do pretty heavy stuff.

And what did you think of album's second single, 'Thrills In The Night'?

That one I don't remember being as into, but I remember it was a really catchy song. I kind of wore out side one with 'I've Had Enough' and 'Heaven's On Fire.' But side two had some really good stuff on it, too. I just remember it was really catchy, and probably could have been a hit. I guess 'Heaven's On Fire' was the only real hit song off that album. I don't know why.

The album closes with 'While The City Sleeps' and 'Murder In High Heels' …

I lived out in the country, in Redfield, Kansas, so any song about the mystique of the big city, I loved … I loved hearing KISS sing about 'Detroit Rock City' and any songs they sang about a city. I had only dreamt of going to a city that had more than fifty people in it—because I grew up in the middle of nowhere. I definitely loved that song.

And 'Murder In High Heels,' I'm a big fan of horror movies, so any song about murder—although I don't remember that's what it's about. Since it has 'high heels' in it, I'm sure they were writing about sex. Any song that mentions 'murder'—I love *Halloween* and *A Nightmare On Elm Street* and all those movies. As a ten-year-old, I was like, *Oh, here's a song with murder in the title ... I have to hear it immediately!*

How do you think *Animalize* holds up, listening to it again all these years later?
I think the music holds up great. The songs are really good—they're heavy. The lyrics don't really hold up for today's political climate, but to me, they remind me of my youth and the kind of risqué nature of the lyrics and being a ten-year-old hearing them sing about sex ... Gene Simmons and Paul Stanley could be considered two of my sex-education teachers! I learned a lot of what I know from those guys and their lyrics, through songs like 'Burn Bitch Burn,' 'Heaven's On Fire,' 'Uh! All Night,' 'Let's Put The X In Sex,' and 'Lick It Up.'

I don't get offended by anything, so lyrics don't bother me. The production, I think, could be a little better. I'd love for Eric Carr's drums to have been louder. On *Creatures Of The Night*, the drums were way up in the front of the mix. I don't think the drums were as loud on *Animalize*. Being a drummer and a fan of Eric Carr, the drums could have been louder for me. But 1984 was a great year for metal, and that was an awesome album. It definitely shaped who I am as a musician and as a music fan. *Animalize* could be up in my top-five all-time favorite KISS albums.

ANIMALIZE: THE TOUR WITH CURT GOOCH

X-rated stage raps. Stage costumes displaying animal print or fur. Gene, Paul, and Bruce riding a lighting truss from high above the stage. All were included in one of the most successful tours of the non-makeup era—for *Animalize*!

For *Animalize*, KISS went to a new production company, Tait Towers, and they designed this really sleek, metal-looking stage that I think served them very well for that tour. I'm talking about the North American leg—for Europe, they just reused the *Unmasked* stage with new set dressing on it. But for North America, they really had a brilliant new stage, which was simplistic but it looked cool. There were ramps that they could run up and down, and they were energetic. I think it was a very good tour, and I think it was also probably KISS's strongest period.

At the end of their set, KISS would perform 'Black Diamond,' and they had designed a lighting rig where a ramp would descend from the lighting rig, the band would ascend up a ramp and then come down on a hexagon or diamond-shaped platform that would descend from the lighting rig and bring them back down to the stage. It looked beautiful on TV, and it looked great in the 'Thrills In The Night' video. It seemed to work—I don't recall any other band from that period doing that. It was very *KISS-like*.

And what people tend to forget is, the last show of the *Animalize* tour was the last time—to this day—that the vintage KISS logo that had been used from *Love Gun* through *Animalize* was ever seen. And nobody knows what's happened to it. With *Animalize*, they went with animal designs and patterns on outfits. It looked good onstage—for the time, at least.

When the *Animalize* tour started in Brighton, England [on September 30, 1984], it was definitely an *Animalize*-heavy setlist. As it should be—because *Animalize* was a point where the songwriting unquestionably shifted, and Paul became the dominant songwriter. You could make an argument that that happened slightly with *Lick It Up*, but Gene did have some credible material on that. And that was mainly due to the fact that he was phoning it in, because he was involved in the production of *Runaway* at that point.

I believe they opened that first show with 'I've Had Enough (Into The Fire),' which I have always thought is easily one of KISS's top-five best non-makeup songs. It's *really* a strong number. And that song—for whatever reason—I don't know if it made it all the way through the European leg or barely into the US leg, but I know that was dropped at some point. I think they even did 'Get All You Can Take' at the first show, but I think that was gone after that. And I forgot 'Burn Bitch Burn' was also played early in the tour—I can't believe they actually played that live. It's funny, because what works in 2018 is obviously not what worked in 1984, and it's funny that they actually tried to pull that off live.

But like on the two tours previous, KISS obviously believed in themselves, believed in the songwriting. And the setlist was very *Creatures*-through-

Animalize-heavy. That changed a little bit over the course of the tour, but not much. When they got to America, they knew they were going to be filming a video for 'Thrills In The Night,' so they did briefly add it into the setlist for a couple of shows in December, just prior to the December 8 gig in Detroit. I think after that, it just did not sound good live, so they dropped that immediately thereafter.

Players that would come into the fold later on would play a prominent role in KISStory at that point, where Doc McGhee—who was successfully managing Mötley Crüe, and had already been able to secure them a spot opening for KISS on the *Creatures* tour—came back with Bon Jovi, and was able to do the same thing, through ATI booking. And Bon Jovi went out and did one of their first tours—they went out with the Scorpions first [in the USA], but I think the KISS tour in Europe was Bon Jovi's first European outing. From what I understand, they were very well received by the audience, and people seemed to like them. It's funny that there was one show somewhere on the *Animalize* tour [October 24, at the Olympen in Lund, Sweden], where Bon Jovi couldn't play—because the stage was so small, they said, 'We don't have room for an opening act.'

Starting with *Lick It Up*, to an extent, but definitely by *Animalize* and *Asylum*, Paul had developed these stage raps that today, are just absolutely *laughable*. And he will tell you the same thing, by the way. He completely agrees. I think he is absolutely embarrassed by those stage raps. But at the time they had a mainly teenage audience, and all that stuff was considered cool, and every other band—for the most part—was doing something similar to that, as well. So they weren't completely out of line with what their peers were doing. But now, it's hilarious.

Even by *Hot In The Shade*, where it had been toned down dramatically, when the *Kissology* DVDs came out, they actually do a lot of censoring of f-bombs and stuff on there—for the Auburn Hills show. It just goes to show you how things changed, because there was a period of time in the 70s … I think [original manager] Bill Aucoin would have *killed* somebody if they cursed onstage! That was never going to happen. Can you imagine, on *Dynasty*, if they were dropping f-bombs with all those little kids there? It would have been a nightmare.

When 'Heaven's On Fire' came out on MTV, the video was actually featured in commercials: they announced the world premiere of the video was pending, and counted down it was next week, later that week, today ... they really went out of their way. And that was an 'MTV Exclusive Sneak Preview' video at the time—which meant that, for thirty days, no other outlet was going to be able to play it. And MTV did put that into heavy rotation, and it did very well for them. Sadly, they were not able to recapture that with 'Thrills In The Night'—which I actually think is a stronger song.

But the tour did really well. And then, in January, MTV aired a *Saturday Night Concert* with KISS from the previous month in Detroit. And that, I think, was another highpoint for the tour. I'm sure that helped ticket sales, because people could get a little preview on MTV, and then they'd go see the real thing.

Animalize was also interesting in the sense that nobody really knew who was in the band. There was a weekly TV series at the time called *Night Flight*, and inside of *Night Flight* there was a half-hour show called *Hit Parader's Heavy Metal Heroes*, and it was first announced on there, in December of '84, that Bruce Kulick was an official member of the band, and Mark St. John was out.

The other thing that people tend to forget about at that moment in time is Winterland Productions—the merchandising company out of San Francisco—worked out a deal with KISS to do merchandising on their next two tours, and gave them a two-million-dollar advance for the privilege. Because of this, there was more KISS memorabilia during the *Animalize* period than at any other time during the non-makeup years. There was actually *a lot* of *Animalize* memorabilia. But they really went all-out for that period.

I think, by the time KISS started *Animalize* and the tour finished, in late March of 1985, they had really gained some serious ground. They were there all of a sudden—they were on the scene. I still think it was building at that point. So *Animalize* was a productive tour for KISS.

GIMME MORE: KATHERINE TURMAN ON MISOGYNY IN METAL

The longtime rock journalist and co-author of *Louder Than Hell: The Definitive Oral History of Heavy Metal* discusses the disturbing trend of misogyny in metal lyrics during the 80s.

Listening back to KISS's non-makeup-era albums today, it's hard not to note that some of their song's lyrics—particularly some of the songs written by Gene—are misogynistic. Perhaps the most obvious example is 'Burn Bitch Burn' from *Animalize*, but also 'Dance All Over Your Face' from *Lick It Up* and 'Domino' from *Revenge*.

It's funny—'Domino' is a song I really liked, musically. And when I heard the line, '*That bitch bends over, and I forget my name*,' I laughed, because I thought he was so lame, silly, and juvenile with it. To me, it was funny—I didn't take offense. But I still thought it was ridiculous. So, not offensive—just lame. And of course, over the years, I've had many encounters with Gene—I even wrote for his *Tongue* magazine, back in the day. But, yeah, that's my feeling about 'Domino.' And I'll ask you … I'm not a huge KISS fan, but I know a fair amount about them—did the lyrics not start becoming misogynistic until this era?

It seemed like in the 80s is when some of Gene's lyrics plummeted to *Spinal Tap*-worthy depths.

Right. [*Laughs*] And that's the thing—I can't really take it seriously, because it is *so Spinal Tap*-y, as it were. I guess there is a reason why a lot of women—or girls, teenagers—didn't love KISS, and it was always like a *guy's band*. Because we didn't want to be dressed-up superheroes. I hate to say that's a difference in the sexes … or maybe because we wanted to be Wonder Woman, I don't know. So that's my take on KISS—they were never to really be taken seriously. Now, they're sixty-year-old men up there in tights, so it's really hard to be insulted. That said, I've had instances with Gene that were annoying and frustrating.

What are your thoughts on the lyrics to 'Dance All Over Your Face' and 'Burn Bitch Burn'?

I have the lyrics to 'Dance All Over Your Face' in front of me. Of course, he calls *her* a bitch. He's the thwarted man, which I think is kind of cool—he's being played, and she's cheating on him. So I applaud that. [*Laughs*] I don't applaud him. I guess you would say 'Dance All Over Your Face' is a threat?

The thing that also strikes me about those lyrics is that they are hypocritical on Gene's part. He was always bragging about sleeping with many women, but if someone cheats on him ... he has a problem with that.

Right. I guess I hadn't thought of that—but that is very accurate. So, no, I guess I'm glad that it happened, the story in this song—that he's disgraced. Because, certainly, that's not a position that he would ever expect to be in—given his ego. That made me think that 'Dance All Over Your Face' may also have a sexual connotation, or the physical punching in the face connotation—which led me to think of 'Pearl Necklace' by ZZ Top. But then I read those lyrics, and I realized that the woman is asking for it in that song. So, it's got a sexual connotation, but she's like, 'I want a pearl necklace,' and he's like, 'Oh, you're a weirdo.' [*Laughs*] I never really realized who the point of view was in that—so, I guess that saves ZZ Top, in that case. But in this case, I think there is no saving it.

And what about the lyrics to 'Burn Bitch Burn'?

'*I want to put my log in your fireplace*'—again, it's hysterical. It's *better* than *Spinal Tap*! It's really hard for me to take any of this seriously, and I am not offended—because I would laugh in their face, and they would be humiliated. I guess it's misogynistic, but I wouldn't take it seriously.

To be fair, KISS were not the only metal band of the era to offer up misogynistic lyrics—Mötley Crüe's 'Live Wire' and Guns N' Roses' 'It's So Easy' come to mind.

It's funny—I saw Guns N' Roses a lot in the early days, and was a big fan of the first record [1987's *Appetite For Destruction*]. Not to be a traitor to my gender, but I loved the way Axl sings those lines, '*Besides, you ain't got nothing better to do / And I'm bored.*' I just love his sass in that. So that doesn't bother me that much.

I think it's more like: words don't bother me. That said, Guns N' Roses did apparently follow it up with actions, because at that time—in the late 80s—Axl was accused of rape, and he had to go in hiding. Do you know about that story?

Yes, that was the lyrical basis for the song 'Out Ta Get Me,' concerning an incident with Axl, right? (Note: these allegations are further detailed in the book *It's So Easy And Other Lies* by GnR bassist Duff McKagan.)
Yeah, I do believe. So, I would say his actions make the words mean a little more. On its own, I think 'It's So Easy' is kind of a good, snotty, rock'n'roll song. But then if the person who wrote those lyrics gets into trouble for treating women really badly, then that casts it in a new light. On its own, it doesn't bother me that much, but when it's tied to a creator who may be misogynistic, then it's bothersome. But I think action and words have to both come together, for me.

And then, of course, a lot of rap artists have been accused of misogyny over the years ...
Yes. I have interviewed Ice-T, who was both metal and rap, and we talked about his Body Count song, 'Bitch In The Pit,' and he tried to spin it as using 'bitch' as an empowering term, and I think he said how it was a true story of how he looked into a mosh pit at a Body Count show, he saw a woman in there, and said, 'Shit! There's a bitch in the pit!' And how cool he thought it was that a woman was getting out there in a mosh pit at a hardcore-metal show. So, this was before #MeToo and everything, and I suppose I missed my chance to jump in and say, 'Would you call your wife and daughter a bitch?' I'm afraid the answer would probably be yes. [*Laughs*] Some kind of term of endearment from him.

Was it ever difficult for you, as a female, to look past the lyrics of certain metal songs that could be interpreted as misogynistic?
No, not really. I remember, again, going to see Poison in the early days. I was slightly offended by the song 'Unskinny Bop.' I don't know if it was so much the words as what I understood it to be about—which was counting up the number of fat chicks you could sleep with. I think they did a spin years later,

where they said, 'No. That's not what it was about.' But that kind of sleeping with women just to get your numbers up, as part of a contest sort of thing—which they could do, because they were rock stars—*did* offend me. And then, to talk about it and/or write about it, I found pretty revolting. In that case, that perturbed me a little bit.

Again, I hate to say this, but most of it is so stupid and brainless that it's hardly worth consideration. It's kind of what you expect, almost, from Mötley Crüe and bands of that ilk. If Bob Dylan did that, I'd say it would be a different story, because he is more of a serious songwriter and storyteller, and he's someone you take seriously. Unfortunately, in the big, wide world, I don't think KISS is taken seriously as a threat to feminism.

Why do you think these types of lyrics and sentiments were considered acceptable in heavy metal and pop culture at the time, but would not be now? That's interesting—I guess you would say times have changed. It's shocking that within not quite our lifetime—but close—that women got the right to vote. When I look back on it and think that, within my mother's lifetime, women hardly had any rights, and birth control wasn't even invented—to me, that sort of thing is just shocking. So I guess times have changed, and women have gained more agency over their bodies, and feel more comfortable speaking out. That time passed, obviously.

Most people say that grunge or Nirvana killed hair metal—which is in a book in and of itself, probably. But I think that Kurt Cobain wearing a dress and being sympathetic to women and talking about an abortion medicine, 'Pennyroyal Tea'—and with alternative musicians in the early 90s, and the culture and riot grrrls—I think that began the conversation, and the feeling that women were going to fight back. And it just wasn't acceptable anymore.

CREATURES OF THE NIGHT

Originally released October 13, 1982. Re-released July 15, 1985.
Produced by Michael James Jackson, Paul Stanley, and Gene
Simmons; three tracks remixed by Dave Wittman for the '85 edition.
US #45, UK #22 (original release). US certification: gold.

SIDE ONE

Creatures Of The Night (Paul Stanley/Adam Mitchell)
Killer (Gene Simmons/Vinnie Vincent)
Keep Me Comin (Stanley/Mitchell)
Rock And Roll Hell (Simmons/Bryan Adams/Jim Vallance)
Danger (Stanley/Mitchell)

SIDE TWO

I Love It Loud (Simmons/Vincent)
I Still Love You (Stanley/Vincent)
Saint And Sinner (Simmons/Mikel Japp)
War Machine (Simmons/Adams/Vallance)

SINGLES

I Love It Loud / Danger (1982, US only, #102)
Killer / I Love It Loud (1982, UK only, did not chart)
Creatures Of The Night / Rock And Roll All Nite (live) (1983, UK only, #34)

★

Some of you may be wondering … just what the heck is a *makeup-era* KISS recording originally released in 1982 doing here? Well, the answer is simple. For the unenlightened: in 1985, sensing that there was a sudden demand for all things KISS in the wake of the platinum success of *Animalize*, Mercury Records decided to re-release the woefully underappreciated *Creatures Of The Night*.

In a crafty move, the original front cover image of four blokes in makeup was now replaced by a more recent, non-makeup pic of the group atop a building with a sunset behind them, as well as a new back cover image (the original 'lightning in the sky' pic replaced by a close-up of someone's tuchus—it's unclear whether it is a man or a woman—in a pair of skintight leather trousers). The other thing that differentiates the original and the re-release is the flip-flopping of two songs from side A to side B ('Saint And Sinner' and 'Killer'), as well as the inclusion of 'remixes' of three songs—the opening title track, 'I Love It Loud,' and 'War Machine'—by Dave Wittman.

The reason I put the word remixes in quotes is because there is barely any difference between how those three tracks sound here and how they did on the original album. When 'I Love It Loud' was remixed once again for the 1988 collection *Smashes, Thrashes & Hits*, it was clearly different (and not in a good way, as all the power from Eric Carr's massive drum kit was completely muffled). Here? The difference is barely detectable. And it's never been properly explained why it was necessary to switch the order of the tracks, as there was nothing wrong with the flow of the original tracklisting.

Now, I've saved the most sly bit for last—replacing the original shot of Ace, Eric, Gene, and Paul with a shot of Bruce, Eric, Gene, and Paul. In other words, both times KISS had an opportunity to include a cover image showing who the heck *truly* played guitar on the *Creatures* album, the ball was fumbled, as Bruce never played on the original recording … and quite possibly neither did Ace, for that matter! The updated, non-makeup cover was for one reason and one reason only—to fool a newly acquired KISS fan into believing that this was a brand new album.

As far as the strength of the material is concerned, however, *Creatures* is undoubtedly one of KISS's best—and *heaviest*—releases. Even the album's sole ballad ('I Still Love You') has a super-heavy part toward the end. *Creatures* was also the first KISS album on which Simmons and Stanley were the only official band members to handle songwriting duties, albeit with a gaggle of outside songwriting help—Adam Mitchell, Mikel Japp (whose name was last spotted by KISS fans on Stanley's '78 solo album), Bryan Adams (yes, *that* Bryan Adams!), Jim Vallance, and Vinnie Cusano (who would soon be rechristened Vinnie Vincent). And with Ace largely MIA from the recording sessions—Gene and Paul claim he doesn't appear on the album at all, but Michael James Jackson says he did—various guitarists offered solos, including future Mr. Mister player Steve Farris (the title track), blues-jazz player Robben Ford ('Rock And Roll Hell' and 'I Still Love You'), and Vincent (the rest of the album).

With KISS's commitment to straight-ahead hard rock/heavy metal wavering during 1979–81 (*Dynasty* contained the disco smash 'I Was Made For Lovin' You,' *Unmasked* was a pop album, and *Music From The Elder* was a lyrically and musically hard-to-digest concept album), the band made the very wise decision to return to 'the metal' on their tenth studio album. And, as I mentioned previously, this resulted in an incredibly strong and consistent listen from front-to-back, 100 percent filler-free, including one of KISS's all-time greatest anthems ('I Love It Loud'); the raging title track; one of Gene's best riff-rockers ('War Machine'); one of Paul's best-ever ballads (the aforementioned 'I Still Love You'); and tracks that, although largely forgotten, remain rockin' ('Saint And Sinner,' 'Keep Me Comin',' 'Rock And Roll Hell,' 'Danger,' and 'Killer').

But despite KISS's glorious return to form on *Creatures*, the record-buying public was not yet ready to forgive the band for their last few misfires. (Also, 1982 happened to be chock full of classic metal albums, including Iron Maiden's *The Number Of The Beast*, Judas Priest's *Screaming For Vengeance*, and Scorpions' *Blackout*, which may have led to *Creatures* getting lost in the shuffle somewhat.) As a result, the album performed far below expectations (managing to reach only #45 on the *Billboard* 200) and the ensuing North American tour (the group's first since 1979) failed to put bums on seats. So from that standpoint, with KISS reconnecting with old fans and/or gaining new ones in 1985, the re-release of *Creatures*, with the goal of introducing this stellar album to a new audience, made sense.

Alas, the re-release and the changes made to the album failed to create any excitement with the record-buying public at the time, as this 'new and improved' version did not even register on the album charts. Over the years, however, *Creatures* has been recognized as the classic album it so rightfully is among both KISS fans and metalheads—the proof being that the album has slowly continued to sell over the years, and was finally certified gold in 1994. Certainly, the re-release bolstered that sales figure.

KNOW THE SCORE: STEVE FARRIS

As well as playing the guitar solo on the title track to *Creatures Of The Night*, Farris tried out as Ace Frehley's replacement. Here, the Mr. Mister guitarist discusses how his KISS connection came about.

How did you get involved in working on *Creatures Of The Night*?

I was playing guitar with a band called The Mambo Jets. It was an original band with Kim Bullard, who is currently playing with Elton John. This was back in '82, and we were playing at a place called the Blue Lagoon Saloon in Marina Del Rey. It was a band that I was featured in and soloing in a lot, and one night I finished a set and walked off, and in the back of the room there was some tall guy standing there. He asked if I would be interested in auditioning for KISS. I'm thinking, *Let's see … I have a Volkswagen Rabbit that won't start unless I push it and pop the clutch, and I'm eating Campbell's Soup every day. Why the fuck wouldn't I want to audition for KISS?!* He said, 'You have the right look. Call this number.'

So I call some girl over in Hollywood, and I have to put together a tape of my playing. I get together with a guy named Tony Paluso, who was the guitar player in The Carpenters, and Tony had become a friend of mine because he was producing at the time, and he always got my guitars to sound just like me, without fucking with them too much. We're talking '82, so this is pre-digital. So I got together all these cassettes, went over to his house, and compiled a thing from songs I played on when I was living in Iowa, some demos in LA, live stuff—just all kinds of stuff that I thought was good playing. Put this compilation together, called the girl, went down to this office on Sunset and

Gower, and she listened to the tape while I was there … and was completely unimpressed. I thought, *That's another day in the life*, and I left there.

About two weeks later, I get a phone call … 'Is this Steve Farris? This is Paul Stanley from KISS. Gene and I listened to your tape last night and we really like it. We want to know if you want to come down to the Record Plant tomorrow—we're letting guys play on this record as sort of an audition.' I said sure—and that's how I started.

What are some memories of going down to the Record Plant?

I wanted to be a hotshot studio guy—a hired gun who could come in quick and be good. I'd been in the Record Plant before, but only late at night. This was the *old* Record Plant that has been torn down now—the Beverly Center sits where it was. There were four studios there. So I go down there, I walk down the hallway, and Tom Petty walks out of one room and into another. Luther Vandross is talking on the payphone. I go back to Studio D, I look through the sliding glass doors, and there's Gene Simmons and Paul Stanley standing there—of course, the first time I ever saw them without makeup. They're standing there, and there's another guy playing guitar, who happens to be Bob Kulick. So Bob is in there playing, and Michael James Jackson is sitting at the desk, producing.

They come in, and they're like, 'Hey man, how are you? Just sit out there—we have another guy playing now.' Finally, Bob comes out and I'm introduced to him. They bring me in, and Paul says, 'I've got a Marshall in the other room. Here's your cord.' I had brought in a volume pedal and something else, and my Valley Arts Strat. He said, 'This is in G, it's an eight-bar solo. We'll scroll up to the bridge and we'll count you in.' So they play the bridge, he gives me the hand signal, I play a take, and they say, 'Give me another take,' and I give them another take.

Gene stops the tape and says, 'Will you dye your hair black?' I go, 'Sure.' He goes, 'Can you wear high heels?' I said, 'I can give it a try.' He says, '*Don't cut your hair*,' and they start flipping out. Michael James Jackson looks up at me and says, 'You're happening, man.' Well, that's the solo that's on the record ['Creatures Of The Night']—the second take of an audition! There were no punches or nothing—that's just when it happened.

This is on, like, a Friday or Saturday. So, they say, 'We'll get together again next week. Don't change a thing.' So, I went the weekend, thinking, *Jesus Christ … I might have gotten the gig in KISS!* I go back and start playing with them more. Then they want to hear me play live with them—set up as a band and actually play. So we go to SIR, I have my gear rolled in, and we start to jam. Eric Carr is there, so it's Paul, Gene, Eric, and me. They say, 'We've got to hear you sing.' I think, *Oh shit. I'm going to sing right now and give it a shot and maybe get the gig … or I'm not going to, and not get the gig.*

So I have the dubious distinction of playing 'Honky Tonk Women' with KISS, with me singing lead vocals! If I had a video of anything, I wish I had *that*. [*Laughs*] We play 'Honky Tonk Women,' we play a little more … and then I never heard from again for weeks. [*Laughs*] Then I get a call out of the blue and it's Paul. He goes, 'Hey man, we decided you're not the right guy for the band, but we love your playing. So we want to hire you to do sessions.'

Mind you, this is the first actual record I'd ever played on. I went on to do a lot of records in my life, and had a pretty good session career. So I go down, and I keep playing guitar for them. And, meanwhile, I had auditioned for Eddie Money. One of my best memories of working with KISS was, I was down in the Record Plant on a Saturday, and I was playing with them until about 2:00, and then I had to split to fly out of LAX, because we were flying to Canada—to play my first gig with Eddie Money. So it was a time for me when all of this shit started happening.

But KISS, to this day … if I run into Paul Stanley or Gene Simmons, which over the years [has happened] many times, they'll start talking about that solo—'We played it for Eddie Van Halen!' and all that stuff. And the odd thing was, we started Mr. Mister, and after a while we became very successful. We were on the American Music Awards—this is 1986—and we were going to play our song that was going to become another #1 hit, which was 'Kyrie' … and there's Paul Stanley backstage. This is the first time I've talked to him since I auditioned for him. He goes, 'Hey Steve!' and gave me a big hug—like we're the best of brothers. 'Gene and I have been watching your career—we're so happy for you.' I was like, 'No shit? *You remember who I am?*' It was kind of a crazy moment. And Paul and I became buddies—we actually ran around together for a while in LA.

Was it just 'Creatures Of The Night' that you played the solo on, or did you play on other songs as well?

That's a question I should know the answer to … and I don't. I just never paid attention. I never played another solo on the record—I know that. But I was playing parts of different things, and, of course, Paul was playing a lot. The rest of it is kind of a blur. And, also, they didn't credit me for years—they just didn't do that. It was all ghost playing. Because a lot of guys played on that while they were auditioning. I didn't know Robben Ford played on it [the solos on the songs 'Rock And Roll Hell' and 'I Still Love You']—God, what a weird pairing. I'm a huge Robben Ford fan, but not in *that* context. And even if I listen to that record top to bottom, I don't know what they used. But that solo has a life of its own.

Did they pay you for that *Creatures* recording session?

They did. But that's part of the contractual thing that they have to do—because the record company is all signatories with the musicians' union, so if they release it, they've got to pay you something. It's not a negotiating deal. It was the first thing I ever got paid for legitimately.

How long after that experience with KISS did you join Mr. Mister?

Well, like I said, Eddie Money kind of overlapped, and then I took off with Eddie Money—which was my first big touring gig—and we did a tour that I want to say was August through Christmas of that year, '82. Then I came back off the road, and, like you do as a musician, you're constantly hustling and trying to find the next gig. And back then, it was a Rolodex—you'd spin through your Rolodex, just networking and calling people.

I happened to talk to a guy called George Ghiz, who had managed a band called Pages. That was kind of a 'musician's band,' and they had three albums out that hadn't taken off. Anyway, Pages was named after their singer, Richard Page, and his partner, Steve George, was the keyboard player. Well, George Ghiz says, 'Richard and Steve are thinking about putting together something new. Are you interested?' I said, 'Sure.' I went to Richard Page's house, and there's Richard, Steven, a bass player, a drummer … and me. We play, and I hit it off with those guys. So we go two months looking for a permanent bass player and a drummer, and we find Pat Mastelotto, and decide to make it a four-piece instead of a five-piece. That's when we started Mr. Mister—so that would have been in the springtime of '83.

KISS were enjoying some MTV success around the same time as Mr. Mister's rise. What did you think of non-makeup-era KISS?

Here's what I think of that *whole* era. When MTV came out … God bless them, because they were a big part of our success. But in that era, *every* act had to be making videos. It was the new thing, and fun, but the odd thing to me was watching The Allman Brothers or someone like that make a video. Here's an iconic band that I was listening to since the early 70s, and weren't video people—they were a fuckin' *Southern rock band* that played their asses off. So the old guard—KISS, everybody else—suddenly, they're making videos. To KISS's advantage, they were always a showboat thing. They're the kings of show—everything is about the presentation. What I thought of them was about what I thought of all of this—you found yourself vulnerable to the commerciality of the video era.

[I remember] the first video we did, for a song called 'Hunters Of The Night,' which was on our first album. They had an iguana brought in. And the rule of thumb is, *never work with children and animals*. Well, I can tell you … never work with children and animals! Because they couldn't get the fuckin' iguana to turn to the right or the left the way they wanted to film it. They spent hours and hours of incredibly expensive time fucking around with the iguana. And then you look at it in the end, and it's this little lizard that's two feet long, and they're trying to make it look like a dragon of intensity. When you get into this contrived sort of ideas of storyboards these guys would write for videos, after you're like, *What the fuck does any of that mean about anything?* [*Laughs*]

Were you aware that *Creatures* was reissued in 1985, with a non-makeup cover photo, supposedly to cash in on the band's commercial success at the time?

I knew that it was re-released. I've signed that record around the world—especially in Japan, where they seem to know everything you've ever done. I was there with Whitesnake, and at every train stop, I'm signing a *Creatures Of*

The Night album. I've come to learn they've credited me on some of the later versions, I think. The Japanese would have known it anyway, because they just seem to know all the lore. It's just part of their culture—they figure out everything. I've signed records in Japan that never were hits. I'm like, *Where the hell did you get this?*

KNOW THE SCORE: WEDNESDAY 13

The Murderdolls singer and solo performer discusses his love for *Creatures Of The Night*, and his thoughts on the non-makeup era overall.

Did you first discover KISS during the non-makeup era?

I was born in '76, and I remember that interview on MTV, when they revealed them all. It was a big deal, because my older brother was into it, so I figured I'd better pay attention to this. I was playing with GI Joes, and then, by about fifth or sixth grade, I started getting into music. I remember *Crazy Nights* was the first new KISS record I got. I heard *Destroyer* on vinyl as a little kid from my brother, but I was watching MTV, and *Crazy Nights* happened to be the album at the time. That got me into KISS, and then I started going back and getting the older records, and then *Creatures Of The Night*. I remember discovering there were two album covers for that, and I always associated it with the one *without* the makeup.

When you first saw the *Creatures* album cover, were you under the impression that it was a non-makeup album?

Yeah, because no one really talked about it. There was confusion, and you have to think back—there was no internet, so you couldn't get online and go, 'What the hell is this?' Then there's people that only saw it and heard it with their makeup off, and go, 'I don't like that record.' Then, when they see the cover with the makeup, they go, 'Oh, it's amazing!' That's just how people are, unfortunately. *They listen with their eyes.*

What did you think of the album?

Well, *Revenge* is my favorite of the non-makeup era, but *Creatures* is a close second. The song 'Creatures Of The Night' is pretty metal. I remember hearing that and going, *whoa! They've gone really metal.* I remember even when I saw them for the first time live, in 1992, it was what they opened with, and I remember just how *metal* it sounded. But 'War Machine'—talk about heavy. Even now, when I hear that song, you can hear the attitude, you can hear the heaviness of it. I was born too late—I don't remember the impact of what that must have sounded like to fresh ears when that record first came out. 'War Machine,' to this day, is *still* heavy. It really is the sister of 'God Of Thunder.' And Paul sings great on 'I Still Love You'—and on the acoustic *Unplugged* thing, he goes off on that. The whole record, it's all killer, no filler.

Do you agree that *Creatures* is one of KISS's more consistent albums from front to back?
I think it's a very consistent record. KISS seemed focused on that—more so than anything they'd done for years previously. They had to reinvent themselves, so you can hear that. For some people, that was a move *too* far. As a musician, I get it—I hear my fans complain when I change my thing up. 'What are you doing?' 'We're growing! Grow with us … or listen to the old records.'

One of the sonic trademarks of *Creatures* is the mammoth drum sound.
That was the big step up. Eric Carr was *a metal drummer*. Peter Criss was a jazz drummer, and played rock'n'roll. Peter set the bar high for a lot of people. But Eric Carr is not given the credit for what he did. That guy was doing Tommy Lee *before* Tommy Lee. He was a powerhouse. He definitely is the foundation and the heaviness and the attitude on that record. You can tell his hungriness in it as well, because that was one of his first shots at it. As a musician, I can smell and see when [something is] honest and when it's not. It seems like I've developed this ability over the years. That's why I try to do everything honest. When someone doesn't, you can see right through it. And that record is honest.

It's interesting that you just mentioned Tommy Lee, because, now that I think of it, I see the similarities between *Creatures* and Mötley Crüe's *Shout At The Devil*—in terms of the sound of both albums.
The big kick drum. Tommy Lee was maybe a little bit more animated, where

Eric Carr was a little more solid. He reminded me of Deen Castronovo, who is actually the father of my drummer [Kyle Castronovo]! Watching his old videos, I see a lot of Eric Carr. I'm not sure if Eric was a fan of Deen or what, but he brought a *sledgehammer* that KISS needed.

Perhaps a fitting comparison to Mötley Crüe's *Too Fast For Love* is Cheap Trick, and *Shout At The Devil* is *Creatures*-era KISS. Plus Mötley Crüe opened some shows for KISS on the *Creatures* tour.

Too Fast For Love was more or less a demo, and a band trying to do what they did. I think they were a band for a couple of years, they saw KISS, and there's no denying—whether they admit it or not—what Eric Carr did, and there's no way that Tommy Lee didn't walk away from that tour going, *That dude's killer. What can I do to step it up?* That's what musicians do—we're always trying to out-do each other. Tommy Lee will tell you that Peter Criss is the guy that made him want to play drums. I bet Eric Carr just put it over the top.

What do you think of KISS's non-makeup-era material when you hear it today?

Early KISS, the classic lineup … whenever I explain KISS to people, I say that they're superheroes to me, with the makeup and everything. I was such a young kid, and just seeing those pictures, I didn't know what I was looking at. Maybe a bit like He-Man figures … but they had long hair. And I lived in the Bible Belt, and my mom was telling me that they're evil, and on TV they're evil. So to see KISS go from what I was told as a kid was 'Knights In Satan's Service,' to see Paul go [imitates opening 'yodel' of 'Heaven's On Fire'] and wearing neon colors … as a little kid, I was going, *What the hell is going on?*

They had killer songs, like 'Lick It Up.' The singles were great. But I do think a lot of those records during the 80s had a lot of filler. They would have their hits, but then the rest of the record … it sounded like they were really grasping at whatever they could to make records. Until *Revenge* came out. Now, *Revenge* to me is the sister of *Creatures Of The Night*, because KISS had to reinvent themselves. They went as far as they could, and people weren't taking them seriously anymore. If you look back at KISS, they're probably the reason why bands started dressing the way they did through that whole era of spandex and neon and all that crap … *it's Paul Stanley's fault!* [*Laughs*] He can take credit for that.

But people forget about that. They go, *oh, KISS with makeup—they started it*. Well, they also started that whole 80s look, too. I mean, all those bands were fans of KISS, so they watched the way KISS dressed *without* makeup, and dressed like that. So that's why you have Dokken and every band … even Slayer were wearing spandex in the beginning. KISS were so influential and people only give the makeup era credit, but they did the same thing with non-makeup. They really did. Name another band that did. They were still KISS. They had the legacy. And then they came out and went, 'All right, fuck you guys—we'll take the makeup off and we're *still* bad-ass!' And we were like, 'OK … *you are!*'

You could say that both *Creatures Of The Night* and *Revenge* are KISS sounding hungry again.
Absolutely. It's undeniable. Compare *Revenge* to any other album—besides *Creatures Of The Night*—and tell me that they tried as hard. Because every single song from beginning to end on *Revenge* is great. And every song on *Crazy Nights* from beginning to end is not. And that's OK—I've got records that have songs that are not good. You're not around those many years and putting out songs that people don't like. But also, if you're around so many years, you get comfortable, and it becomes difficult to live up to your legacy.

When you're on top of the world for years and you fall a bit, the rest of your life you're trying to climb back up to that level again. And KISS have done it multiple times and have done it better than all the bands, and still, every single band—from the black-metal bands to the heaviest of metal bands—you get those guys with a couple of beers in them and you mention KISS, and it is *on*. Singing at the top of their lungs. I've seen members of Crowbar, Type O Negative, Lamb Of God, myself included, with all those dudes … KISS is one of those things that unites a lot of musicians my age and older. They really were—and are—one of the greatest rock'n'roll bands of all time. They set the bar high, and they're game-changers.

GIMME MORE: RON KEEL ON GENE'S PRODUCTION WORK

Since there was no tour in support of the *Creatures* re-release, let's take this opportunity to have singer Ron Keel discuss what it was like to have Gene produce two albums of his band, Keel, in the 80s, as well as recordings by other artists during this era that Gene produced.

How did you first cross paths with Gene, and how did the idea for him to produce Keel come about?

When Keel signed our major-label recording contract with Gold Mountain/ A&M Records in the summer of 1984, the label presented me with a list of potential producers. And the list was basically a who's who of the hotshot rock producers of the day—Max Norman, Michael Wagener … it was the A-list. It was cool that I got the input, because I was a brand new artist on the label, and for them to give me the opportunity to at least have a say on who was the producer, was amazing.

I looked at the list, and Gene's name was on it. I'm obviously a KISS fan, and Gene's name really popped out on the page. Looking back, I wish I could take credit for that being a brilliant career decision, but I did not look at that scrap of paper with the thought that *Gene is going to help me sell a lot of records.* I really wanted to meet him and talk to him about producing Keel, because he was an artist that I looked up to and admired and had enjoyed.

Now, looking back on it, it was a great move, because the KISS Army embraced us. Gene hadn't produced a whole lot of acts at that time—I think Wendy O. Williams [1984's *WOW*], and a co-production credit on some of the KISS albums. He was pretty new to that side of the mixing console. So the KISS fans really embraced Keel when that *Right To Rock* album came out, in January of 1985. We sold ninety thousand albums the first week. I attribute that to Gene—the hype that came along with having Gene produce the record was huge. The media buzz, the advertising campaign, the fact that the KISS Army knew who we were by the time the album came out—and they bought it because Gene produced it.

The label set up a meeting at the Beverly Hills Hotel. I walked up to the lobby, and there was a man sitting on the bench out front, before you entered the lobby. A nice-looking gentleman—a big guy, clean-cut, short hair, business suit. He looked up at me, and said, 'Ron Keel? *I'm Gene Simmons.*' I didn't even recognize him! He had cut his hair for the role in the film *Runaway*. I was used to the fire-breathing, blood-spitting Gene Simmons that I saw onstage. We went up to his room and talked about music. He asked me some questions. And we listened to the song 'The Right To Rock,' which didn't have any vocals on the cassette that I played for him—it was just a jam tape, basically. And I sang the lead vocal to his face. He pushed stop on the cassette player, looked at me, and said, 'I'm going to produce this record … *and we're going to start on Tuesday.*'

What are some of your memories of working with Gene on *The Right To Rock* and *The Final Frontier*?

There are a lot of great memories—both in the studio and out. Gene really took us under his wing. It wasn't a job to him. To this day, I'm not sure if Gene even got paid for those records. The business arrangement was out of my hands. He didn't treat it like business—he treated it like *music*, and he became the sixth member of the band. A side of Gene that most people don't ever get to see—the fact that he loves music. He's got an affinity for the history of rock'n'roll and the bands that influenced him—the Stones, The Who, and those 60s bands that he grew up listening to, and had a profound impact on him.

He tried to pass a lot of that love of early rock'n'roll on to me. We'd sit and listen to Leslie West and Mountain. He *loved* 'Mississippi Queen'—he probably thought that was the greatest rock song of all time. He would sit and play KISS songs for me, and then he would play the Who song or the Stones song that he stole the riff from! He told me, 'Ron, *only steal from the best.*' That's a lesson I took to heart, and I still practice what Gene preaches—to this day. He was a big brother to us.

I think Gene would tell you now that he didn't know what he was doing—he was in over his head when it came to producing records. He had *been produced.* He had seen people on the other side of the glass help him create—with Bob Ezrin and all the great producers KISS worked with. But when you got on the other side of the glass, it's a whole different ballgame. And a lot of people probably don't even know what a producer does. Basically, in a nutshell, it's the director of the film or the coach of the football team. It's the guy who is in charge of everything.

There are two kinds of producers: *hands-on* and *hands-off*. Guys like Michael Wagener can engineer their own recordings. They can work the gear, they can dial in the tones, they can choose the microphones and determine mic placement. Gene was not that guy. Gene was the coach of the team, and he would hire engineers to get the tones. And then you'd have to relay to that engineer in verbal terms what you're looking for. Gene even allowed me the latitude to bring in *my* engineer on that *Right To Rock* session [Mike Davis], because I think we were really pressed for time.

Once he decided he was going to produce *The Right To Rock*, he had to work that around the KISS schedule. We got signed in August of '84—around the same time *Animalize* was about to come out, and KISS were going on tour. So he had to get the record done *right now*. We had a really accelerated pace—in fact, we were working with Gene before the ink was dry on the recording contract! We did preproduction in one day, went into rehearsals and arranged some intros and endings … in fact, we didn't even have enough songs for a record. We were just finishing up our debut independent album [1984's *Lay Down The Law*], and all of a sudden we were signed. We were not ready to make a record by a long shot. We were not anywhere near prepared. It all happened in a span of days. We didn't have any new songs, so Gene gave me a tape of a lot of songs that did not make it to *Animalize*, and he offered to let us record three of his compositions. And I chose the three that ended up on the album—'So Many Girls, So Little Time,' 'Easier Said Than Done,' and 'Get Down.' And I wrote a couple of quick tunes, like 'Electric Love,' and we re-recorded three songs off the independent record and ended up with nine songs on the session.

Before producing Keel, Gene produced Wendy O. Williams's *WOW*.
At the time, I listened to it, because, *OK, Gene is going to produce us. Let's check out what else he's done.* I listened to the Wendy O. Williams album, and I've listened to it a few times through the years. Gene would bring his KISS buddies to the party, and he'd bring his non-KISS buddies to the party as well.

That Wendy O. record, you're very much going to hear the KISS influence. I think if I produced a lot of hard-rock bands, they would end up sounding like me or like Keel. It's just in your nature—it's how you work. It's your style, it's your trademark.

The Wendy O. record had massive drums—Gene would always look for the biggest room he could find, whether it was a church or an auditorium or some big room, and we would cut the drums in the biggest room available, and try to get that massive 80s drum sound. Simple guitar riffs, and you could tell the vocals are doubled on that Wendy O. record. Gene would have me do a lead vocal and then double it, which is extremely challenging for a vocalist, to duplicate exactly what they just sang. You can tell on the KISS records—Gene and Paul do a lot of that. I haven't heard it done in a long time—I haven't done it since *The Final Frontier* [in 1986].

Every annunciation, every vowel, every consistent—you double that, and it thickens up the vocal. It makes it sound a little artificial, but it also hides a lot of the imperfections, as well. You can really mask a lead vocal by putting a double on it, and they will cancel each other out, in terms of if the note is flat or sharp—it beefs everything up. It's very difficult to do, and a very dated style of producing—nobody does that these days. But Gene taught me to do that. And Wendy's doing that on that album—you can certainly tell her vocals are doubled.

Gene also produced two Black N' Blue albums, *Nasty Nasty* and *In Heat*. On the former, you sang on the song 'Best In The West' with Peter Criss.
Peter and I went in the studio and kind of sang around Jaime St. James's vocals. They're not actually background vocals—background vocals to me is when everybody is singing the chorus together, or doing harmonies, or *ohhs* and *ahhs*, or yelling the title of the song. These were screams, basically, and ad-libs—scat vocals. David Lee Roth–ish, if you will—to make it sound like we're having a party in the studio. I'm very proud to have contributed some really sick screams to that Black N' Blue track.

Gene also produced the self-titled debut by the Japanese metal band EZO.
I did not sing on the record, but I was involved in the EZO sessions to some

extent—just welcoming them to America, have fun, kick ass, pep talk, and whatever. EZO ended up going on tour with Keel to support that first album, and they were our opening act when we became a headliner in some of the smaller venues. I know Gene had changed their name—they were called Flatbacker, and Gene was instrumental in changing their name to EZO. And, of course, another innuendo—a theme that runs through Gene's work is sex. In fact, you can hear it in Black N' Blue's *In Heat*; on *The Right To Rock*, with 'So Many Girls, So Little Time'; and EZO's 'House Of 1,000 Pleasures.' That sexual innuendo is a common thread in a lot of KISS records and the albums that Gene produced, as well. Gene was a strong proponent of sexual content in lyrics and rock'n'roll.

Why didn't Gene produce Keel for a third time?

It was time to do the third major label album, the self-titled Keel release, which came out in 1987—Gene came to me and we talked about doing the next album together. Gene had given me a lot of latitude on *The Final Frontier*—he really let me call the last shot. Basically let me co-produce that record with him. He believed in my vision and supported it. And, to a certain extent, it didn't work. Not because of the content, but because of the choice of singles, I think. The label chose [a cover of the Patti Smith/Bruce Springsteen composition] 'Because The Night' as our first single, and that was a career-killer for me. If we knew they were going to choose that as the first single, we wouldn't have cut it and put it on the record. That's not Gene's fault, that's not my fault, but for whatever reason, the album did not reach the multi-platinum expectations we had.

When it came time to do the third album, Gene said, 'OK, Ron. We did it your way last time. This time, we're going back to doing it *my* way. And 90 percent of the lyrical content has to be sexual.' And, at that time, I had just had enough of sex, drugs, and rock'n'roll. I thought there was more to say, frankly, and I ended up moving on from Gene to working with Michael Wagener. But those few years we spent with Gene left a strong impression on me—and, I think, an impression on Gene, as well. Every time we see each other now, there's a friendship and a big bear hug, and a mutual respect and admiration. I think he admires the fact that I have survived in this business and managed to carve out a career for myself. And the fact that I've always acknowledged his contribution to my career—both from a business standpoint and from a production standpoint.

I've made many records between then and now, but Gene's lessons are still with me. In the studio, he would try to be prepared as possible. He taught me how the kick drum and bass guitar are supposed to work together. I never really realized that until the *Right To Rock* sessions. He was very attentive to that foundation of bass drum/bass guitar—that relationship between those two instruments, and how to build on that. And be prepared to be well rehearsed and ready—don't be afraid to take a chance or to go off on a tangent. Don't be afraid to be creative in the studio. He encouraged me to try *anything*. But a lot of those lessons he taught me are in every session I do.

Gene produced Doro's self-titled release, plus House Of Lords' self-titled album and *Sahara*—the latter pair coming out on his own label, Simmons Records.
I did sing on [*Sahara*] as well—on a song called 'Chains Of Love.' Like I mentioned earlier, he brings friends to the party. On the Doro record, Tommy Thayer was involved in the production, songwriting, and guitar playing. When I went to sing on the House Of Lords record, there was Andy Johns … and Gene sitting right beside him. What an intimidating duo!

Andy Johns was obviously a hall-of-fame producer and legendary in our business [having previously worked with the likes of Led Zeppelin, The Who, Blind Faith, Free, and Humble Pie]. And to credit Gene, Gene was smart enough to say, 'I need to bring in a heavy-hitter on this project.' He brought in Andy, and I was not real privy to how they worked together as a production team, but they were there at Sound City in LA, where I was living and rehearsing at the time. So I was there, outside the sessions on the compound, and Gene said, 'Why don't you sing on the record?'

In terms of sonic quality, that album still holds up to this day. That record sounds fantastic. You get the balance of Gene calling some of the songs' shots, and Andy Johns taking care of the sonic duties—a pretty deadly combination. That was probably the best *sounding* record that has Gene Simmons's name on it as producer.

Gene also managed the recording side of Liza Minnelli's career for a while, too ...
That's Gene. He's a showman. It's *show business*—it's not just rock'n'roll. Whether it's TV, big-band tunes ... I saw Gene do big-band tunes once on a solo a tour. Knowing Gene and his love of Cher, show tunes, I could certainly see him doing that. And, once again, it goes back to his nature—he's not afraid to try anything. He's not afraid to fail. I think he's written that in some of his books. You're not going to succeed in everything you do—whether it's his magazine [*Tongue*] or his production career.

Now, was his production career a success or a failure? You tell me. But he made some great records, he made some real lasting impact on people's lives, like myself and Black N' Blue. If he hadn't produced the Black N' Blue records, would Tommy Thayer be the lead guitar player in KISS today? That's a big part of rock'n'roll history.

I am thankful for what Gene taught me in life—in business *and* in the studio. He was a mentor. He would take me in Manhattan from the studio to a restaurant, and tell the limo driver to go by this building or that building, and he would say, 'Ron, do you see that building? *I own that building.* There are four units per floor, I get X-amount of dollars per floor—how much per year do you think I make off of owning that building?' It instilled in me a desire to succeed not only in music but in business. So, I'm really thankful for those lessons and that relationship, and the good times.

After we'd get done at the restaurant, he'd say, 'Ron, come over to the house.' I think he lived on Eighth Avenue—right next to Central Park. His house overlooked Central Park, and you could go up the elevator to the eighth floor, and he'd put in a special key that took you up to the rooftop. You'd get out and you'd be in Gene Simmons's entryway, with marble floor and columns. We'd go into his house, eat ice cream and popcorn, and watch movies. He'd even show us KISS videos—I remember watching *Kiss Meets The Phantom Of The Park* with Gene! I think he could watch that movie over and over again. We'd sit there and watch movies, until he'd have the limo driver take us back to the hotel, and we'd pick up the session the next day. So a lot of good times, a lot of good memories—and a lot of good music came out of that.

GIMME MORE: GENE'S ACTING CAREER IN THE 80s

During the 1980's, quite a few musical artists tried their hand at acting, including Sting, Prince, Madonna, Phil Collins, David Byrne ... and Gene Simmons. Unlike many of those names, who just appeared in a film or two, Gene seemed more serious than most, starring in a total of five movies and two television programs, before turning his attention back to his music career by the dawn of the 90s. Here is a guide to Gene's flicks.

RUNAWAY (1984)

Gene's first film role was in the 1984 action/crime movie *Runaway*, also starring Tom Selleck (who was quite the sex symbol at the time, thanks to his role on the TV show *Magnum PI*), Cynthia Rhodes (who had appeared in *Staying Alive*, would later appear in *Dirty Dancing*, and would eventually marry and divorce pop singer Richard Marx), and Kirstie Alley (before she found fame in *Cheers*). Gene plays a bad guy, Dr. Charles Luther, who proves to have a fondness for miniature spider-like robots that sting you with acid, and also heat-seeking bullets fired from a handgun.

Selleck and Rhodes play the two cops (Sgt. Jack R. Ramsay and his partner Karen Thompson) who do battle with the dangerous Luther, while Alley plays Jackie Rogers, a former lover of Luther's. Be warned: if dangerous heights and spider robots scare you, the film's ending may prove problematic. Also of note—Gene cut his hair for the film, introducing a look that he would keep for most of his other acting roles.

Not a bad B-movie, *Runaway* fits in well with such similarly styled if better-known titles of the era as *Robocop*, *Cobra*, and *The Terminator*. It was shown quite a bit on HBO back in the day, resulting in it being probably Gene's best-known film.

MIAMI VICE (1985)

Perhaps no other TV show screamed *80s!* more than *Miami Vice*, which was aimed straight at MTV viewers and spawned a particular look that has become synonymous with the era, courtesy of actor Don Johnson's five o'clock shadow, pastel-colored blazer, and shoes with no socks. And while Johnson and Philip Michael Thomas (as undercover detectives James 'Sonny' Crockett and Ricardo 'Rico' Tubbs) were the show's main attraction week in and week out, a wide variety of special guests were featured, many of them coming from the rock'n'roll world, including Phil Collins, Frank Zappa, Glenn Frey, Ted Nugent … and Gene Simmons, in the episode 'The Prodigal Son,' which aired as the show's season-two premiere on September 27, 1985. Gene plays the role of Newton Windsor Blade (quite a name, eh?), a Miami-based drug dealer who apparently has a weakness for flaunting his wealth via wild parties aboard his yacht. Although Crockett and Tubbs have tried and failed to bust Blade in the past, the drug dealer is kind enough to provide the handsome cop duo with a connection to a New York–based drug ring—which leads them on a wild goose chase through NYC. And here's an interesting observational tidbit for ya—along with the film *Red Surf*, this is one of few 80s roles in which Gene sports his KISS-like long hair.

THE HITCHHIKER (1986)

Gene continued his television work with a role in HBO's nighttime series *The Hitchhiker*, which ran from 1983 to 1987 before being resuscitated by the USA Network from 1989 to 1991. Each episode features a chap simply known as The Hitchhiker (played by actor Page Fletcher), who sets up the show with an opening monologue and then reappears at the conclusion. In between, a whole new cast would tell a tantalizing tale.

In the episode that originally aired on January 28, 1986, entitled 'O.D. Feelin',' Gene again plays a drug kingpin: Mr. Big, the proud owner of a much-cherished yet dangerous bag of cocaine, which exchanges hands quite often throughout the course of the episode (passing through Sandra Bernhard and Michael Des Barres, among others), before ultimately finding its way back to him. Though Gene only appears toward the end of the episode, his role is a good one, and he even manages to model one of his trademark demonic stares.

NEVER TOO YOUNG TO DIE (1986)

You could make an argument that, for the most part, Gene was a bit typecast in his 80s acting roles, as either a drug kingpin or a murderous villain. But while he once again assumed the role of villain in the film *Never Too Young To*

Die, you have to give ol' Gene some credit for at least putting a unique spin on it—by playing a *hermaphrodite* villain.

Starring John Stamos (as Lance Stargrove) and Vanity (as secret agent Danja Deering), *Never Too Young To Die*'s storyline revolves around Stamos's character trying to avenge the death of his father (who was *also* a secret agent). And who is the dastardly devil that committed this heinous crime? It's Gene's character, of course—Velvet Von Ragner.

Of all of Gene's 80s flicks, this one is probably the hardest to sit through, due to the dreadful acting and awful dialogue. But at least the God Of Thunder's Vegas-like wardrobe is there to provide a cheap thrill or two. On second thought … Gene's over-the-top flamboyant fashions here aren't too far from KISS's *Asylum*-era neon-electric wardrobe!

TRICK OR TREAT (1986)

Of all the films that Gene appeared in, the one that's closest to the heavy-metal/hard-rock vibe of KISS is undoubtedly *Trick Or Treat*. And while Gene's role isn't all that prominent, he does an A-OK job as a motormouth radio DJ who goes by the name Nuke. The storyline focuses on a doomed heavy-metal singer, Sammi Curr (played by Tony Fields), and his #1 fan, Eddie Weinbauer (played by Marc Price, best known for his role as Skippy on the TV show *Family Ties*), with lots of glitz and fantasy along the way—in a way that could have only happened in the 80s.

Truth be told, the best—and most memorable—part of the movie is a cameo by none other than Ozzy Osbourne, who plays the role of evangelist and moral crusader Reverend Aaron Gilstrom (keep in mind, this was during a time when televangelists and the PMRC were regularly targeting metal acts for the 'questionable lyrical content' of their songs). And for those keeping score, this is one of few roles in which Gene doesn't die in a ghastly manner at the end. In fact … *he doesn't kick the bucket at all!*

WANTED: DEAD OR ALIVE (1987)

Landing action-adventure roles was Gene's primary focus during his 80s acting career, and he continued as such with the 1987 flick *Wanted: Dead Or Alive*. I will be bold to say that this may be the best and most realistic film that Gene ever appeared in, largely due to a strong supporting cast, including Rutger Hauer (best known for his role as android Roy Batty in *Blade Runner*) and Robert Guillaume (best known for his role as Benson DuBois on the TV shows *Soap* and *Benson*). In one of his better displays of acting, Gene plays the role of terrorist/murderer Malak Al Rahim, who ends up with both bounty hunter Nick Randall (Hauer) and detective Philmore Walker (Guillaume) on his tail after blowing up a movie theater. (In case you were wondering, *Rambo* is being shown that night.) Lots of action and a surprise or two are included, including an ending that will blow your head off.

RED SURF (1989)

'One last big score' has been the basis for countless films over the years, so why not another in the year 1989?! Two members of a surfer-gang (who, let's be honest, *do not* resemble gang members whatsoever), Attlia (played by Doug Savant) and Remar (played by George Clooney, years before becoming one of Hollywood's leading men), are caught up in the world of drugs and crime. But when one of the lads gets his super-attractive girlfriend Rebecca (played by Michelle Pfeiffer's sister, Dedee Pfeiffer) pregnant, they hatch the aforementioned plan for one last big score before resuming life on the straight and narrow.

Predictably, it doesn't go exactly as planned—when will criminals ever learn? And how does Mr. Simmons figure into all of this, you ask? Good question. He (briefly) plays the role of a chap simply named Doc, who offers aid to the two unsavory lead characters. While you could classify *Red Surf* in the same B-movie (or perhaps *C-movie*) category as *Never Too Young To Die*, it proves to be more watchable, probably due to its slightly better acting.

ASYLUM

Released September 16, 1985. Produced by Paul Stanley and Gene Simmons. US #20, UK #12. US certification: gold.

SIDE ONE

King Of The Mountain (Paul Stanley/Bruce Kulick/Desmond Child)

Any Way You Slice It (Gene Simmons/Howard Rice)

Who Wants To Be Lonely (Stanley/Child/Jean Beauvoir)

Trial By Fire (Simmons/Kulick)

I'm Alive (Stanley/Kulick/Child)

SIDE TWO

Love's A Deadly Weapon (Stanley/Simmons/Rod Swenson/Wes Beech)

Tears Are Falling (Stanley)

Secretly Cruel (Simmons)

Radar For Love (Stanley/Child)

Uh! All Night (Stanley/Child/Beauvoir)

SINGLES / EPS

Tears Are Falling / Any Way You Slice It (US #51)

Tears Are Falling / Heaven's On Fire (live) / Any Way You Slice It (UK #57)

★

With *Lick It Up* and *Animalize* successfully reestablishing KISS as one of the top bands in the hard-rock/heavy-metal kingdom—and with new guitarist Bruce Kulick on board for his first recording as a full-time member—the fellas set out to keep their winning streak going with *Asylum*. Paul Stanley once again occupied the producer's throne, but this time Gene Simmons joined him.

The album's cover image makes it seem like a distant relative of *Dynasty*, albeit with a painting of the four members' faces rather than a photograph. And hardcore fans probably noticed that each member's lips represent the 'aura colors' of the four KISS members' 1978 solo albums. There was one itsy-bitsy problem, though—Ace and Peter were no longer in the band. So why have Bruce and Eric represent these colors? Or perhaps this was a precursor of things to come years down the road, when Tommy Thayer and Eric Singer would assume the Spaceman and Catman makeup designs and personas. OK, OK, perhaps I'm being a bit nitpicky—let's continue …

While *Asylum* was indeed a success (another Top 20 album that spawned an oft-aired video on MTV and earned gold certification), it was the first KISS album in a few years that did not outperform its predecessor. And there were several reasons for this. The most obvious reason is that *Asylum* is comprised of material that is not as strong as *Lick It Up* or (for the most part) *Animalize*, and includes more than just a few throwaways. But when the material clicks, it clicks mightily—at least one certified KISS klassic resides here, 'Tears Are Falling,' which contains a killer opening chord progression, instantly memorable/melodic vocal melodies, and one of Bruce Kulick's best ever guitar solos.

Speaking of KISS's newest member, he should be given kudos for being one of the few rock/metal guitarists of the era to know when to shred and when *not* to, unlike quite a few other guitarists of the era (cough … *Vinnie Vincent* … cough). And unlike Mark St. John, Kulick was immediately called upon to lend a hand in the songwriting department, co-penning three tunes (and going on to steadily increase his songwriting workload on subsequent KISS records).

Another prevailing criticism of *Asylum* was that it was not as heavy as their previous offerings. And while there is some basis for this claim, you can't deny that the songs that kick off sides one and two—'King Of The Mountain' and 'Love's A Deadly Weapon,' respectively—are pedal-to-the-metal rockers, custom-made for headbangers. But that said, KISS did continue the troubling post–*Lick It Up* trend of filling space with unmistakable 'padding,' in the form of songs that were never even *attempted* on the concert stage (see: 'I'm Alive,' 'Secretly Cruel,' 'Radar For Love,' et cetera).

Once again, outside songwriters-for-hire were enlisted, with Desmond Child making his presence felt throughout the album ('King Of The Mountain,' 'Who Wants To Be Lonely,' 'I'm Alive,' 'Radar For Love,' and 'Uh! All Night'), while Jean Beauvoir returned in both a songwriting and 'bass ghosting' capacity (co-penning 'Who Wants To Be Lonely' and 'Uh! All Night' with Stanley and Child, and thumping the four-strong on both tracks for good measure).

Clearly taking their cue from such glammed-up chart kings as Mötley Crüe, Ratt, and David Lee Roth, KISS went overboard with the eye-popping, Vegas-y wardrobes and 'femme' makeup onstage and in music videos around this time. Simmons and Stanley have said in interviews over the years that in KISS's pre-recording years, they had attempted to copy The New York Dolls' androgynous image, but failed miserably due to their height and build. Yet here they were, committing the same flub again, all these years later. As a result, their look during the *Asylum* era was unquestionably *not* one of KISS's finest.

The quartet also had set their sights on conquering MTV, with *Asylum* being the first KISS album to spawn three music videos ('Tears Are Falling,' 'Uh! All Night,' and 'Who Wants To Be Lonely'). Of the three, 'Tears Are Falling' was the only clip that MTV really put any muscle behind, spinning it regularly upon the album's initial release; it then enjoyed a second wind in early '86, when it was regularly featured on the station's *Dial MTV* program (where it camped out at #2 for what seemed like ages … but was always held off the top spot by Mötley Crüe's 'Home Sweet Home'). Strangely, the multiple airings of the video did not translate to singles-chart success, as 'Tears Are Falling' only managed to peak at #51.

If you ever want to get a feel for 'The Big 80s' within the realm of rock videos, by all means, re-watch the three *Asylum* clips, which feature such memorable moments as a certain band member swinging on a vine, a guitarist playing a solo in the shower, a woman ripping down dusty drapes, scantily clad females being spritzed with water, and ladies in negligee pushing beds done up as cars in unison, among other eye-popping delights. And no, I can't tell you which videos contain these segments … that would spoil all the fun before you sit down and revisit them!

Looking back on it today, *Asylum* can be viewed from a glass half-empty/glass half-full perspective. It is true that the album wasn't as strong as the previous three KISS studio offerings, and the tour wasn't as hot a ticket as their '84–85 arena jaunt. But, that said, the 'Tears Are Falling' video kept the band's rapport with MTV intact, Paul and Gene's mugs seemed to be on all the hard-rock mags every month, and they had finally found a permanent replacement for Ace Frehley on the six-string. And to think—just a few years before, KISS would have *killed* to have scored an album as successful (from both chart and fan-reception perspectives) as *Asylum*.

KNOW THE SCORE: JEAN BEAUVOIR

The co-author of 'Thrills In The Night' (*Animalize*) and 'Who Wants To Be Lonely' and 'Uh! All Night' (*Asylum*), Beauvoir also supplied bass on several KISS tracks, as well as playing with Little Steven & The Disciples Of Soul and The Plasmatics.

How did you first cross paths with KISS?
Paul and I actually met at a club called Heartbreakers. It was like the popular club in the city, downtown. I forget the street, but it was where everybody went—actresses, actors, rock guys. Celebrities went there to hang out. One night, Paul actually came over to me and said, 'Hey, you're the guy from The Plasmatics.' And I said, 'And you're Paul Stanley from KISS!' I did recognize him.

We talked that night and exchanged numbers, and then, from there, I just started getting involved in things they were doing—and him as well with things that I was doing. I believe at that time I had just left The Plasmatics, and I started doing stuff with Steven Van Zandt, and I was looking to do a solo thing. From there, I just started spending time with the band—with Paul and Gene.

How would you compare your experiences of co-writing and playing on songs for *Asylum* and *Animalize*?

The experience was similar. Paul and I used to spend a lot of time together back then. We both lived in New York at the time, and we would just hang out. We actually became friends before we started writing. And then it just so happened, we were hanging out one day at his house, and he said, 'Let's mess around with something here.' We just picked up a guitar, he had a four-track on his table, and we started messing around with some ideas. And then, from there, a song came out of it. That was the first record, and 'Thrills In The Night' came out of it.

Asylum was a similar situation, but for the second one, we planned it out—that was the difference. We knew we had done work on the first one, so when the time came, he said to me, 'We're getting ready to make another record.' I was pretty much in the loop with everything they were doing, because we would spend so much time together—I was always in the studio [and would go] to rehearsals. That came pretty simple. I was just hanging out in the studio, and Paul said, 'Why don't you play bass on these tracks?' Because I had played bass on the demo, and he liked the feel [of my playing]. It just felt like, *Hey, why don't you just play bass on this? Just go for it.* It was really casual.

At the time, it wasn't something that was credited or anything. You know, those days—we didn't credit those kind of things. You just went in the studio and did it, almost like we weren't paying it much mind. It was not until later on that I actually saw it for the first time, on Wikipedia and all these different places—that I actually played on the songs.

Let's discuss each song that you co-wrote with Paul.

On *Animalize*, it was 'Thrills In The Night,' and I played on 'Get All You Can Take'—because Mitch Weissman was a friend of mine, as well—and 'Under The Gun.' And then, for *Asylum*, I played on 'Who Wants To Be Lonely' and 'Uh! All Night'—which were both songs that I co-wrote. The melodies and the actual musical parts of those songs all happened very quickly. I think Paul and I had a very quick sense of melody, so we would just start playing a riff and messing around a little bit, and all of a sudden it would just come. I can't remember which one of the songs, but I just kind of walked into the bathroom

83

for a second, and I heard a melody, I came back out, and said, 'How about *this?*' He said, 'Yeah, that sounds good'—and then he would add to it.

The lyrics always took longer. We spent a lot of time on lyrics. It might not appear so, because you listen to it and you think the lyrics might seem simple, but actually KISS—and Paul—were very particular about his lyrics, and how things were worded and how things were said. We would actually wind up on the phone together, sometimes for hours. We would be going through lyrics and trying verses … *OK, let's see … that one's not good enough. How about if we say this?*

I remember it was a pretty long process … I'd be at my house, laying on my couch—and I think Paul was doing the same—just going back and forth, back and forth, until we had it right. At one point, we brought in Desmond—who is a great lyricist, and was really good at those catchy metaphors and interesting rock things. So we'd get his take on some things, and add to some of the material.

What stands out about working with KISS in the studio?

It was easy. Gene is really easy to work with in the studio. He just liked whatever I would do, so he never really had many comments or anything—he'd just be like, 'Great job! Sounds good!' Since I had played on some of the demos already, the parts were kind of mapped out, so I knew what I was going to do. I was a pretty proficient bass player at the time—I still play bass—so it came really easily to me. It would be just a couple of takes, and that would be it. Then we'd have the song. But it was quite easy to play on those records, and the band was a great band—so it was really easy to play to the drum tracks. No problem.

An obvious question—how come Gene didn't play bass on those songs?

I've seen all kinds of things written about it—he was too busy doing business, doing this and doing that. I don't think it was any of that. I just think he felt I had a good feel for those songs, and he was completely fine with it. I was really close to the band, so Gene didn't have any kind of ego or anything like that—he was just like, 'If Jean sounds good playing that part, I like his feel on that, so, just play.' That was it. I think they both felt that was best for the song.

Were you ever self-conscious, playing bass in front of Gene in the studio?
No. To tell you the truth, it was pretty relaxed. Before that, I was playing with Little Steven—I was the bass player in The Plasmatics first, and then jumped from The Plasmatics to playing with Steven. So I found myself in the studio with all the guys from Springsteen and The E Street Band—all these fantastic musicians. At that point, I was very comfortable. I was honored that Gene would have me play those bass parts.

It's just that, since I wasn't being credited for it, I didn't really take it that seriously—because I just thought it would be something that would lie in the background. But when I finally found out [I was] getting credited on these songs is when I started looking at it and saying, 'Wow. I actually played bass on these KISS songs. *That's pretty hip!*' There are not a lot of other bass players that had the opportunity to play bass on one of the biggest bands in the history of rock'n'roll's records.

Paul is credited as the sole producer on *Animalize*, and co-credited with Gene on *Asylum*. How would you compare Paul and Gene as producers?
First of all, they've been doing it for so many years—they know exactly what they want. They're *meticulous* producers … it's very well organized. When they lay down tracks and the drum track goes down, they're really mapped out. It's not, like, off the seat of your pants. It's like, these are our days to work on drum tracks, this is going to be ready by then, bass is going to happen then, it's going to be at this studio. It was a really professional operation, with professional experience. They're seasoned producers, these guys.

How would you compare the actual recording sessions for both albums?
It wasn't very different. It wasn't like it was a completely different experience. How many records did KISS release? Quite a few. So they really had their 'formula' down. They'd go into preproduction for their records—I think it was SIR they went in—and would really map out the songs to get everything ready. I remember it happened the same way for both records.

I remember being in the rehearsal studio, going through the tracks, and Paul was being pretty picky about the parts—'*Play this.*' Not me, but the drum tracks. That's the main part of being in the studio—making sure the drum tracks were perfect. Because you can overdub some of the other stuff, but the drum tracks, back in those days, it was like ... *that's it.* That's the whole structure and basis of the record.

The costumes that KISS wore on the *Asylum* tour were quite glam and over-the-top. Why do you think that era of rock music was this way, fashion-wise?
For one thing, that's one of the things that Paul and I had in common—we *really* loved wild clothes. As a matter of fact, we'd spend a lot of time going shopping together. We'd always go looking to try and find cool stuff. And he had some great people that would make clothes for him. The same thing with me—I had a blond Mohawk, and I always really liked glam-y leopard prints and all kinds of things like that.

I just think that we had the feeling that rock'n'roll is about fantasy—it is about bringing people to a different place when they come to a show. They're not supposed to feel like they're going to work. It's supposed to take them to a completely different place, and give them an experience that really takes them away from their everyday life. And I think that's one of the great things about the 80s: the 80s were about taking people away and being over-the-top. I think that's what made it a really great time.

Why didn't you continue writing with KISS, beyond those two albums?
I moved away—I moved to Sweden, and I got signed as a solo artist, so I started making my record [1986's *Drums Along The Mohawk*] in Sweden, and I was gone. I wasn't really in the States anymore. I rarely saw them—whereas before, I was sitting in New York, we hung out every day. That's probably the reason—I disappeared for a bit. And we didn't reconnect again until I came back to LA, around '92, when I started working on the Crown Of Thorns stuff. And that's when I got involved with Paul again.

It's not like I hadn't spoken to them, because in '89, I was hanging around New York, and I had a band called Voodoo X at the time—Paul co-wrote a song for that record [1989's *Vol. 1: The Awakening*] called 'A Lover Like You.' And then Paul and I actually did more writing, come to think of it—other demos that we never did anything with. I have some cassettes of three or four other songs that Paul and I wrote. So we did do some more writing. It wasn't for KISS because, at that point, Paul was doing his own thing and wanted to get involved in just writing. With me, I was writing for a lot of other people plus my own projects. So we started writing for the publishing company and doing demos of stuff. I think we wrote another three or four songs that we did demos of, plus a song for an Australian artist named Craig McLachlan, and then he co-wrote a song on my Voodoo X record.

Are you still in contact with Gene and Paul?

Yes. I emailed back and forth with Gene about four months ago. I saw them in Vegas about a year ago—I went to their show out there, and saw them both. Here and there. Not as much as before, but I keep in touch here and there.

Do you still see royalties from your writing on those two KISS albums?

Yes, I do, actually. These days, records don't sell like crazy anymore—with Spotify and everything. It's not a lot of money, but I do receive payments, and I do have publishing—I get paid for my contributions.

What are your thoughts on *Asylum* and *Animalize* today?

I really like those records. Not to sound pompous because I was involved with them, because there were other songs that I loved on those records—'Tears Are Falling' is a song that I *really* loved, and I didn't write that. But I think they're some of their best records. And I think it was a good departure and change to make—to give them a chance to reflect a little bit on what they wanted to do, and where they wanted to go. And I think those records fit nicely into their catalogue.

KNOW THE SCORE: BRENT FITZ

Drummer Brent Fitz—known for his work with Gene Simmons, Bruce Kulick, Union, Alice Cooper, Slash, and Vince Neil—on why *Asylum* is one of his all-time favorite KISS recordings, and the overall appeal of the non-makeup era.

How did you first discover KISS?

My discovery of KISS was probably *Love Gun*, and then I went backward. But that was the first KISS record I ever bought on my own. I was locked in pretty early. I remember when they came through on the *Love Gun* tour, but I was just a little too young. I remember being super-bummed I couldn't go, but I was just a little under the wire there. I saw them on the *Crazy Nights* tour, and I was lucky to see *Animalize*. The *Animalize* tour was a big deal, because I'm from Winnipeg, and that's a small Canadian city, so most of the bands didn't come through. To have KISS, even in the 80s, was a big deal.

It's so weird, because that was right when Bruce joined the band, and the record had been out a little while, with Mark St. John. But the Bruce stuff was kind of new, like, *Oh … there is a new guitar player?* I had seen Bruce early on, in his first bunch of shows. At the time, we were like, *OK. What's going on? There's a new guitar player in KISS?* We were just so excited to see KISS. There was some juggling of guitar players at the time, but look at how things transpired many years later, when I ended up in LA and started a new band with Bruce [called Union]. I never would have expected that, seeing Bruce back in '85, or whenever it as.

I was definitely invested in KISS with the *Love Gun* album. It changed my life. It started with the 70s era, and, basically, I went backward. Every kid in my neighborhood had a favorite KISS record. Like, my best friend and I, we were *Love Gun* fanatics, and the guys two doors down, who were a couple of years older, were *Destroyer* fanatics. And down the street, my other friends were like, 'Oh, you've got to check out *Alive!*' So I kind of went back to the earlier KISS stuff. But *Love Gun*, at eight years old, was what hooked me. And from then on it was just obsession, from all the action figures that came out, the notebooks—we were the perfect age to get hooked on this band. They were our Beatles.

And then, afterward, as it got into *Dynasty*, for some reason, that was a weird record for a lot of people, because of the disco era. But I knew the songs were really good on that record—like 'Sure Know Something,' and of course 'I Was Made For Lovin' You' was a big hit. But I loved everything on *Dynasty*. And then around that time I had a little brief time where I discovered Cheap Trick, too, and I was kind of almost more into Cheap Trick and Van Halen in the early 80s. But when *Animalize* came out, I was kind of back into that very visual, video era of KISS, where their faces were visible without the makeup.

I mean, I thought *Lick It Up* was fucking awesome, and then *Animalize*—they were so MTV-oriented, with 'Heaven's On Fire' and everything. I played *Animalize* a lot. But I got *Asylum* when it first came out, and I was *really, really* into *Asylum*. I played that record over and over. And I still have the original copies of all my KISS records.

What do you recall was going on with KISS circa *Asylum*?

The good thing about the *Asylum* record was that it was our first chance to get to know Bruce on a KISS record, and see his face on the cover. And, video-wise, I think that was a peak time for KISS. When we look back as fans—and maybe KISS might even admit—some of the stuff that they were wearing was crazy. Like, *so* colorful and flamboyant. But at the time it was still KISS. We were like, *Well … this is ridiculous*. But I loved it. I loved the videos and I loved the songs. Always great melodies. I thought 'King Of The Mountain' was such a wicked song to open a record, and killer drumming. You'll argue with KISS fans [about] who had the better songs on certain records, but each guy always shone on at least one or two songs.

Every song had a catchy chorus on *Asylum*. I don't think there is a bad chorus on the songs. They are all songs that stick in your head. But I like 'Trial By Fire'—that was my guilty pleasure. Certainly, 'Tears Are Falling' was very strong—and *still is* strong to this day, and has held up really well. I thought 'Radar For Love' was cool—it had a Zeppelin kind of vibe. And 'Uh! All Night' was obviously a big video song, and it was very tongue-in-cheek, and I was kind of like, *Oh my God, these are crazy lyrics*. But again, I was invested. At the time, I would have been fifteen years old when that record came out. And I was just embracing the 80s era of KISS. They were very visual, but still with great, catchy songs. It was a different band than the 70s, but I never judged them in the same way. And Ace Frehley was solo around then, anyway, and Peter Criss wasn't in the band, so it was like [it was] is a new band.

I thought Eric Carr brought a totally different energy to KISS—a different feel. And a lot of the songs were very up-tempo. The 80s were very exciting. If you remember the *Animalize Live Uncensored* video, I burned that thing out! I played that thing a million times, back in the day. But, the songs and the tempos … I've played with Gene most recently on tour, and little things come up in discussion. And I remember Gene mentioning that things were pretty fast back in those days. Even for the old stuff, like 'Love Gun,' the band had *so much* energy. But I think Paul's best singing was in the 80s. I think the stuff he put on record, his voice was never better than in the 80s, for sure. He was *untouchable* in the 80s.

And something to note also: on *Asylum*, the band moved from the E-flat tuning to 440. I think Gene had mentioned that they had brought it up because E-flat is a little dark-sounding, and the 440 tuning brought it more melodic—maybe a more 'pop' sense. It actually changed a lot of how their sound was, because they weren't in that half step down—they went half a step up. Bands usually go *down* half a step—they went *up*.

Why do you think the tempos of the songs were so much faster live than on record in the 80s?

I don't know if that was a band suggestion, but it seemed like Eric Carr was a very … the drum kit was big, and larger than life. The KISS sign was massive at those times, too. I remember, on the *Crazy Nights* run, how big the KISS logo was. Well, it's always big with KISS, but things were escalating through the 80s. And the era of the 80s was just *big*. Everything was over-the-top. So KISS was doing the best KISS in the 80s—which was being over-the-top, in a different era. It was a different show they presented then—there was no black leather. Very little black onstage for the 80s with KISS.

A lot of it started to change back on *Revenge*—you can see how the whole look of KISS completely changed back to a dark, black-leather look around *Revenge*. Of course, you had leopard prints and animal prints on *Animalize*, and then just layers of color in the 80s, from *Asylum* on. And maybe *Hot In The Shade* was tamed a little bit, but still in that same very visual timeframe.

Let's talk a bit more about the tracks on *Asylum*. You mentioned that 'Trial By Fire' is a favorite.

I think the chorus is killer. Bruce co-wrote that with Gene, and Bruce co-wrote 'King Of The Mountain.' I like to guess the influences of some of the outside writers on KISS songs, because Desmond Child certainly had his stamp on a lot of great melodies and choruses among the Paul Stanley songs on KISS records. 'King Of The Mountain,' again, [has a] very strong chorus that comes out swinging right away. That's probably my standout song on the record, even though the hits are 'Tears Are Falling' and 'Uh! All Night.'

'King Of The Mountain,' the drum stuff was like, *Holy shit! This is wicked.* But let's go down the list … 'Any Way You Slice It' is kind of a weird Gene song—it's catchy, but there's a breakdown section with a little electronic Simmons kind of drum sound in the middle there. Again, cool chorus. 'Who Wants To Be Lonely'—amazing song. That's definitely a Desmond Child co-write, and Jean Beauvoir is on there, too. Those are two cats that *really* know how to write great choruses. I do love that song. That is sort of another guilty pleasure—'Who Wants To Be Lonely.'

'Trial By Fire' is a very cool song. 'I'm Alive,' I think, is the lesser of the fast, up-tempo, double-kick songs—'King Of The Mountain' stuck out a little better for me. But Paul sang *the shit* out of 'I'm Alive.' Holy shit! That's a great Paul song—very, very strong vocal. 'Love's A Deadly Weapon' is a great Gene song. There are really up-tempo songs up to there. And then 'Tears Are Falling' is just a *huge* song—it's great and different-sounding. And talking to Bruce about how they did that, I think they used a capo, because it's in 440, but they actually capo'd up, so it's in F. So, it's actually *really* high, and so high for Paul to be singing in that key. But it really brought up the feel and melody of that song—bringing that song into F. A strange, strange key. The drums were cool in that, too.

That whole *Asylum* record, in the choruses, there is an extra thump of the two and the four—it's, like, snare and floor tom. I don't know if that was a direction from someone outside of the band, but it really gave the choruses a sexy punch. The whole overall record had it. And you can hear it when there is a lot of snare and floor tom at the same time. It's a very different-sounding feel—I guess you could say it's a stamp—that Eric Carr would use a lot of double-kick. But those choruses, and the way they laid them in, was a really neat drum effect—instead of just [on] the two and four, there was a snare and the floor toms played on a lot of things. There were very syncopated drums in the middle of different sections, too—it was very clever, I have to say. At the time, I would have been overlooking that, but now that I look back, those were very clever, well thought-out drum patterns, that are very cool.

'Secretly Cruel' is another cool Gene song. That's a rarity on an 80s song [for Gene to write on his own]. I can listen to *Asylum* in its entirety. I can listen all the way through, and I wouldn't skip that song. 'Radar For Love' I love. It's a super-cool guitar riff—great playing from Bruce on that. The pre-chorus is huge on that. Lots of killer vocals. And then 'Uh! All Night' has just got *hit song* written all over it. It's a massive chorus. Then again, it has that really signature drumbeat in the chorus, with the floor toms and the snare—it's really cool.

'Tears Are Falling' was written solely by Paul—not with Desmond.

I've never thought that Paul or Gene couldn't write one of my favorite songs on their own. Certainly, it was their choice to have outside writers. But I was a fan of those guys as musicians, and I know Gene very well now, after touring and being in a band with him. He's one of the best musicians I've ever worked with—best singers, best bass players. Just as a musician, overall, the guy is three-dimensional. He's just super-talented, and knows melodies and knows cool parts, and keeps things simple, because when you make it complicated, sometimes you overthink it.

But certainly, involving outside writers, you can see where … yes, Desmond Child has a very great ability of making that chorus that just hits you and you can't get it out of your head. He's written *so many* great songs. But what about 'Rock And Roll All Nite'? There are no outside writers on that song, and that song will stand the test of time over any KISS song. I'm sure there are others early on, too, but I don't discredit Paul or Gene as writers on their own—I just think that they chose to write with other people. Sometimes, it's good to have a little bit of back-and-forth. I've written songs with many people, and having the ability to bounce an idea off of somebody sort of gives you the feeling of … sometimes you don't know what you're doing by yourself. It's nice to have somebody to bounce the ideas off of.

I agree with what you said earlier, about Paul being an underrated singer and Gene an underrated bassist …

Yep. What you said about Gene being very active in other roles outside of KISS at that time … Paul I would say definitely became the leader of KISS in the 80s. And maybe Gene would admit that, too. But as far as musicality on the record, and performance-wise … do we know if Gene played on those records? I know he was a busy guy. He certainly sang great on *Asylum* and *Hot In The Shade* and stuff, but did he even play a lot of bass? I don't know. I wonder who played bass on 'Forever'? Was it Gene or somebody else? But *Asylum*, for me, I'm good with the whole record. It's not that long of an album, and I listened to it straight through, over and over, a million times.

What did you think of KISS's glammed-out look circa *Asylum*?

With KISS, I would say I rode it through the 80s and was still a fan, but … it seemed a little like the whole presentation was a different thing. There were bands like Bon Jovi that were big at that time, and it was almost like every band in the 80s was jockeying to outdo Bon Jovi or Whitesnake, or all those MTV bands. I always thought, *Well, KISS is maybe taking a look at the other bands and comparing themselves, and maybe conforming a little bit*. But I never looked at it as a bad thing. I just realized, *OK, they look more like an MTV band. They're just adapting to the times*. They were adapting to the times, and it affected the visual side of KISS. They were evolving. And that's not a bad thing. The band didn't sound the same all the way through. The band in the 80s era had its own thing. And it was just as successful. They were getting all new fans in the 80s, too—probably from the visuals of MTV.

Let's discuss the KISS shows you saw during this era.

They only came through Winnipeg on *Animalize*. That was the first time I saw KISS—with Bruce Kulick on guitar. Dokken was opening. *Crazy Nights* came through in '88—I was eighteen at the time and very much myself playing in bands, regular gigs around town. I started to play in club bands when I was sixteen. At that time, on the *Crazy Nights* tour, I worked at a music store in Winnipeg. I was a teacher there. And the bands I saw in *Circus, Faces, Creem, Hit Parader*—all my favorite magazines—they just all didn't come through Winnipeg. They'd play Toronto, they'd play Vancouver. But Winnipeg was not a regular stop, so I had to live vicariously through a lot of these magazines.

Of course, we could buy the records, but we didn't get to see the bands.

So KISS came through the next time on *Crazy Nights*, I'm working at this music store, and the cool thing was, once in a while, the music store—Drums Unlimited was what it was called—would get calls from touring bands coming through, saying, 'Can we order some spare heads? Can you send them down to the arena?' It happened a few times, and the owner knew that these were my favorite bands, so I actually dropped off a bunch of drumheads for Eric Carr!

I met Eric Carr's drum tech during the day, and they invited me in—before Eric was there. The drum tech invited me onstage, to check out Eric's drums—it was early in the afternoon, before soundcheck—and he let me play Eric's drums! And what was even cooler was, as I was playing them—and of course, I'm a little bit taken that this is my favorite band, and I'm getting to sit behind the drums—I look over, and Eric Carr came up right behind me! So I met Eric while I was sitting on his drums. It was really cool—we took a photo. I didn't see KISS in the early days, I didn't meet the early KISS in makeup, but I met Eric Carr. I didn't meet Bruce Kulick that day—I saw him during soundcheck. I went to the show, and I had after-show passes. I was eighteen years old, and that was a pretty big deal, for being in Winnipeg. If I only knew I'd be in a band with Bruce several years later … who would have known?

When I spoke with Eric that day, I was probably commenting about how cool his kit was, because it was chrome. I think we discussed something about electronic drums at the time, too. In his solo, he was doing Simmons Drums, and that was still a little bit early on with electronic drums. It was cool that he had the massive drum kit, and then had the electronic drums. We had drummer talk. I was just trying to be cool, and I wanted it to be loose—I didn't want to be a *KISS fan*. I wanted it to be drummer-to-drummer, and make the conversation relaxed. I remember he was wearing a black jumpsuit. He just looked cool—with super-long hair and sunglasses.

Why does there appear to be a new appreciation of 80s-era KISS?

I think it's maybe because the fans have just as much visibility for the 80s … but maybe [they're] a different generation than the early KISS fans. It seems like maybe those fans are getting older, and most people go, 'Well, my first KISS was 1985, and I didn't like KISS in 1978—*because I wasn't born yet!*'

ASYLUM: THE TOUR WITH CURT GOOCH

The most flamboyant and glammy look of KISS's entire career occurred during the *Asylum* era, and its supporting tour took the glowing glitz to a whole new level …

On *Asylum*, something really interesting happened. Gene and Paul went to meet with Fleur [Thiemeyer], to see her designs and assemblies of the first outfits. And when they saw the outfits, they were sort of laughing, because they thought she was playing a joke on them. And she actually burst into tears and started bawling, and they realized she was serious … and wore the outfits out of pity! [*Laughs*] They were actually *embarrassed* to be in the *Asylum* outfits—at least according to Fleur. So, the *Asylum* outfits were meant to be over-the-top, but I don't think either Gene or Paul realized quite how over-the-top they were going to go. *Asylum* was certainly the height of the 80s fashion faux pas. KISS definitely went overboard.

That being said, there's something about that period of time—and, in particular, the *Asylum* tour—that fans seem to love, and it really seems to resonate with the fan base. More so than *Lick It Up*, *Animalize*, or even *Crazy Nights*—there's something about the *Asylum* period of time that was just absolutely *magical* for the fans. And most people, when I talk with them about that tour, they go, 'The *Asylum* tour, oh … *I saw six shows.*' People love that.

I have a theory that most people will probably not understand or agree with, but I'm pretty certain I'm right: the last day of the *Asylum* tour was the last KISS concert ever. And what I mean by that is, if you watch the last known video of the *Asylum* tour, and you look at that band, they're hungry, they're on fire, they're running around the stage, they're energetic, they're happy to be there. Then, go watch the earliest known video of the *Crazy Nights* tour, and that is not the same band. They're standing in place, they are not running around, they're phoning it in. *Nothing* compared to what came prior to that. The energy level never came back after *Asylum*. There was an unbelievable drop—I want to say of, like, 75 percent, from *Asylum* to *Crazy Nights*.

In September of '85, when *Asylum* was released, MTV did a great job of embracing KISS at that point. Paul Stanley came on and was interviewed by

Martha Quinn, Paul hosted a show they had called *Heavy Metal Mania*, Paul did a guest VJ spot, Eric Carr was on a USA Network show called *Radio 1990*, Gene was on *Miami Vice*—KISS were very high-profile at that point. They were on TV in the fall of '85 probably more consistently than at any other point during the non-makeup years. And that definitely helped sales of *Asylum* in the beginning.

The tour wasn't doing great—it was doing OK. But something happened mid-tour that doesn't really get a lot of credit. In January of '86, MTV started a new show called *Dial MTV*, and it was a thing that eventually became *Total Request Live* or *TRL*. *Dial MTV* was something where people could call in and vote for their favorite videos. And, every day, 'Tears Are Falling' was on that top ten—and usually somewhere in the top five. And having that daily exposure—between Mötley Crüe, Ratt … and Whitney Houston, believe it or not—I think dramatically helped the profile of that album. Because 'Uh! All Night' had already been released as a video, and that wasn't doing jack-crap on *Dial MTV*—it was the previous single, 'Tears Are Falling,' that seemed to resonate with the fan base and do something on the network. So that one thing, I think, really helped the second half of that tour. I think it really helped their bottom line.

Now, the *Asylum* tour—as far as the staging goes—is interesting, because there was not one, not two, but *three* different versions of the stage set that was used throughout the course of the tour. Tait Towers—who had designed the previous *Animalize* set—was so crazed about working with KISS that they literally stopped designing the stages with the artists and just [started] building. The very first stage lasted only eight shows—supposedly because the floor was too slippery. That had the *Asylum* album cover on the floor. So they did a lot of promotional filming and all kinds of key shows that had happened during that period were bootlegged with that floor, and it made it appear that that's what you were going to see on the tour. And I remember seeing my first KISS show—which was Norman, Oklahoma, [on February 21, 1986], toward the end of the *Asylum* tour—and it was the third production by then, and it was dramatically altered. The second production was a rehash of the *Animalize* stage—kind of a taller version of the *Animalize* stage. The third version was just the hollow amps—that's what I saw. And I was so disappointed, because the staircases weren't there, and the ramps weren't there—it was just the amps, a drum riser, and the giant logo, basically.

Plain and simple, it was down to economics. Chris Lendt, in his 1997 autobiography, *KISS And Sell*, really does a fantastic job of detailing how they simply had too many trucks out with the production, and if they didn't scale it back, they were going to lose money. So they scaled it back. But then, guess what? *Not enough.* So they had to scale it back a second time—in order just to get to a point where they were going to be making money or not losing money. And I think between that second scale-back, and the bump they got from exposure from *Dial MTV*, really helped bring that second leg of the tour home.

Asylum—much like *Lick It Up* and *Animalize*—had been a *build*. KISS were definitely stronger when that tour ended in April '86 than they had been in September of '85. They definitely gained momentum and were bigger. They were more high-profile. It had done what a tour was supposed to do—it made the band more successful.

The *Asylum* tour—much like its predecessors—started out very heavy with an *Asylum*-skewed setlist. However, unlike on the previous tours, that changed pretty quickly, with 'Tears Are Falling' and 'Uh! All Night' really being the only two songs that made it into the setlist on a consistent basis every night, although 'King Of The Mountain' was played, and later on in the tour, they did bring back 'King Of The Mountain.'

The tour had some interesting surprises. This was probably the low point for KISS's 70s songs. There might have been only two or three or four 70s songs in the entire setlist. And with them doing four [unaccompanied] solos and mostly *Creatures* and newer material, a lot of the old fans were turned off. Some people complained. But I actually loved the *Asylum* setlist and period—I really think it was valid, especially at that point.

But one thing they did—that they had never done before, or since—is, for some reason, they decided to do a cover. They decided to cover The Who's 'Won't Get Fooled Again.' They even split up the vocals, so Gene, Paul, and Eric all sang a verse of it. And it actually went over very well, I thought. I was happy to see and hear it. But there were definitely people complaining: *Why are they doing this, when they should be doing another KISS song?*

KISS were at a point where they had done album-tour, album-tour, album-tour for five years. And now they made a very interesting decision: to hold back and wait to get the right producer. They were a little displeased, because *Asylum* did not go platinum, only gold. And they waited to get Ron Nevison—who had done an unbelievable job with Heart and Ozzy Osbourne, and turning their careers around. And they thought—and probably rightfully so, at the time—that he could do the same thing with them. And he must have agreed, because he signed on to do the album, but they had to wait for him to finish a cycle with some other band. So there was a long period of time, April '86 through September '87, where there was no new KISS album, and the only thing that came out from KISS during that period was [the home video] *Exposed*.

What a lot of people forget is that this was really the best time to be a KISS fan, because all of a sudden, there was Frehley's Comet, Vinnie Vincent Invasion, Mark St. John's band White Tiger, Gene was in three or four movies during that time—there was so much to collect and do. As a KISS fan, there was never a shortage of things to buy during that period of time. There was always a new movie to go see or a new album to get, or go see Frehley's Comet or Vinnie Vincent Invasion. There was a lot going on during that period that people forget. As KISS fans, it was a very rewarding and interesting time, and exciting, looking forward to *Crazy Nights*.

GIMME MORE: K.K. DOWNING ON METAL VETS SOFTENING THEIR SOUND

Original Judas Priest guitarist K.K. Downing looks back on the short-lived phenomenon of when such veteran acts as KISS, Ozzy, and Priest modified their metal for the mainstream.

Why do you think so many veteran hard-rock and heavy-metal acts lightened their sound around the same time in the 80s?

You get to the late 70s, and you start to see a lot more arena bands and arena tours. We jumped on some—supporting Led Zeppelin, Alice Cooper, Foghat, KISS. But I think it's fair to say, by the time we see the 80s, we see MTV coming along, which broadened a massive spectrum. Radio stations got bigger and more powerful. Every car that was driving down the street had the radio pumping. When we got to the mid-80s, there was such a feel-good factor. We would come over to America, and we would do 138 shows—*in North America alone*. We would go all the way around the country and Canada, have a break of two weeks, and then go all the way around again, playing the secondary markets. And even the secondary markets were notable places to be, for bands like us.

But what is very important is that bands were going to the people. People were not having to spend a fortune or having to travel overnight to see bands in major cities, so they could spend more money and see more bands at this time. It was harder to do that before, and it was certainly harder to do that afterward. Most bands stopped going into the secondary markets, because we were told they had become 'non-lucrative' areas. Which was sad. Because we would go to Boise, Idaho; we'd go to Little Rock, Arkansas; we would go to Biloxi, Mississippi, and play these towns—Midland-Odessa. I remember going to Midland-Odessa with Judas Priest, the Scorpions, and Def Leppard! That's great for the people, and it's great for the radio stations, and it's great for the media who are not in Los Angeles, New York, Chicago, and St. Louis, for example. So it's great all around.

I think we saw the most positive and productive period in music history in the mid-80s. And I think it's fair to say they were the 'big hair' days. We would see bands—Scorpions, Judas Priest, Dokken—all go to the hairdressers. But it was all good, because the whole rock and metal genre became more colorful. These were just magical times. But did it become a fight for positions on MTV and radio stations? Probably it did.

We played the US Festival [on May 29, 1983], and Ozzy went on before us, Quiet Riot went on before us. And then, before we know it, Quiet Riot do an album, and they sell six million records [1983's *Metal Health*]. Before we know it, Def Leppard come out of the box and sell six million records [1983's *Pyromania*]. And Def Leppard's follow-up album [1987's *Hysteria*] sold over *ten million* records! And then you've got Van Halen [who also had a ten-million seller with 1984's *1984*]. So, suddenly, you start to see mixes of tours, where you could get any mixture of any bands. It's a mix-and-match, but everything is good, and everything is in the genre. And I think, with Judas Priest, we probably started to think—consciously or subconsciously—that we haven't had our day yet. All of those other bands have had their day with these big-selling records. Judas Priest seemed to be one of the biggest bands around at the time, but our biggest-selling record was, like, two million records [1982's *Screaming For Vengeance*]. Not to be greedy, but we were thinking, *Our support bands are having these massive-selling records. If you create the songs, you've got the media outlets with radio and television now. You can have these big records—you just have to put the songs together.*

Hence, probably, why Priest decided not to do a double album with the *Turbo* album, which was originally going to be called *Twin Turbos*. What we decided to do was condense everything down, and put out an album together that had good continuity, a good flow, but also was pretty much a radio-friendly album. We attempted it once, and kind of failed, because it didn't happen for us. The producers from *Top Gun* wanted a song from the album to put in the movie, and that didn't happen—our fault. Otherwise, it could have been very, very different for the band.

We had an opportunity—it just didn't click for Judas Priest. They wanted the song 'Reckless' [for the *Top Gun* soundtrack]. That probably would have done it, because it would have been all over the radio, I suppose, if it was in the movie. We thought 'Turbo Lover' and 'Locked In' were going to do it for us, but they didn't. The tour was very successful, the album was successful, but it wasn't the big-selling album that we hoped for. I think quite a lot of that went on with the acceptability and success of a lot of other bands that you would look at on MTV. Even *Ozzy* went to the hairdressers!

So that was what was going on in the mid-80s. But it was a wonderful time. We would drive up to a show, and there would be at least a hundred girls forming a line outside the backstage area. We did see more girls at the concerts on that *Turbo* tour. If you look at the video [1987's *Priest ... Live!*], it's totally apparent. But it didn't quite click in the big way that we thought it was going to. I think that's the crux of it—about bands lightening up a bit in the mid-80s. *It did happen.* Everybody was in a happy place—the musicians, the fans, the media. It was a good time economically. It wasn't really until the Gulf War happened that it started to decline. Wars are bound to have an effect on how people feel, and the economy. We had five years or so—maybe more—of great times, of everything getting to where it had been headed, for quite a long time. Because punk and the new-wave thing had gone, and there was an acceptance of what we were doing. Our 'art' became accepted by the masses. Even though we had to suffer court cases and the PMRC—there is always a battle to fight when you do what we do. But over the years it lasted, it was good.

Judas Priest would play with Heart, Journey, Sammy Hagar—you name it. It was a great mix-and-match situation, and, for Judas Priest, we were happy with that, because we were always a band to experiment and to try to expand and widen the boundaries of rock and metal. And to popularize it. And it seemed to all come together in the mid-80s.

Did the radio/MTV success of such bands as Mötley Crüe and Ratt, and later Bon Jovi, turn the tide?
Yeah. MTV and the radio stations—once you got big hits and numbers there, potentially you could have that big-selling album on your hands. We seemed to get plenty of coverage and play, but it didn't quite fit, for some reason. Maybe it was just quite simply the name 'Judas Priest.' I don't know. It's difficult. But it was a great place to be, because you could check into a hotel virtually anywhere in the US—any major city—and there would be *lots* of bands in town.

Some guys would be playing the arenas, some guys would be playing theaters, and some people would be playing clubs. One time I was in Chicago, and I saw Michael Schenker in the coffee shop in the hotel! I remember being in Seattle, and we had a party in our hotel—it was us, Van Halen, Heart, and I think UFO. I can remember quite a few instances like that.

Priest, KISS, and Ozzy wore quite over-the-top fashions on tour in 1986, in support of their respective albums—*Turbo*, *Asylum*, and *The Ultimate Sin*.
I think rock musicians had this awareness by then that if you could be attractive—or *seemingly* attractive—to the female audience, then you would be more successful. I think there was a lot of truth in that, in that particular time. Because it seemed to me that the female fraternity now seemed more comfortable going to concerts and getting out there—more so than in the 70s. I mean, when we first went to Japan, it was a 95 percent male audience.

And then, it turned around—by the mid-80s, it would probably be 80 percent female. Massive, massive turnaround.

'Hair metal' is the term often used to describe this era, which is fitting—Rob Halford even grew his hair long at the time!

Everybody had cute-looking chicks in their videos. Scantily clad women. And I think a lot of the girls thought, *I want to be in a video with a rock band.* And, of course, we would use girls in our videos—mud wrestlers, you name it. Fit-looking girls. In that 'Locked In' video, I think we had a total of about thirty-six girls. And that video cost our record company—if my memory serves me well—$360,000. We got caught up in that. We'll never see those days again. But I must be right about what I'm saying about it reaching its pinnacle—if you think about those video budgets, it's absolutely insane. I think bands spent a million dollars on their video—I'm *sure* they did.

But the main thing is, we reached a point where everybody was in a good place. It seemed that people were happier and enjoying life better. And people were enjoying music a lot more than they ever did. Everybody as a whole—it was seriously big. Those massive record stores that we used to go to—doing in-stores, playing shows. There were a lot more bands around for the people. And now, unfortunately, so many fans have to travel so far to see a band, because there are less tour dates. It's a big investment to see a band these days for lots of people in the States.

Interestingly, Priest, Ozzy, and KISS all returned to heavy metal during the early 90s and issued albums that are now considered metal classics—Priest with *Painkiller*, Ozzy with *No More Tears*, and KISS with *Revenge*.

Well, certainly for Priest, we saw that particular time come and go with the *Turbo* album. It didn't work for us, so we went back to where we were. We did the *Ram It Down* album, which was pretty cool. But there was a sense of change. Because there were bands like Slayer, Metallica, Megadeth, and Pantera, and there was a movement of other things that started to come in—the grunge thing. There are lots of things happening. Everything started to get a little bit more disrupted. There were a few more world threats happening—obviously, the Gulf War. So, after *Ram It Down*, we were getting back to heavy metal. I guess we just got caught up in the wave of everything that happened in the mid-80s.

You go through different periods of your life. You go through changes—as a band, as a person. Economics, politically—changes happen that bring about how the world is in that particular time. And you do get affected and influenced. As I just mentioned, there was a case of [needing] to get back to what we do best. Otherwise, other bands are just going to take the mantel and run with it. Musicians get affected by it, record companies, and managers. Everything that surrounds a band is affecting what a band does as well, because there are all of these influences. People saying, 'Maybe you should do *this*, maybe you should do *that*.' Not as if you always listen, but sometimes, maybe, you do.

Priest toured with KISS in 1979. Did you keep track of their career during their non-makeup era?

I followed it some, but obviously we were doing our thing. But I will say that it was quite an experience, doing the KISS tour. Those guys looked after us—they treated us well. They're good guys. We played at this old theater in New York, and I know the guys came down and saw us, and they told their management they wanted us on tour with them. Gene Simmons would come to a lot of our shows—if ever it was in the area. He's a good guy—I like him.

It was quite an eye-opener, doing that tour. I can remember one night in Chicago; all of those girls were lined up outside. They would let all those girls in, and line them all the way up from the dressing room to the stage, if they wanted an autograph. I was there one night, and I swear to God, all those girls lifted up their T-shirts, and those guys came out of their dressing room, and signed those girls' boobs all the way to the stage. My eyes were popping out of my head. I'm thinking, *This is America?!* [*Laughs*] Fun times, fun times.

CRAZY NIGHTS

Released September 18, 1987. Produced by Ron Nevison.
US #18, UK #4. US certification: platinum.

SIDE ONE

Crazy Crazy Nights (Paul Stanley/Adam Mitchell)
I'll Fight Hell To Hold You (Stanley/Bruce Kulick/Mitchell)
Bang Bang You (Stanley/Desmond Child)
No, No, No (Gene Simmons/Kulick/Eric Carr)
Hell Or High Water (Simmons/Kulick)
My Way (Stanley/Child/Bruce Turgon)

SIDE TWO

When Your Walls Come Down (Stanley/Mitchell/Kulick)
Reason To Live (Stanley/Child)
Good Girl Gone Bad (Simmons/Davitt Sigerson/Peter Diggins)
Turn On The Night (Stanley/Diane Warren)
Thief In The Night (Simmons/Mitch Weissman)

SINGLES

Crazy Crazy Nights / No, No, No (US #65, UK #4)
Reason To Live / Thief In The Night (US #64, UK #33)
Turn On The Night / Hell Or High Water (US did not chart, UK #41)

★

For quite some time, keyboards and heavy metal did not go merrily together. In the early 80s, keyboards were mostly associated with *pop* and *new wave* acts. But as soon as Van Halen were bold enough to feature keys on their mega-selling *1984* album (and, specifically, their #1 single 'Jump'), it seemed like every hard-rock/heavy-metal band was eager to jump on the bandwagon. Heck, even *Iron Maiden* took the plunge! KISS seemed to hold out a bit longer than most of the other bands, but even they eventually fully embraced the keys on their 1987 offering, *Crazy Nights*.

When it was announced that Ron Nevison had signed on to produce the album, it seemed like a slam-dunk that the album would match the mega-million sales numbers that recent albums by Van Halen and Def Leppard had racked up. After all, Nevison was fresh off producing such blockbuster hits as Heart's self-titled album and Ozzy's *The Ultimate Sin* (not to mention engineering classic recordings by The Who, Led Zeppelin, and Bad Company back in the 70s). And since it took longer than usual for KISS to follow-up their last album—1986 was the first year since their debut that there was not a single new release by the band (not even a bloody compilation)—fans grew increasingly eager to hear the fruits of the KISS/Nevison union.

The album's near-title track, 'Crazy Crazy Nights,' whetted fans' appetites by being issued as a single and video a full month before the album dropped, and certainly served as a faithful preview of what was to follow—a kinder, gentler, and *poppier* KISS. But unlike their last true *pop* offering, 1980's *Unmasked*, this time around the lads wisely made sure that their trademark hard rock could still be detected beneath the glossy sheen. And the move paid off, chart-wise—at least in the UK, where both the feel-good anthem single and its parent album rocketed to #4 on their respective charts. Stateside, the single and album did little better than KISS's past few offerings, chart-wise, but sales-wise *Crazy Nights* did out-perform its predecessor, successfully returning KISS to the platinum-selling promised land.

With such a long layoff between albums, you would assume that adequate time had been spent on songwriting, and that the end result would be a throwaway-free album, à la *Creatures Of The Night*. Unfortunately, this proved not to be the case, as evidenced by such largely forgettable fare as 'My Way' (no, not the Paul Anka–composed tune of the same name ... actually, a KISS cover of the tune Frank Sinatra made famous would have been an improvement!), 'Hell Or High Water,' and 'Good Girl Gone Bad.' In fact, now is as good a time as any to state the obvious: in terms of his songwriting contributions to the past few 80s-era KISS records, Gene Simmons was getting further and further away from his former *god of thunder* persona. Which, looking back on it today, was a major flub on his part (and something he would regret, before eventually returning with a vengeance on the fittingly titled *Revenge* album).

That said, not all of Simmons's offerings on *Crazy Nights* were strikeouts— the album-closer, 'Thief In The Night,' is an overlooked rocker, co-penned with Mitch Weissman (the last time his name would be found in the credits of a KISS recording), that originally appeared on Wendy O. Williams's *WOW* before being re-recorded here. Another Simmons standout was the Kulick shred showcase 'No, No, No,' which also served as Eric Carr's seemingly requisite one-tune-per-album co-songwriting contribution. (It has always befuddled yours truly as to why the drummer was not awarded more songwriting space per KISS album, as his tunes always proved to be inspired standouts: see 'All Hell's Breakin' Loose,' 'Under The Gun,' 'Little Caesar,' et cetera.)

Second only to 'Crazy Crazy Nights,' the other best-known tune on the album is the power ballad 'Reason To Live.' As with 'Tears Are Falling,' the video clip for this song enjoyed a prolonged presence on *Dial MTV*, yet frustratingly, once again this did not translate to chart success Stateside, with 'Reasons To Live' registering only a single slim digit higher than 'Crazy Crazy Nights' on the *Billboard* Hot 100, at #64.

The other tune to enjoy the music-video treatment was the oh-so-poppy 'Turn On The Night,' which has never been played live by the band, even though the video shows the band lip-synching the tune onstage … in front of an audience. In fact, it turns out that the crowd that evening—January 27, 1988, at the Centrum in Worcester, Massachusetts—had been subjected to seeing the band mime to the song *four times*.

Once again, songwriters-for-hire came out in force for *Crazy Nights*— the trusty Desmond Child racks up three credits this time, including 'Bang Bang You' (was it really necessary to seek help for a tune that contained such dazzling lyrics as 'I'm gonna bang, bang you / I'll shoot you down with my love gun, baby'?), 'My Way,' and 'Reason To Live.' Also lending a hand once more was Adam Mitchell ('Crazy Crazy Nights,' 'I'll Fight Hell To Hold You,' and 'When Your Walls Come Down'), as well as the renowned Diane Warren ('Turn On The Night') and future Polydor and EMI label head Davitt Sigerson ('Good Girl Gone Bad'), among others.

The *Crazy Nights* album cover did at least offer one of the better images of KISS's non-makeup era. Each member is 'reflected' in a mirror, showing both close-ups of their mugs plus more distant shots of each of them from the chest up (as well as both a yellow KISS logo and the album title in each corner of the cover, making it rather reminiscent of the setup for the *Rock And Roll Over* cover). It looks like the thought behind the cover image was capturing the end result of a wild and crazy night … *geddit?*

Was *Crazy Nights* the pop-metal-crossover-blockbuster that KISS had hoped for, to be mentioned in the same breath as *1984* and *Hysteria*? No. Did it succeed in keeping the KISS locomotive chugging along into the latter part of the 80s, while measuring up to the majority of other successful rock acts who were mining similar sonic territory at the time? Sure, why not.

KNOW THE SCORE: RON NEVISON

The producer of *Crazy Nights* weighs in the making of the album, and his association with KISS.

How did the idea come about for you and KISS to work together?

The *Crazy Nights* album was recorded from March '87 to June '87. I was in talks with them in the fall of '86. And I know that because during the Labor Day weekend of '86, my then-girlfriend and I went to Aspen—she had a modeling assignment. We were there for a few days, and I hiked while she was modeling. We said we would get a place for Christmas and New Years—for a skiing vacation in Aspen. So I got a house for ten days—from December 19 through January 2, or something like that. And the reason this is relevant is that, right around the end of October, my girlfriend and I broke up.

I was in conversations with Paul Stanley, and I mentioned to him that I had a house in Aspen that I had paid for, and if he would want to come and share it with me—or he offered, or something. We ended up going to Aspen together for ten days. We had had a relationship in the 70s—I had a meeting with him and Neil Bogart at Casablanca, about doing his solo record. For whatever reason, it didn't happen. But I guess with the success I had with Heart in '85, '86, I was a 'hot producer.' So they contacted me, probably through my manager.

How were the songs selected for *Crazy Nights*?

Paul sent me his good stuff. He collaborated with Desmond Child and different writers—he had some really good stuff, including a ballad that I thought would really put them over the top ... which ended up not doing that: 'Reason To Live.' He had written that with Desmond Child, and I thought it [would be] great as a single.

Paul sent me his songs in demo form, whereas Gene sent me ... twenty things. Gene just sent me *everything*. He didn't sing as many songs as Paul did on the record. And Gene is a headbanger kind of guy, right? He sent me *all* of his songs, whereas Paul *selected* his. I had to do more picking with Gene than I did with Paul. I remember a song title that Gene sent me was 'I Want To Put My Log In Your Fireplace.' It obviously wasn't on the album. [*Laughs*] But those were the kind of songs that he sent me. The demos of Gene's songs weren't as polished as Paul's songs.

How would you compare working with Paul and Gene in the studio?

Whenever you have a drummer like Eric, and a bassist like Gene ... Gene wasn't the world's best bass player, but he was solid. Once the cutting of the tracks is finished, unless they have any other things to do—like add vocals—they're basically finished on the first day. Whereas a guitar player or a keyboard player adds layers of overdubs, rhythm guitars, acoustic guitars. The keyboardist I used was Phil Ashley, and also Paul played some keyboards [as did Bruce]. But obviously KISS had two great guitar players. So that's how we proceeded.

How was working with Bruce Kulick and Eric Carr in the studio?

They were dream guys. Working with them was great. Very sad about Eric.

How would you describe Gene and Paul's relationship at that point?

I thought they were getting along fine. Really, Gene used to come in the studio at Rumbo, and would sit in the back of the studio and read *Variety*. So, yeah, I guess Paul saying Gene was focusing more on acting [in *Face The Music*]—he *was* back there reading *Variety*.

Was it a conscious decision on the band's part to make a 'pop-sounding' album?

Yeah, I guess, a little bit. The mid-80s presented a different situation—MTV had taken hold, but you also had two separate formats of radio that were very important: AOR [album-oriented rock] radio, which had been around for a long time, and then you had CHR [contemporary hit radio], which was what drove single and album sales. Just to get on the rock stations didn't really penetrate the whole country. The rock stations would just play rock, and CHR stations were playing lighter fare.

You had to do ballads as a rock band. And we had a ballad, which I thought would take them over the hump, as far as that side. But I didn't make the conscious effort to make a softer record. It might have had a little more keyboard presence than KISS fans would like—after all, they didn't like it when Bob Dylan put on electric guitar! My biggest thing after listening back to it a few years later was, I thought it could have been a harder rock mix. I think the production is there—maybe the mix isn't.

In his first book, Paul's main criticism of this era is that he felt that Gene wasn't fully focused on KISS, but rather was trying to launch an acting career and other interests. And, as a result, the quality of his songs suffered. Would you agree that Paul's songs were stronger than Gene's at this point?

Oh, Paul's songs were *twice as strong* as Gene's songs. There were a couple of things that I thought were interesting, but if I had had to do an album with *just* Gene's songs, I wouldn't have done it. But I didn't really know the history of [their] relationship, so I had nothing to compare it with. Whereas Paul and Gene had been working together—and are *still* working together—so he would be an accurate judge of that. I do know that Gene didn't participate in the album too much. Like I said, once you've done your bass parts and a vocal or two … I had situations with Heart, where I didn't see the bass player, Mark Andes, for the whole album, once he did his bass tracks—except maybe at the end of the album, for mixing. Either they come in and hang out and listen to see what's happening, and all things were formulating … or they don't.

Paul was always trying to sing higher than his range was. And there's really nothing I can do about it—that's the way rock singers think they should sing, right? And he was always straining a bit. He didn't have the kind of chops of say … the guy from Journey [Steve Perry] or the guy from Yes [Jon Anderson]—singers with super-high voices that were clear. But Paul was adequate. I thought the album should have had more commercial success, but it didn't. But it's platinum, you know?

What are your thoughts on *Crazy Nights* today?
I thought it didn't pack enough punch. The guitar, bass, and drums weren't as prominent, and the vocals maybe should have been tucked a little bit, and the keyboards tucked a little bit. KISS fans are a particular breed—they know what they like. And this didn't fit into their format.

2017 marked the thirtieth anniversary of *Crazy Nights*. That would have been a golden opportunity to remix and reissue the album.
That would have been great. I wish we did. I would definitely make it sound more like I wanted it originally to sound. I rarely get called to do stuff like that—to redo stuff. It's a shame. But I would love to do that.

KNOW THE SCORE: CHARLIE BENANTE

The drummer for Anthrax, who covered 'She' on the *Kiss My Ass* tribute album and other KISS tunes over the years, looks back on the period when the thrash band opened for KISS for portions of the *Crazy Nights* tour.

What do you remember about Anthrax getting the opening spot for KISS on their US tour from March 1 to April 2, 1988? Were you excited about it, since you were a KISS fan growing up?
I have to say that the level of excitement when we heard about it was … *Wow!*

Totally stoked. And again, people who read this and know my fascination with KISS, it's always going to be from the '73–78 period. That was it, for me. That was a magical time. When they took the makeup off, I wasn't really into it as much, but I still loved them. I loved Eric Carr—his playing and him as a person. He was such a fucking awesome dude. I remember he wasn't doing so good on that tour—I remember he was having some physical problems, and there was a concern there. We didn't know anything else, but he was having some problems.

The first person who made us feel welcome was Gene. The first person that *didn't* make us feel welcome was John Harte, their security guy. I'll never forget the first or second night: we were going onstage, and we were waiting on deck, and he was like, 'How long do I have to listen to your noise for?' But after that, he was awesome. We would talk to Gene almost every day—there would be fan-boy moments. It was awesome.

I'll tell you a funny story—it was probably two weeks into the run, and we were talking to Gene. At this point, Paul wasn't as friendly as Gene. Maybe he was just shy, or whatever it was. One of the guys in Anthrax said, 'You're so nice to us … and Paul has been a bit of an asshole to us. He doesn't acknowledge us, he doesn't say anything, he doesn't say hi or anything like that.' And as this was being said, who comes by walking by … Paul. Gene stops the conversation, and he's like, 'Paul, Paul. These guys want to know why you're being such an asshole—come over here.' Paul comes walking over, and in typical Paul fashion is like, 'Why am *I* an asshole? What does that mean? Maybe it's *you guys* who are the assholes, and didn't say hi to me?' It was uncomfortable for a minute, but then it was cool. After that, the air was cleared, and it was great.

What kinds of things do you recall discussing with Gene?

My main concern was talking to Gene about inside stuff that only I wanted to know about: 'Who played on *this*? I've always heard *this*, I've always heard *that*.' He would always tell me that on side four of *Alive II*, some of it was Peter playing, and some of it was not Peter playing. He was like, 'I think you can tell in the songs which ones he was playing on.' I definitely took that into consideration, and then went back and dissected each one of those songs! Like,

This has got to be Peter. This isn't Peter. Stuff like that. And he would tell us how Ace didn't show up [to a recording session]—Ace had a card game that was more important than coming to the studio.

Did he ever reveal who it was that played the drums on side four of *Alive II*?
He told me it was Anton Fig, and also Carmine Appice. But he couldn't remember which one was which.

Did you watch KISS's performances on that tour?
I watched them every night. It was a different band—a totally different band. The mystique, that element of KISS was not *this* KISS. It was that time where everything was very Bon Jovi–looking. *Glitzy.* But I understood that they felt like they couldn't take the makeup thing any further than they did, and they needed to reinvent themselves. And that is exactly what they did. The surroundings they were in, too, were kind of dictating to them: *I think it's time for a change.*

How did Anthrax go over in front of KISS's crowd on that tour?
It didn't matter—we were just excited to be on that stage. But I do remember having good shows. You have to remember that this was the period where our *Among The Living* album did really well, and now we were in the midst of the *I'm The Man* EP blowing up. So this was a whole different crowd for us. And there was such good momentum that nothing could stop it. I remember saying, 'I wish this tour was longer.'

Later that summer, Anthrax played additional shows with KISS as part of the Monsters Of Rock tour of Europe (August 27–September 10).
Right. But before that, we were recording our *State Of Euphoria* record at Electric Lady in New York, and Gene came down to hear 'Parasite' [which Anthrax were recording for a B-side] and to play ping-pong with us. It was one of those magical moments. The friendship started there, and I think he took a liking to us. But yes, we did the Monsters Of Rock, and that was awesome. And we became friendly—I became very friendly with Eric. It was definitely a good time.

How would you compare playing with KISS in arenas to big outdoor stadiums?
Over there [in Europe], it was a totally different vibe for us. We were blowing up over there, so it wasn't like we were opening. It was a festival—people were there to see everybody, and they treated you as the headliner. It was a great vibe. I wish some of those shows were done over here.

The Monsters Of Rock tour had a great lineup that also included Iron Maiden and David Lee Roth, among others. Were KISS able to hold their own?
Oh, yeah! *It was KISS*. I mean, it's not every day that KISS goes to Europe, you know? Especially that lineup.

CRAZY NIGHTS: THE TOUR WITH CURT GOOCH

The very Vegas-y wardrobes of the *Asylum* tour were toned down somewhat for the *Crazy Nights* arena trek—which eventually signaled the return of 70s-era classics back into the setlist …

By the end of the *Asylum* tour, Paul was very frustrated—they were blaming this on business manager Howard Marks—that KISS had not broken big. So they decided to wait on Ron Nevison, and do the album they thought would be perfect.

Had *Crazy Nights* come out a year earlier, it would probably be thought of a lot differently than it is. But *Crazy Nights* had the unbelievable mistiming of coming out post–*Appetite For Destruction*, which was an absolutely game-changing album for the industry. And once that happened, that Ron Nevison poppy sound was—virtually overnight—eliminated from the conversation. And *Crazy Nights*—in my opinion—suffers from an overly slick production. I've heard the demos for *Crazy Nights*—and in particular, the song 'Crazy Crazy Nights'—and they're actually really good. A lot better than what's on the record. It got so overproduced and so polished that it lost all of its edge.

For *Crazy Nights*, the stage set was minimal at best. They just recycled the *Asylum* logo, and the stage looked like a bootleg version of the *Animalize* tour. It was very minimal, and very in keeping with the nature of the setlist—the length of the setlist. And the costumes they were wearing on the *Crazy*

Nights tour … they certainly worked at the time. I don't know if you would look at them now and say they were embarrassing, like some of the *Asylum* outfits—Paul was wearing Body Glove stuff. It was quite a way from the Day-Glo gloves of the *Asylum* tour. But they definitely toned down the look and became a little more 'street' for the *Crazy Nights* tour. And I think that trend continued, look-wise, to the *Hot In The Shade* tour.

The *Crazy Nights* tour started on November 13, 1987, in Jackson, Mississippi, at the Mississippi Coliseum. The setlist included 'Black Diamond' on the first night, and then that was dropped. And the setlist was unbelievably *Crazy Nights*–heavy. Six songs from *Crazy Nights* were there in the beginning—'Crazy Crazy Nights,' 'Bang Bang You,' 'No, No, No,' 'Hell Or High Water,' 'When Your Walls Come Down,' and 'Reason To Live.' And then, over the course of the month, that got pared back to four. But oddly enough, they cut the two better songs ['Hell Or High Water' and 'When Your Walls Come Down'] and kept two of the worst songs on the album, with 'Bang Bang You' and 'No, No, No,' which I don't think had any appeal—even at that point.

The *Crazy Nights* tour—especially at the beginning—is considered to be the band's worst tour up to that point. The shows had gone from ninety and a hundred minutes during the *Asylum* tour down to seventy-five minutes. Ultimately it made it up to eighty minutes, but still, that's very weak for a rock band of their stature at that point. All of their peers were doing longer shows. But by that point, when 'Crazy Crazy Nights' did not take off as the big single in America, they were having a hard time booking shows and getting that tour to even happen.

The *Crazy Nights* period can be defined in two eras—pre–'Reason To Live' and post–'Reason To Live.' Once again, *Dial MTV* really had a huge impact on ticket sales for that tour … *Crazy Nights* went platinum based on the fact that 'Reason To Live' was scoring so high on *Dial MTV* for months and months. So that really helped the tour, big time. But it didn't help the shows, which were still seventy-five minutes in length. And KISS made a very bizarre choice by allowing the set opener to be 'Love Gun.' 'Love Gun' may be a KISS classic, but it is in no way, shape, or form an opening song. Who thought of that, and why that was allowed … I have *no idea*.

At some point in January, they brought 'Shout It Out Loud' back in the set, and that was the first time since *Creatures* that 'Shout It Out Loud' had been played—and that was a big surprise for people who were seeing the show. But then the band went overseas, to Japan, and proceeded to put all kinds of rare material back into the set—'Deuce,' 'I Was Made For Lovin' You,' 'Calling Dr. Love.' Things that hadn't been played in years.

It's funny, because [in] the bootlegs and the TV appearances from Japan and Europe, [KISS] seemed to be more popular than when they had been here, months earlier. It seemed like people liked the band a lot more, because now they were doing better material in the set—70s tunes. That definitely woke Gene and Paul up—they had to have been aware of that, because when you get to the next album and outing, *Hot In The Shade*, this is where non-makeup KISS go to their *zenith*.

In 1988, KISS were invited to do the Monsters Of Rock tour—I believe it was five shows throughout several countries in Europe. And this was the first time since 1975 that the band actually opened for somebody. This time, they were opening for Iron Maiden, who had previously opened for KISS in 1980. Whether they liked it or not, there was no denying that Iron Maiden were a bigger band in Europe than KISS … that was just the way the cookie crumbled. But the audience for Donington '88, I think still to this day is the record-winner—I'm pretty sure that audience was never that big again. [Note: one reason for that is that tragedy struck when two audience members were crushed to death when the enormous crowd surged forward during Guns N' Roses' daytime set.]

Also, the *Crazy Nights* tour was the first time in KISS's history that they brought in keyboards—they had an offstage keyboardist by the name of Gary Corbett. Gary was there for part of the *Crazy Nights* tour, and then they decided to cut back costs and got rid of [him]. He was there for certain shows and not other ones. They brought him back for Europe, but then part of the North American tour was without him. But Gary definitely helped fill in some notes while Paul was swinging his arm or doing some kind of move—there would be a note that would get missed, and Gary would fill in.

GIMME MORE: BRUCE KULICK ON THE *CRAZY NIGHTS* DEMOS

Seemingly more so than for any other KISS album, quite a few demos of songs considered for *Crazy Nights* that did not make the final cut have surfaced over the years. Here, Bruce gives us a guided tour of the material, and what he remembers about each song.

'Sword And Stone' (Bruce Kulick, Paul Stanley, Desmond Child)

Nevison didn't want it—he didn't *hear it* for the record. I was pretty shocked. I think he was dead wrong—it belonged on the record. What else can I say? We did a great demo for it. Other people covered it [Loverboy's Paul Dean, and the band Bonfire]. And Desmond really loved it—he didn't understand why it wasn't on the KISS album. I have plans for myself to record it in the future. I think I played the bass on it. If not me, it would have been Paul.

I liked the KISS version better [than the covers]. In fact, I was playing the Paul Dean one for my wife recently, and she went, like, *What?!* But I was very flattered it was covered. The Bonfire one is probably closer, but they do it so *German*. I mean, it's not easy to imitate Paul Stanley. He really *owned* the song, emotionally. I'm hoping whatever version I cut in the future could be strong—but that demo was amazing. And it's on YouTube, and people share it—it's out there. [Note: when I asked him about this song in an interview for this book, Nevison had no memory of it.]

'Dial "L" For Love' (Eric Carr, Gene Simmons, Adam Mitchell)

Adam is a good songwriter, and he worked hard with Eric and Gene on that. I might have been involved with the demo, but I wasn't a writer on it. It just never got chosen for anything. It ended up on the *Gene Simmons Vault*, and it was on Eric Carr's *Unfinished Business*.

'Are You Always This Hot' (Gene Simmons, Adam Mitchell)

It wasn't one of my favorites. They kept pushing it, and it didn't get used. I didn't really love that one. I probably have a demo of that, but it is not for 'public consumption.' [Note: this track was also eventually included on *Gene Simmons Vault*.]

'Time Traveler' (Paul Stanley, Desmond Child)

That was done at exactly the same time as 'Sword And Stone.' And it was really interesting that they put it on *The Box Set*. I like the song, but I thought 'Sword And Stone' was stronger—that's why I'm still even more confused as to why they didn't use 'Sword And Stone.'

'Hide Your Heart' (Paul Stanley, Desmond Child, Holly Knight)

I think the demo existed way before *Hot In The Shade*. And by the time other people covered it, and we were ready to do *Hot In The Shade*, it was obvious to the band—meaning Gene and Paul—we need to put it on *our* record. It became a video and everything. I think, once again, if Paul writes a song, he is going to have the definitive version—rightfully so.

'Boomerang' (Bruce Kulick, Gene Simmons)

The demo probably would have sounded similar [to the version that appears on *Hot In The Shade*]. As much as I'm a co-writer on it, my mindset of that was just *fast guitar riffs*. Gene liked that kind of stuff, Paul didn't. And *Hot In The Shade* was very much a compromise between the two of them: *Well, I'll let you do that song … and you've got to let me do this song.* When I listen back to that now, I'm like, *I get it.* We were just doing the *fast guitar riff/double bass drum/manic rock tune* here. And Paul never had a really big affection for that. I understand that, too, but that was very much the genre of hair-metal bands back then.

'X Marks The Spot' (songwriters unknown)

I remember the title, but I don't remember [the song]. I knew exactly what Paul was hoping to get covered, and the only ones that didn't make it were 'Time Traveler' and probably 'Sword And Stone.' It was probably a Gene track.

'Scratch And Sniff' / 'What Goes Up' / 'Hunger For Love' / 'Dirty Blonde' / 'No Mercy' (songwriters unknown)

I don't remember anything about those songs. I might have played on one of Gene's demos. Now, keep in mind, I do have cassettes [from] when the band was like, *Check out these songs.* A lot of the stuff I've archived—not all of it. So there may be titles there. But since it wasn't created by me, I didn't co-write it with Gene, or I never even worked on the demo he did with whoever he did it with—which sometimes was just him and a drum machine, and sometimes guys that would do the work or co-write with him—I don't remember them.

Why were there seemingly more songs demoed for *Crazy Nights* than for any other non-makeup-era album?

I think the answer is simpler than you think. Gene always has more material than is necessary—which is why he has the *Vault*. Paul, though, got involved with a publishing deal, so it was in his benefit to create a lot of material, because generally Paul likes to write for an album. And even though I have a lot of unfinished things and ideas with Paul that I have on tape, generally, only if you really feel strong about an idea does it get to that demo stage, where it's a real recording that everybody can learn from and then do in the studio.

When you have a publishing deal, you can't get a song covered unless you have a proper demo. And that's why I think Desmond certainly was the one that ran with 'Sword And Stone.' Paul didn't go knocking on doors and say, 'Cover my song.' Look at 'Hide Your Heart.' That was another one that was in that very fruitful era where Paul was writing a lot of material, because he did have a publishing deal, and he introduced me to one of the guys that helped him sometimes—this guy Curt Cuomo, who wound up co-writing some of the things on *Carnival Of Souls*. So that worked in our benefit. You see how that dynamically affected things a little bit.

SMASHES, THRASHES & HITS

Released November 15, 1988. Produced by Paul Stanley, Gene Simmons, Eddie Kramer, Bob Ezrin, Michael James Jackson, Kenny Kerner, Richie Wise, Vini Poncia, and Neil Bogart. US #21, UK #62. US certification: double platinum.

SIDE ONE

Let's Put The X In Sex (Paul Stanley/Desmond Child)

(You Make Me) Rock Hard (Stanley/Child/Diane Warren)

Love Gun (Stanley)

Detroit Rock City (Stanley/Bob Ezrin)

I Love It Loud (Simmons/Vinnie Vincent)

Deuce (Simmons)

Lick It Up (Stanley/Vincent)

SIDE TWO

Heaven's On Fire (Stanley/Child)

Calling Dr. Love (Simmons)

Strutter (Stanley/Simmons)

Beth [with Eric Carr vocal] (Peter Criss/Stan Penridge/Ezrin)

Tears Are Falling (Stanley)

I Was Made For Lovin' You (Stanley/Child/Vini Poncia)

Rock And Roll All Night (Stanley/Simmons)

Shout It Out Loud (Stanly/Simmons/Ezrin)

SINGLES

Let's Put The X In Sex / Calling Dr. Love (remix) (US #97, UK did not chart)

(You Make Me) Rock Hard / Strutter (remix) (US/UK did not chart)

★

In the wake of KISS's first best-of collection, *Double Platinum*, being released in 1978, several more comps were issued in specific territories throughout the world—the best known among them being the Europe-only *Killers* (1982) and the Japan-only *Chikara* (1988)—but there were no follow-ups for the US market. By 1988, ten years had passed since KISS last issued a compilation in the USA, and with eight albums, several lineup changes, and their unmasking having taken place during that timespan, it certainly made sense to issue another. The result was *Smashes, Thrashes & Hits*. As on *Double Platinum*, and in an effort to attract both fans that had already purchased the previous albums *and* more casual listeners, quite a few of the selections on *SM&H* were remixed, while there were also two brand new tunes exclusive to this collection.

The two new tracks, 'Let's Put The X In Sex' and '(You Make Me) Rock Hard,' were both sung and co-written by Paul Stanley, with Desmond Child once again earning a writing credit on both, and Diane Warren joining the duo on the latter. Stylistically, neither song would have sounded out of place on *Crazy Nights* (although, musically, 'X In Sex' bears more than a passing resemblance to Robert Palmer's 'Addicted To Love'). And, like the videos from *Asylum*, the clips for both new ditties could have *only* come out of the 80s. Paul Stanley does not play guitar in either clip, but there are plenty of shots of skyscrapers, and fashion models marching in time or swinging on a trapeze … I think it's best if you watch them to get the full effect!

Instead of picking up where *Double Platinum* left off and focusing solely on material recorded from 1979 to 1987, the fifteen-track *ST&H* combines the best of the 80s with the 70s. Actually, it's more fitting to say *70s with the 80s*, as there are more tracks from the makeup era than the non-makeup era. Overall, there can be no complaints about the tunes plucked from KISS's golden period ('Love Gun,' 'Detroit Rock City,' 'Deuce,' 'Calling Dr. Love,' 'Strutter,' 'Beth,' 'Rock And Roll All Nite,' and 'Shout It Out Loud'), but there is much to be said about the *versions* of the songs that are included.

First off, the remixes of these songs have an unmistakable 80s sheen to them, especially in the drum department. (Give 'Deuce' a listen and then compare it to the original to see what I mean.) And while the new drum sound is not as extreme or distracting as, say, what ZZ Top did on their *Six Pack* collection around this time (for which they were heavily criticized for replacing all the drums on their classic albums with a newly recorded, contemporary-sounding drum machine), most KISS fans will undoubtedly agree that the originals are far superior.

Another misstep that occurs here—and on most other KISS comps—is that the studio version of 'Rock And Roll All Nite' is included instead of the far superior live version. After all, it was the *live version* that served as KISS's breakthrough hit way back when. And I've saved the biggest faux pas for last—having Eric Carr replace Peter Criss's lead vocals on the hit ballad 'Beth.' That's not a slight against Carr's vocal performance—he was quite an underrated singer, as heard when he sang lead on such tunes as 'Black Diamond' and 'Young And Wasted' in concert, or on 'Little Caesar' on record. It was the overall idea that fell flat, because the song had become Criss's trademark—both lyrically (an early version dated back to his pre-KISS band, Chelsea, and was supposedly inspired by events from that time) and vocally (especially live, when the Catman would come out to the front of the stage to sing it). Perhaps a version of 'Black Diamond' with Carr's vocals would have been a wiser choice? I guess we'll never know. A valid argument could also be made that the song 'New York Groove' should have been included here, since it was a sizable hit single from Ace Frehley's 1978 solo album (yes, it was off Ace's *solo album*, but for all intents and purposes, 'Beth' was a Peter Criss solo tune, since no other KISS members played on the original).

The selections that represent '79–87 here include 'I Love It Loud,' 'Lick It Up,' 'Heaven's On Fire,' 'Tears Are Falling,' and 'I Was Made For Lovin' You.' But by opting to include only five tracks from this era, the band completely ignore three albums: 1980's *Unmasked*, 1981's *Music From The Elder*, and 1987's *Crazy Nights*. While it's understandable that they would skip over the first two albums (they have since gone on record in saying that they consider both stylistic missteps—not to mention the fact that neither album exactly set the charts alight Stateside), it's hard to come up with a reason why they would not have included at least one tune from *Crazy Nights*. Or, to further entice longtime fans and collectors, a *live* version. After all, two of the songs from *Crazy Nights* enjoyed some degree of success—the UK Top 5 hit 'Crazy Crazy Nights' and the MTV hit 'Reason To Live.' And, to add insult to injury, the former *was* actually included on the UK version of *ST&H*, which makes you wonder why the heck it could not have been squeezed in on the US version as well. But the biggest gripe is how they totally neutered the gonzo drum sound of the opening of 'I Love It Loud'—which was such a huge part of what made the song a sing-along arena-rock anthem in the first place.

Despite its shortcomings, *Smashes, Thrashes & Hits* has gone on to become one of KISS's steadiest and biggest sellers, earning double platinum certification (with, as of this writing, the only other double platinum releases of their career being *Destroyer* and *Alive II*) and seemingly becoming the go-to release for many newcomers, since more eras of KISS's career are represented here than on the majority of single-disc comps on the market.

KNOW THE SCORE: BRUCE KULICK

The longest-tenured KISS guitarist of the non-makeup era shares his thoughts on *Smashes, Thrashes & Hits*.

When *Smashes, Thrashes & Hits* came out, it coincided with KISS starting to bring songs from the 70s back into the live set.

I was always aware of the strength of the makeup era. And to the record company—in their own brand-name connection of the makeup era—it was always in their benefit to in some way remind people, or include it, and not separate it. You know, does Van Halen separate the Sammy Hagar years from the David Lee Roth years? Maybe, but to me, they're *all* Van Halen. That's an example maybe nowhere near as extreme, because KISS is the only band that ever had such an important footprint on the music world as almost like a superhero/comic-book band ... and then turning into a hair band.

Them not letting go of their past, or not including it in with something that was really a greatest-hits album with new material, it didn't get me thinking, like, *Uh oh*. But I was always aware. Every couple of years, I was like, *[They] could easily just go back into makeup ... or not*. It didn't affect me too much, that way. I was not surprised. I was just excited that we would be doing a couple of new tunes—even though they were very much Paul's mood then. They were that vibe. I was surprised by how successful the album was, actually. It showed that a lot of people wanted a combination of everything.

What's funny is that *Smashes, Thrashes & Hits* went double platinum, whereas *Double Platinum* itself only went platinum.

It wasn't that long ago that I [found out] that *Smashes* went double platinum, and I wanted it, so I did get a double platinum award for my wall, which is always nice to have.

The album had two new songs, 'Let's Put The X In Sex' and '(You Make Me) Rock Hard' …

We went in and knocked them out one day. I was so excited to rehearse those songs for the KISS Kruise in 2018. I had a real strong [hope] that, as much as they're not talked about a lot—and maybe they were very *pop* for KISS—that they would go over incredibly. And they did. I just think it was Paul's thing—Gene was probably still knee-deep in his movies and whatever he was up to. By working with Desmond Child on 'Let's Put The X In Sex,' and with Desmond and Diane Warren on '(You Make Me) Rock Hard,' you know Paul was looking for his A-team to put out some singles. And we did videos for both of them.

That was Paul being real *pop* with a couple of tunes, and with Desmond and Diane being such great writers, I never had a problem with those songs. It's interesting—they don't get talked about a lot, but clearly they were related to more pop music than rock music at the time. Especially 'X In Sex' having a bit of a Robert Palmer vibe … but not done completely like that. I did notice we used keyboard elements—that was not so common, but not so unusual after *Crazy Nights*, because Nevison was into that, because that was definitely [of] that era.

What were your thoughts on Eric singing 'Beth,' and how did he feel about it?

He was very torn about it. I understood him being uncomfortable with it, but I didn't think it was the wrong thing to do. So he did it, and Paul really enjoyed producing him. If you think about the big picture, they didn't use Eric as much as they could have, because he was such a great singer. The live stuff proves that.

See, I didn't have the complete history of what happened with Peter and those guys, because I wasn't around then. Plus I think there were some contractual things related to that song with Peter—because Peter just felt like it was *his*. I guess it was a way to share it with everybody—but with the current drummer, and him doing a fine job. I'm sure [some people thought it was] blasphemy, or, *That's cool that Eric's singing that song*. It almost seems like there are five sides of the story, as to why it's going down the way it is. But I still thought it was positive for Eric to do it. I doubt if it gets any radio play … but he did a good job.

There were no songs from *Crazy Nights* on the US version of *ST&H*, yet the song 'Crazy Crazy Nights' was included on the UK version.
There are different song lists, and I purposely went out of my way to get a UK copy, because it had more of my era on it. I think, in some ways, my era was more revered in Europe than in America—or at least that was the perception of the record company.

That's an interesting point, because the album *Crazy Nights* and the song 'Crazy Crazy Nights' both peaked at #4 on their respective charts in the UK— far higher than any 70s-era releases did there.
And then the most recent greatest-hits record, *KISS World*, opens with 'Crazy Crazy Nights.' And it has quite a few songs from my era: four, which is pretty big [the others being 'God Gave Rock And Roll To You II,' 'Tears Are Falling,' and 'Unholy']. I know it came from England originally. So I find that remarkable— that that's what they're going to put out. But all that makes me happy.

KNOW THE SCORE: MITCH LAFON
The host of *Rock Talk With Mitch Lafon* analyzes the lone compilation KISS issued in North America during the non-makeup era.

Let's discuss *Smashes, Thrashes & Hits*.
Before *Smashes, Thrashes & Hits* came out in November of '88, in May of that year, KISS in Japan had released an album called *Chikara*, which in English means *power*. I actually had a chance to purchase it locally in a store in Montreal. And what was always exciting about *Chikara* is that it had the

twelve-inch single version of 'I Was Made For Lovin' You.' So, it had this long, eight-minute version of the song that had not been made available since the late 70s. The *Creatures Of The Night* songs were remixed for that album—or certainly that was the rumor. It had focused a little bit on the non-makeup era, and had 'Heaven's On Fire,' 'Thrills In The Night,' 'Who Wants To Be Lonely,' and other non-makeup era tracks ['Lick It Up,' 'All Hell's Breakin' Loose,' 'Uh! All Night,' and 'Tears Are Falling']. And, like pretty much anything in Japan, it did exceptionally well, because Japanese fans—especially at that time—loved CDs and unique products just for their country.

And that leads us to *Smashes, Thrashes & Hits*. The band had put out *Crazy Nights*, and it had not set the world on fire. When you're looking around, and you're seeing Bon Jovi, Def Leppard, and Mötley Crüe having success, and you're KISS, and you go, *We're going to put out an album that sounds like those bands*, and it doesn't set the world on fire … [then you] put out *Smashes*. They put out two new songs on there … in fact, it's *three* new songs, because 'Beth' was redone with Eric Carr on vocals.

It's an interesting compilation, because I guess they were trying to look at where they could find success. New, fresh albums weren't happening, so they went back to this, and I think, at the time, there was a lot of disagreements going on with Ace and Peter about back catalogue, and so on and so forth. They put songs like 'Heaven's On Fire' and 'Lick It Up' on this thing, and then they remixed some of the older tracks, and I'm not really sure what led them to the remixes—was it better technology that could reveal a few extra seconds of 'Deuce' or 'Shout It Out Loud,' or was it really to try and trick the fans into thinking, *Hey, these are new versions?*

But they had added some stuff—there seems to be some added keyboards to some songs, or some added rhythm guitars or effects. It's interesting that it came out that way. In fact, a lot of fans will say that 'Love Gun' or 'Shout It Out Loud' on *Smashes, Thrashes & Hits* are better than the album versions. And the two new tracks have gotten a lot of hate from the KISS world, but I'm a fan of 'Let's Put The X In Sex' and '(You Make Me) Rock Hard.' I think they are exactly what KISS is and was: *mindless fun*.

I don't mean that in a disparaging way at all. I think if you look at KISS and you look at KISS lyrically, it's not about solving world hunger or saving the whales—it's about *rock and roll all night and party every day*. And 'Let's Put The X In Sex' and '(You Make Me) Rock Hard'—and I say this lovingly—are as goofy as anything else. That's what it's supposed to be.

Contextually, in '87, '88, not a lot of bands were saying real deep things, whether it was the pop scene or the rock scene. The metal scene sometimes wants to think it says important things … and a band like U2 always thinks they're saying something important, but 90 percent of the music back then was, *Hey baby, let's have some fun*. And that's what this was.

What were your thoughts on Eric Carr singing 'Beth'?

Well, I've always been a fan of that version. I've always been a fan of bands doing [new] treatments and repurposing of their songs. I mean, right now, in my iPhone, I have a 350-song playlist of Foreigner, and, yes, a lot of the songs repeat—you've got a lot of 'Cold As Ice' and a lot of 'Urgent,' but there's the orchestral version, there's the acoustic version, there's the acoustic version with Lou Gramm, there's the acoustic version with Kelly Hansen. So, when it comes to KISS and other bands—Metallica—I like when they do that.

I thought it was interesting, because Eric was there, he was the drummer, and he was almost sort of like the hidden drummer. Fans, as we look back, go, *Oh, Eric Carr was a great drummer*. But in the 80s, a lot of us were like, *When's Peter coming back? When's Ace coming back?* We didn't give Bruce or Eric their due. And having Eric sing 'Beth' sort of gave him a validity that had been missing. Bruce didn't get to be 'Bruce' until *Revenge*. Up until *Revenge*, I think Bruce was just *the guy that wasn't Ace*. And then *Revenge* came out, and they were like, *Oh … that's Bruce Kulick*. I think we sort of had the same, thinking of Eric Carr, like, *Well, that's not Peter. Peter can still play—why can't Peter be in this band?*

And then he sings 'Beth,' and you're like, *Well, OK, he's the drummer, and he's doing the drummer's song*. And then we sort of go back and go, *Oh, and he used to sing 'Black Diamond' and 'Young And Wasted' … good on him*. I think that kind of gave him a validity: *Yeah, he's the drummer, and now, he's doing the drummer's song*. I know some fans hate *Smashes, Thrashes & Hits* because of the remixes. I like it.

What do you think of the fact that the US version had no material from *Crazy Nights, Unmasked*, or *Music From The Elder*?

Well, having nothing from *The Elder* to me made sense, because it really *isn't* that great of an album. And some of the songs on that album—whether it's 'A World Without Heroes' or 'Dark Light'—OK, you can say they're good songs, but they're not singles. And *Smashes, Thrashes & Hits*, to me, suggests *singles*: 'This is a smash song,' or 'It's a hit.' And nothing there was a hit.

As far as *Unmasked*, I found that kind of strange, because you look at a song like 'Shandi,' which gets a huge reception in Australia—and I know this wasn't an Australia-specific release, but you would think they'd want to polish it up and say, *A lot of you might have jumped ship when we put this out. Hey, listen to it in context with these other songs. It works!* And I think they could have done something with that.

I don't think that's a condemnation of *Crazy Nights*. I think they were sort of anticipating fan pushback in North America: 'We just bought *Crazy Nights* six months ago … now you're making me re-buy the songs?' It seemed to me that it was complementary, filling a void between *Crazy Nights* and *Hot In The Shade*. Now, in the UK, 'Crazy Crazy Nights' was a massive hit. So it was included. But the American market—to me, as a Canadian—is sometimes fickle, and fans don't like to feel like they're being ripped off. And if you put a *Crazy Nights* song on there, they might have felt ripped off. Now, of course, it's just my opinion. But I think that's the marketing angle.

When you mentioned KISS trying to 80s-ify some of the 70s tunes on *Smashes, Thrashes & Hits*—to be fair, other veteran rock bands were doing similar maneuvers at the time, such as ZZ Top with *Six Pack*.

And it doesn't just stop there. A couple of years later, bands did *Unplugged*, and then *everybody* did *Unplugged*. And then there were the orchestra albums, and a lot of the bands did orchestra albums—including KISS and Metallica. And then there were remix albums with a little *oom-pah-pah* … the market dictates fads, and a lot of bands jump on the bandwagon. So, yeah, you look at all these different bands, and you can even look at pop bands who put out 'rock remixes' of their songs. It happens. And KISS does good business, and the reason they do good business is because they're on top of the business, and when the business is changing, they change with it. It's totally normal and expected, and it makes sense. It didn't light the world on fire, like they might have expected, but it served its purpose.

What did you think of the album cover for *Smashes, Thrashes & Hits*?

Not a lot, quite frankly. And I don't want to be dismissive of KISS, because they had some great artwork—especially in the 70s. You look at *Destroyer, Rock And Roll Over, Love Gun*, even *Alive!*—there is something magical, even though it's just a pose of four guys on a stage. *Smashes, Thrashes & Hits* looks like a kindergarten project. It really does. It looks like somebody said to a couple of grade school kids, *Cut out some pictures of your uncles and aunts, and present them to the class*. Which is too bad, because, like most things, had you given it a nice cover—had you spit-shined the shoes on this one—it probably would have been taken more seriously. Even though you had those couple of new songs that folks thought were a little bit too sugary-sweet, I think, properly packaged, it would have had an impact.

You look at the band Ghost—they are doing melodic rock. If they showed up on a stage in T-shirts and jeans, they would be signed to Frontiers Records, playing bars in Sweden, never making it to North America. And yet they've created this mystique through image. And I think KISS, with *Smashes, Thrashes & Hits*, and with other bands, sometimes the image has to go with the music. And I think, had they made a little more effort on this cover and made it a little more special, it probably would have done a lot better. Especially had they gotten Ken Kelly—the guy who did those albums [*Destroyer* and *Love Gun*], it would have been magical. It could have been better. But the summertime art-project look … *not great*.

Did you ever notice that one of the 'hands' looks like it's touching Gene's private parts on the cover?

I had not noticed it, but I am looking at it right now, and I see that. In fact, there is another hand on the other side that looks like it's touching not only Paul's behind, but also *his* private parts! There are two hands, sort of boosting up Paul's tuchus. *That's expected.* I've never noticed it, because, listen … it looks like a summer-camp art project, so I've never spent time studying it, nor

128

do I think that the time to study it is valid. But yeah, that's typical. And the double-entendre or whatever makes sense.

PAUL STANLEY SOLO TOUR WITH CURT GOOCH

With KISS off the road during the time of *Smashes, Thrashes & Hits*, Paul opted to tour solo—performing several tracks off his 1978 solo album onstage for the first time ever, among the expected and not-so-expected KISS klassics …

Smashes, Thrashes & Hits had come out, and the band, for whatever reason, just were not going to tour in support of it. So Paul decided, perhaps in response to all of Gene's extracurricular activity, that he was going to go and do a solo tour. Much to the dismay of Eric Carr, who wanted to be the drummer on the tour and was not allowed to do so. Paul went out and started doing clubs—mainly clubs, and maybe in a couple of markets theaters. He played songs off his '78 solo album that had never been played live before up until that point. It was absolutely a diehard KISS fan's dream to see those shows and hear that setlist—to hear songs like 'Goodbye' and 'Tonight You Belong to Me.' To hear those live after eleven years of never being able to do so was pretty special.

Paul Stanley's solo band consisted of Bob Kulick on guitar, Dennis St. James on bass, Gary Corbett on keyboards, and Eric Singer on drums—who, of course, wound up becoming KISS's future drummer. But that whole period was bizarre—Paul was dating Samantha Fox, KISS were all over MTV with 'Let's Put The X In Sex,' and to a lesser extent with '(You Make Me) Rock Hard.' It was a bizarre moment in time that I didn't see coming at the time. And, looking back, I don't really understand why it ever happened in the first place!

GIMME MORE: RICHIE RANNO ON THE BIRTH AND RISE OF KISS CONVENTIONS

The New Jersey KISS Convention is often credited with being one of the first of its kind. Certainly, it served as the precursor for the KISS expos and conventions that exist today worldwide. Here, its co-creator, Starz guitarist Richie Ranno, explains how it all started.

How did you come up with the idea to do the New Jersey KISS Convention?

In the fall or winter of '86, I got a letter from the IRS, saying that I owed $75,000 back taxes—from 1977. I thought, *That's kind of weird … I didn't even make that much money in '77! How can I owe them more than I made?* I found out there was some kind of problem from the filing from our manager's accountants, and instead of getting in touch with me all those years, they just let interest and penalties build up, and they deleted all expenses, or something like that—I can't remember what it was. Whatever it was, it was a little alarming. And they said that every member of the band Starz was going to get the same letter, but mine went out too soon—they shouldn't have sent it out right then, they were going to send them all out together.

I was the first one to get it, so I called Brendan Harkin, who was the other guitar player in Starz—even though we had split up a number of years before—and I said, 'Hey, you're going to be getting this. I don't know what we should do … but we've got to figure something out.' So he tracked down Bill Aucoin's files—Bill managed my band, Starz. We just wanted to get the files from 1977, so we could prove to the IRS that we didn't owe them anything. We found them at a warehouse in Manhattan. We contacted the warehouse, and the warehouse said, 'Bill did not pay his bill'—for a whole period of time. The warehouse got a warehouseman's lien against him, and now owned everything in his storage facility there. But if we would pay the back rent— which was $5,000—we could have everything in there, including those files. So we did that—we went there, paid the money, and got everything out.

By actually paying them the money, we had the storage unit for a month or two in our name, and we cleaned it out. And what we couldn't clean out, we threw out. So we got all the files we needed, and eventually we cleared it up with the IRS. But they had a bunch of stuff there—some interesting stuff—and we wanted to sell it. To get our money back and, hopefully, make some money.

Not long after that—I think that spring—there were two people up in New England who said they were running a KISS convention in Boston. A friend of mine had a table, and they said, 'They're looking for another dealer. If you want to come up and bring some of that KISS stuff with you, maybe you can sell it.' So we did. It was just a little room at a Holiday Inn. A meeting room, but a *tiny* meeting room that you could only fit about ten tables in. It was crowded, and we thought it was a nice idea. The other dealer, Marv Pritchard, who sadly passed away [in March 2018], said to me, 'I think we should talk to these people, and have them do one down in the New York/New Jersey area. And we can help them out if they want.' I said, 'That sounds like a good idea.' But they didn't want to do it. So, then we said, 'OK. Well then, *we're* going to do it.'

So we ran what we called the New York KISS Convention, in June of 1987, in a little suburb of New Jersey called Cranford. And it went over like gangbusters. It was really great. A lot of people showed up, and we had a great time. And then we moved it to a bigger hotel, at the Crown Plaza [originally called the Meadowlands Hilton], in 1988 and 1989. It went well, and we just kept doing it every year. I ran it until 2008.

It seems like the New Jersey KISS Convention was one of the first big ones, which led to other conventions throughout the world.
The Jersey one was the first big one. I think, by the second one, we were already having special guests and bands—we took it to a pretty high level.

What were you able to acquire from the warehouse? Any rare KISS items?
Mostly a lot of gold and platinum records awarded to either Aucoin Management or Rock Steady Productions for all those early albums. I didn't save any of them. We sold them pretty cheap, to be honest with you—I just wanted to make the money back, and maybe make some money here and there.

What are some of the cooler KISS pieces that you've seen being sold at the Jersey KISS Convention over the years?
We had the actual People's Choice Award, and we sold that. But what other people had? People had *so much* stuff. It was insane. People were just crazed

about the makeup years. And then we had Bill Aucoin as a guest. We had him as a guest more than once. But the first time we had him as a guest, I explained to him what I just explained to you, that we got the warehouse, and that's how this whole KISS Convention thing came about. He said, 'I'm glad it went to someone I like.' But we did pay for it! When KISS got back together in '96, Bill said, 'This is because of your KISS Conventions. They realized the value of putting the makeup back on.' I don't know, but he stood by that.

Who were some of the other guests throughout the years?
I think Peter Criss was the first big guest. [Original Frehley's Comet second guitarist] Richie Scarlet was the first guest, then Peter Criss, Ace Frehley, Vinnie Vincent, Mark St. John. And then we started branching out, and we had Dee Snider and regular rock guys—in addition to the KISS guys.

Did you ever reach out to Gene and Paul, or vice versa, and did they ever want to get involved with the KISS conventions?
No, they did not want to get involved. I think part of them coming up with the idea of running their own [was that] they sent someone to videotape one year from start to end—one of my conventions. And then, about a year later, they were running their own convention, and now they knew how to do it, because they videotaped *my* convention. I played on Gene's solo album, so we were friends going way back.

You mentioned that you go way back with KISS. When did you first cross paths?
Long before I was in Starz, I was in Stories. We had [Kenny] Kerner and [Richie] Wise producing us, and they produced the first two KISS albums [1974's self-titled and *Hotter Than Hell*]. When we were recording some singles over at some studio, Richie Wise showed me that KISS album cover, and said, 'This is the band I just produced.' And I said, 'I don't understand … is that a cartoon or something?' He said, 'No, that's the guys! They put makeup on.' I said, 'What kind of music is it?' He said, 'It's hard rock. It's *really good* hard rock. Here, take my copy.' It was about two weeks before the album came out. And I absolutely loved it. I made this cassette of it, and Stories went on the road for a while, and I was playing the cassette all the time.

We went from San Francisco to LA, and we pulled into the hotel in LA—a Ramada Inn, I believe, on Sunset Boulevard. We were checking in at the desk—it was about midnight. And this girl walks in from the outside pool area: 'I'm lookin' for some cups. Ya got any cups?' She had the *heaviest* Brooklyn accent I'd ever heard. And I said [*impersonating a Brooklyn accent*], 'Where ya from, Brooklyn?' She said she was, and she was here with her husband, Peter Criss. I said, 'I love KISS!' She said, 'They're in the swimming pool now.'

So we walk into that area where the pool was, and all four guys from KISS were standing in the pool—waist high—in their leather outfits. And Paul was holding a serving tray, and it had champagne glasses on it. I said, 'Are you guys nuts, or what? What are you doing?' And they said, 'We're celebrating that we're making a new album.' I told them how much I liked their first album, and they liked that, because not too many musicians liked KISS back then.

The next day, I woke up and went over by the pool, we all hung out, and they came to see us play the Whisky—we did a five-night stint there. Kenny Aaronson was the bass player, and Kenny and I went to the studio with them and hung out, because we were good friends with Kerner and Wise. I remember Ace playing a solo, and going, 'Richie, what do you think of this solo?' We were just having a good time, and we got to be good friends with them. While sitting around the pool, they introduced me to Bill Aucoin, and he said they were looking for another rock group for them to manage: 'You should quit Stories and put a *real* rock group together.' I said, 'I'm not quitting a group with a #1 record [a cover of Hot Chocolate's 'Brother Louie'] … but thank you!'

Actually, when Stories split up, I did try to put a group together, but I just couldn't get the right guys. The irony is, my former guitar roadie from Stories lived in New York City, and he told me there was a *Village Voice* ad for a guitar player for a band managed by Rock Steady Management. I called up and I got the gig. That was Fallen Angels, then we switched around one member and became Starz.

And you played on Gene's solo album from 1978.
That's a whole weird story. Starz went to Detroit—we had no album out yet—to spend a couple of weeks out there, doing gigs. Sean Delaney spent the two weeks with us out there, and I had this bizarre dream that I told him about: 'I had this

vivid dream that Gene put a solo album out. But those guys will never put solo albums out. It's weird, don't you think?' Then 1978 comes along, and they're doing four solo albums, and I told Sean, 'Sean, my dream is coming true!'

They mixed the album, and they didn't include me on it. They came back over, and Sean [who co-produced Gene's solo album, with Gene] called up one day, and said, 'We're not satisfied with the guitar playing on "Tunnel Of Love." Joe Perry did it, we didn't like it. So we had Jeff Baxter overdub it, we didn't like that either. Gene wanted Nils Lofgren to do it, and he was going to fly up, and he wanted a limo, he wanted this, he wanted that. I just told Gene, 'Why are we wasting our time trying to get Nils Lofgren? Let's just have Richie come in, and he can do it in five minutes.'

So I went in at the last minute. It didn't take but five minutes. It was great—Gene stood with me, and he was looking for a theme for the solo. He worked with me on it. I got a platinum album for it, and got paid pretty well for it—it was very nice of him.

What are your thoughts on the famous clip from 1994 of Gene and Paul going into a KISS Convention in Troy, Michigan, and taking back vintage costumes?

They were just making a big deal about it because they wanted to publicize themselves. I can't remember who was running it, but I think they really just wanted to make a publicity stunt, because they were getting ready to run their own convention. I've heard through the years that various employees sold costume parts. Whether that's fact or not, I don't know, but that's what they made it seem like. And whoever ended up with them was at the short-end of the stick—by having it confiscated.

What do you think about the KISS conventions of today?

I don't pay attention to it. I did twenty-two years of that, and I'm so burnt out on it that I won't go to another one again. I don't want anything to do with all that stuff. I don't go to any of those conventions. I got back into music around 2003, when we reunited Starz. I got more and more away from the whole memorabilia thing and the KISS convention thing. It really just started to become an annoyance to me—it was a lot of work, and it started getting [to be] not as much fun.

HOT IN THE SHADE

Released October 17, 1989. Produced by Gene Simmons and
Paul Stanley. US #29, UK #35. US certification: gold.

SIDE ONE

Rise To It (Paul Stanley/Bob Halligan Jr.)

Betrayed (Gene Simmons/Tommy Thayer)

Hide Your Heart (Stanley/Desmond Child/Holly Knight)

Prisoner Of Love (Simmons/Bruce Kulick)

Read My Body (Stanley/Halligan)

Love's A Slap In The Face (Simmons, Vini Poncia)

Forever (Stanley/Michael Bolton)

Silver Spoon (Stanley/Poncia)

SIDE TWO

Cadillac Dreams (Simmons/Poncia)

King Of Hearts (Stanley/Poncia)

The Street Giveth And The Street Taketh Away (Simmons/Thayer)

You Love Me To Hate You (Stanley/Child)

Somewhere Between Heaven And Hell (Simmons/Poncia)

Little Caesar (Eric Carr/Simons/Adam Mitchell)

Boomerang (Simmons/Kulick)

SINGLES / EPS

Hide Your Heart / Betrayed (US #66, UK #59)

Forever (remix) / The Street Giveth And The
Street Taketh Away (US #8, UK #65)

Rise To It (remix) / Silver Spoon (US #81, UK did not chart)

First KISS ... Last Licks (promo only)

★

After releasing some of the most pop-sounding recordings of their entire career (*Crazy Nights* and the two new tracks off *Smashes, Thrashes & Hits*), KISS made a very wise move on their next studio offering, 1989's *Hot In The Shade*: *they cut the crap*. In other words, they attempted to return to a much more hard-rocking, direct sound. But while the move was admirable, and the resulting album at least successful in moving the band's sound closer to the KISS that most fans knew and loved most from a sonic standpoint, the material wasn't always quite up to snuff.

In an effort to get back to basics, Gene Simmons and Paul Stanley were the album's sole producers. And to give fans the most bang for their buck, *HITS* was one of the lengthiest KISS studio albums ever, lasting nearly a full hour (or 58:39, to be precise), with fifteen tracks total. But while they kept the production 'in-house,' outside songwriters returned in full force—including some familiar names (Desmond Child, Holly Knight, Vini Poncia ... yes, *that* Vini Poncia, who produced Peter Criss's self-titled solo album, as well as *Dynasty* and *Unmasked*) and some new ones (including one that would later figure prominently in the KISS story, Tommy Thayer).

But the biggest story to come out of *HITS* was KISS's first Top 10 single in the USA since 'Beth'—the acoustic guitar–driven power ballad 'Forever.' By the late 80s, it had become a proven formula that for rock bands to score a hit single/video, they should momentarily turn down the Marshalls—as evidenced by such #1 hits as Guns N' Roses' 'Sweet Child O' Mine,' Def Leppard's 'Love Bites,' Poison's 'Every Rose Has Its Thorn,' and so on. And certainly, KISS coulda-shoulda been added to that list with 'Reason To Live,' but it wasn't until 'Forever' that a Top 10 hit single actually became a reality for the band.

Co-penned by Stanley and pop star Michael Bolton (also Bruce Kulick's former bandmate in Blackjack), 'Forever' wasn't that far removed from the aforementioned chart-toppers—especially in what it had to say lyrically. (With most power ballads, bands took a break from their usual smutty lyrics and exposed their sensitive sides.) But an interesting twist that made 'Forever' stand out from the rest of the competition was the guitar solo—instead of going electric, Kulick offered up another one of his standout/trademark solos ... but on an *acoustic* guitar, bringing to mind the early Zeppelin classic

'Thank You.' The video was also memorable, as probably the most tasteful clip of KISS's non-makeup era, showing the band playing to each other in a circle, rehearsal-style. It was shot mostly in black-and-white, with a gold hue lighting the room via sunlight through the windows.

That was it for the 'tender moments' on *HITS*, however, as by and large this was a *rawk* album, with seven songs co-penned by Simmons and seven more co-penned by Stanley. Several of the Simmons tunes showed the former demon was *finally* starting to find his niche in the non-makeup years ('Betrayed,' 'The Street Giveth And The Street Taketh Away'), while the best of Stanley's compositions included the kickass album-opener 'Rise To It' (which contains some surprising bluesy guitar doodling at the beginning) and 'Hide Your Heart.' Another of the album's surprising highlights was the Eric Carr–sung 'Little Caesar' (sadly the only song he would ever sing lead on for a non-compilation KISS studio album), which contains a sturdy Zep groove but manages to avoid the 'Zep clone' virus that was plaguing rock music at the time.

Returning to 'Hide Your Heart' for a second, there turned out to be an interesting tale behind the tune, which as previously discussed had been demoed for *Crazy Nights* but was not released until *HITS*. With its instantly memorable chorus, the song, written by Stanley with Child and Knight, had already been circulating in fan tape-trading circles, and was even performed by Stanley on his solo tour of '89. But the zaniest thing about it was that it must not have been a forgone conclusion that it was going to be included on *HITS*, as it was shopped around to other artists to cover. As a result, in 1989 alone, *four* artists recorded the song and included it on their respective albums. The best-known version was of course KISS's, but alert rock fans could have also spotted the tune included on albums by Molly Hatchet (*Lightning Strikes Twice*), Robin Beck (*Trouble Of Nothin'*), and … Ace Frehley (*Trouble Walkin'*)!

Not all of *HITS* was worthwhile, however. A case in point is 'Read My Body,' an oh-so-obvious rewrite of Def Leppard's mega-hit 'Pour Some Sugar On Me' (specifically the chorus)—so much so that it wouldn't have been too far-fetched if the Leps had cried plagiarism in the court of law. Elsewhere, while listening to such tunes as the album-closing 'Boomerang,' you can easily picture the lads saying, 'We need another song to fill out the album … got anything handy?'

So, while *HITS* was not on par with *Lick It Up* or *Animalize* among the best KISS non-makeup studio efforts, it at least showed that the group were slowly regaining their focus, and finally realizing that they were at their best with the amps cranked to ten, with no extra-added studio gloss. And on the supporting tour, they wisely began re-airing classics from the 70s that hadn't been played in ages, mixed in with the best of the 80s. Sadly, just as it appeared that the Simmons/Stanley/Kulick/Carr lineup was truly coming into its own, it came to an end: *HITS* would be the last KISS album that Eric Carr appeared on.

KNOW THE SCORE: EDDIE TRUNK

Eddie Trunk returns to discuss the entire *Hot In The Shade* era.

What are your thoughts on *Hot In The Shade*?

I think there's some great stuff on that record. I think it should be about five songs shorter—because it's a long record, and there's some real filler on there. Five songs less would have made it a better record. And I also don't like the mix *at all*. I think it's a very thin-sounding mix. I know for a fact that Eric Carr played electronic drums on it, because he told me when they were recording it. And I know they recorded that record on the cheap—in a demo studio in LA. Some of it was demos that they ended up staying with. So I think, sonically, it doesn't sound like it should, and I think there are four or five songs that could easily be cut, and would make it a better record.

What are some of your favorite tracks?

'Hide Your Heart' is a *great* song. That was a whole interesting, crazy story, because that song had been around, and that song should have been on *Crazy Nights*, but it wasn't. But I would have loved to have heard that song with *Crazy Nights* production. I remember going to the listening party for *Crazy Nights*, and going up to Paul and Gene, and saying, 'How is "Hide Your Heart" not on this record?' And they were shocked that I knew the song even existed, because I had a demo of it. But I was happy to see that turn up on that record—although I thought the production and the mix should have been way better, it still is a great song.

'Rise To It' is kind of old-school KISS. That was a huge video for KISS fans, because it opens with them putting makeup on, and that got people really crazy, because it was like, *Whoa, what are they doing? Are they putting the makeup back on?* I remember the video for that being a big deal. 'Forever' was obviously a huge song for that record, and, interestingly enough, to prove my point about the mix being pretty shitty on that album, when it was serviced to radio, 'Forever' was remixed. I actually have a CD single 'radio mix' of that, where the song was completely remixed for radio and video—as was 'Rise To It.' There's a remix of 'Rise To It' called the 'Full Power Guitar Mix' that is way punchier.

They probably recognized after they made that record kind of on the cheap that when they were going to bring it to radio or video, they'd need to punch it up a little bit. And they did. The other thing I will say about that period is that is my favorite non-makeup/non-original lineup of KISS—the Kulick/Carr lineup. And I think the *Hot In The Shade* tour was by far the best KISS lineup, stage production, and setlist that they had with the non-original band.

How would you say *Hot In The Shade* fits in with what was going on at the time with hard rock and heavy metal?

Well, when you look at the KISS history through the non-makeup years, *Creatures Of The Night* and then to some degree *Lick It Up* were total responses to the fact that KISS had gone so far away from hard rock. So they ended up going, basically, *metal*. To me, KISS was never a metal band. KISS was always a *hard-rock* band. And with *Creatures* and *Lick It Up*, those were direct reactions to *The Elder*, *Unmasked*, and *Dynasty*—to replant the flag as a hard-rock band. So much so that the promo poster for *Creatures Of The Night*, the headline just said, 'THE LOUDEST BAND IN THE WORLD.'

So, in that period of time, they were very much about trying to establish themselves as a heavy-rock band, and let everybody know they were back to that. And then, as they progressed through the 80s, *Animalize* was some of that, too—*Animalize* had some fast, shred-y stuff. Whereas *Crazy Nights* was completely glossy and poppy—they were chasing a Bon Jovi/slick-production deal with Ron Nevison—on *Hot In The Shade*, I think they finally found the right balance. They figured it out. They had just sorted themselves out. They figured out how to sound, they found a balance between rock, hard rock, and metal—but it was more of a rock'n'roll record.

If you listen to 'Rise To It' and 'Hide Your Heart,' they are straight-up rock songs. They weren't trying to blow your head off and be the fastest players or the hardest players. I think, earlier on, they were, because they were trying so hard to fight against the backlash. So, to me, *Hot In The Shade* was them really finding their skin, really getting into a comfort zone of how to act, how to look, how to *be* without makeup. They embraced their past a lot more than they ever had—in terms of introducing a lot more 70s songs into that tour.

With Bruce, they had a guy that could respect the past *and* do his own thing. And Eric had been there for a while at that point. I think, without question, Eric Carr is the most loved non-original member of KISS. He had been there and planted his flag, and people really loved him. *Hot In The Shade* featured the first-ever lead vocal from Eric, which I know was a huge thing for him—I knew Eric personally very well, and we talked a lot during that time. So I thought it was really good, healthy time for KISS. Their stage production was great—that sphinx and all that sort of stuff. They cut out those really long, extended solos, and they concentrated on playing *songs*. *Hot In The Shade* wasn't a great record by any stretch, but it had its moments.

The one thing with KISS is, during the 70s, KISS were innovators on a lot of things. But throughout the 80s, to me, KISS were followers—in a lot of ways. They copied a lot of bands, they borrowed from a lot of bands. There are moments on those records where you can hear KISS trying to do Bon Jovi, [or] KISS trying to do Def Leppard. They knew what was going on.

The 80s in general were *brutal* for 70s bands trying to assimilate and figure out what to do. And a lot of them looked to what was going on at that time. The big bands at that time, in some cases, were bands that once opened for these groups, like Bon Jovi once opened for KISS. So you saw a band like KISS, at that point, really looking at what was going on around them, and some of these bands that were blowing up on MTV, and what they looked like and what they sounded like, and these guys were eight to ten years younger than they were, so they were going to do everything they could to relate to that audience.

There are some interesting songwriting credits on *Hot In The Shade*, including Vini Poncia, who had produced Peter Criss's solo album, as well as *Dynasty* and *Unmasked*.

I didn't even realize that. The big co-write that everybody knows about is Michael Bolton on 'Forever' with Paul. And if people don't know that story, that's kind of interesting, because Bolton was in a band with Bruce Kulick, before Bruce joined KISS, called Blackjack, and there was a lot of history there. Michael Bolton at one point actually did do hard rock. So that was one that jumped out at me.

I don't remember all the co-writers for that record off the top of my head. I just know that in the case of 'Little Caesar,' that was a moment for Eric Carr. Eric Carr was *ecstatic*. Eric Carr had been fighting forever to get a lead vocal on a KISS record. He had been a lead singer in his previous band, and he sang live when they did 'Young And Wasted' from *Lick It Up*, and he did so many backing vocals. He was a great singer, and he really wanted the opportunity to have his own song and have a moment where he sang lead vocals in KISS.

Additionally, Tommy Thayer is listed as co-writer of the song 'Betrayed,' so that's his first 'foot in the door' with KISS.

Yeah, and that would have just been looked at—at the time—as them writing a song with the guy from Black N' Blue. Who, of course, opened for KISS on the *Asylum* tour.

I remember you once telling me a funny story about introducing KISS at a show on the *Hot In The Shade* tour.

That was at the Meadowlands in New Jersey [then called the Brendan Byrne Arena] on June 30, 1990. At that point, I was on great terms with KISS—Eric was a close friend, I certainly knew Gene, Paul, and Bruce, and I had done some stuff with them. KISS were still … even though their records would go gold and platinum, even though they were on MTV, they still were not anywhere close to what the big, big, big bands were doing at the time. Their shows—they still needed help selling tickets. I mean, look at the opening acts—on the *Hot In The Shade* tour, it was Slaughter and Winger. At the time, those were two *really* big bands who were really doing great business. They

141

needed that—that wasn't by coincidence. To go into an arena, *they needed that.*

I remember going to the Meadowlands—which would have been my local show—and it was a big deal that they were playing the Meadowlands again. I remember being backstage, and, at that time, I was working for a local rock station in New Jersey. Everybody knew that I was the KISS flag-waver. I remember being backstage, and I was in the hall, and I'm pretty sure, at the time, Larry Mazer was managing them. I went up to Larry and one of the guys at PolyGram and we were talking, and I remember busting their balls in the hallway, going, 'You know, I'm the only one who actually plays this band on the radio, beyond one song. This is my hometown gig, this is where my radio station is … *you should let me go out and introduce them.*' They didn't immediately say no. They kind of shrugged their shoulders a little bit: *Yeah, we'll see, we'll check with the guys, I don't know.* If I remember correctly, they went back into the KISS dressing room, and they came out. I think it was Larry who said, 'You can do it if you want.'

And then Eric comes out—and if anybody knows anything about Eric Carr, they know he was a total prankster. He was a ballbuster. He comes out, and he's like, 'So, I hear you're going to introduce us tonight buddy, huh? What are you going to say? What are you going to do? There are *a lot* of people out there.' He was making me more nervous! He's like, 'Well, start thinking about it … showtime is coming up soon!' He went away and came back out, and said, 'Make sure your voice is good. Here, knock back this cup of water, to make sure you're hydrated.' It was a big red Solo cup. I took a big chug, and it wasn't water—it was, like, Chivas Regal or something! I almost blew it all over the wall. So he was fucking with me. And he goes, 'Come on, man, that will take the edge off—finish that off.'

Then, when I got the cue that it was time to walk up to the stage, he walks with me, and he's in my ear, messing with me behind the curtain, saying, 'You're going to do great, buddy. Don't worry about it. There's only probably, I don't know … *everybody you ever knew in your hometown out there.*' Really messing with me. And there was a curtain on the stage, so we're behind the curtain—no one can see us. They give me a flashlight signal, and say, 'Go out and say what you're going to say.'

I remember I walked out to the front of the stage, and whatever the hell

I said to the crowd—'Get ready! *KISS!*'—it was just some sort of typical rev-up-the-crowd moment. It was awesome, but I felt stuff hitting me in the back while I was on the microphone. Usually, you look for somebody to throw something at you from the front. I felt stuff hitting me in the back of my legs and my back. I turn around, and in the corner of my eye is just Eric's arm and half his head coming out of the cut of the curtain, and he was taking drum sticks and guitar picks and flicking them at me while I was talking! I was so nervous that when I turned around to leave, I was, like, floating on air. I got back behind the curtain, and Eric put his arm around me, gave me a big hug, and goes, '*You did great, man!*'

KNOW THE SCORE: BRENT FITZ

Brent is back! And this time, he's voicing his likes and concerns about *Hot In The Shade*.

On *Hot In The Shade*, it seems like KISS were trying to get back to basics.
I remember first seeing the album cover, and it didn't jump out at me. The KISS logo was really small on the cover. I remember seeing the 'Rise To It' video and thinking that was cool—with the little hints to the makeup. I thought that was clever, to have that. What I didn't like—which was strong to me, as a musician and a drummer—that it seemed a little bit *cookie-cutter*, as far as [how] the music was recorded. I learned later and figured it out that some of the drums were programmed.

I don't think Eric Carr was ill yet, but there were some programmed drums going on. But that was big at the time—a lot of the drums on a lot of mid-to-late 80s records had these … technology-wise, drummers were getting screwed, and drum machines were taking over. And you can definitely hear it on the record. It just sounds like someone else programmed the drums—not necessarily Eric Carr. I don't know if [that has been confirmed], but I'm pretty sure something was going on there, that didn't give the album an organic feel. And it's pretty long—there are *a lot* of songs on that record.

And in '89, for me personally, I was now doing my career as a musician, and as a fan, still invested in KISS and always happy when a new record comes out, but as far as going the distance and spending a lot of time listening to the record ... I remember I bought *Hot In The Shade* on cassette. I was a traveling musician at the time, and I remember listening to it a lot in the van, driving around. But that was the first KISS record I did not buy on vinyl. I had a cassette of it because it was easy, but I still to this day do not have a vinyl copy of *Hot In The Shade*. I still listened through to the songs and have my favorites, and I think there are several songs on the record that were standouts—and several that really got relegated into the backseat, if you know what I mean.

Let's discuss the individual tracks.
I love 'Rise To It.' I think it's super-catchy. And I love the video that went along with it. A great Paul vocal on that. I love when Gene and Paul sing together and harmonize. And in the verses, when Gene's voice comes in with Paul, I think it is really cool that they complement each other. That's one of my favorite things about KISS—when both lead singers sing together. 'Betrayed,' that's a Tommy Thayer song, right? That was a cool Gene vocal. I would say a good song, but not sticking out as one of my favorites. But I thought 'Hide Your Heart' was great—obviously Desmond Child on there, and Holly Knight. A very strong song, and a very intense video at the time, too—with the storyline to go along with the lyrics.

'Prisoner Of Love' is a Bruce song—very cool that Bruce had a co-write with Gene on that song. Again, just a cool Gene song, but not a standout 'hit.' 'Read My Body,' that one may be where a lot of people go, 'Oh my gosh, *Paul is rapping*,' or, 'This is an anomaly of a song.' But it's still got catchy parts, and a little bit of interesting drum programming—with a cowbell, which again, was a late-80s sort of drumbeat. It gets kind of shelved into the middle section of the record. 'Love's A Slap In The Face' is another cool Gene song, but probably not one of the standouts on the record.

And then you come to 'Forever,' which is definitely one of the best KISS songs ... it's different, and I think Bruce played such a great acoustic solo. That's a really special, standout song on a KISS record. Even though it's a co-write with Michael Bolton, no doubt it's a real strong song, and a great video—I really like how they created the vibe, with the music stand and sitting down and playing. I thought the band looked really cool.

RIGHT Covering up: Paul gives us a hand on a 1983 cover of *Kerrang!*, while the band were photographed in all their unmasked glory inside.

BELOW The short-lived *Creatures/Lick It Up* lineup. *Left to right*: Eric Carr, Gene Simmons, Vinnie Vincent, Paul Stanley.

TOP Letting off some steam: KISS meet atop a tank for one of the *Lick It Up* tour's standout numbers, 'Black Diamond.'

ABOVE AND LEFT Japan appeared not to be sold on the idea that KISS's naked faces could sell product … hence the choice of covers for the 'Lick It Up' single (*left*) and its parent album (*above*).

RIGHT On at least one occasion during the *Lick It Up* tour, Vinnie would shred … and Paul saw red.

BELOW One of the few holdover concert gimmicks from the makeup daze: Gene breathing fire.

TOP Who is that mystery man behind Gene? Mark St. John's replacement, Bruce Kulick, learning on the fly during the *Animalize* tour. **ABOVE** Standing tall: Eric Carr and his leopard-skin jumpsuit.

ABOVE RIGHT Paul forgets his shirt for a 1984 *Kerrang!* cover. **BELOW RIGHT** KISS edited Vinnie out of the *LIU* artwork for this Euro *Animalize* ad and replaced him with Mark, despite Mark not playing any of the dates! Whatever happened to the opening act?

RIGHT Might as well jump: Paul tests out his snazzy *Asylum* stage duds.

BELOW The folded-out front and back covers of the *Asylum* tour book (*left*), which included an advert by Paul for BC Rich Guitars inside (*right*).

OPPOSITE PAGE A grand entrance: 'Detroit Rock City' was the set opener on the *Asylum* tour, which featured the biggest KISS logo yet.

TOP Eric standing tall: part deuce. ABOVE Paul rockin'
a double-neck BC Rich, while sportin' Body Glove
attire (I didn't know he surfed?).

OPPOSITE PAGE KISS's last remaining original members,
Paul and Gene, during the *Crazy Nights* tour.

ABOVE LEFT Ticket stubs for four non-makeup-era events attended by this book's author! **ABOVE** Bruce solos on his ESP 'Banana' guitar (note Chiquita sticker below the strings on the body). **LEFT** KISS have been the subject of countless comic books ... but few feature the non-makeup era as prominently as this one.

OPPOSITE PAGE A whole lotta hair: KISS meet Vixen. *Left to right*: Vixen guitarist Jan Kuehnemund, MTV VJ China Kantner, Gene and Paul, bassist Share Pedersen, singer Janet Gardner, drummer Roxy Petrucci, singer-songwriter Richard Marx.

ABOVE Another grand entrance, this time via the mouth of a sphinx (!) on the *Hot In The Shade* tour.

LEFT Gene gets a chuckle out of Pantera singer Phil Anselmo in Dallas, Texas, October 1991.

LEFT Ace is back, and he told you so: Frehley adorns two *Kerrang!* covers, from 1985 and 1987.

BELOW Spaceman sighting: Ace, a flashy silver jacket, and his trademark sunburst Les Paul, during the 90s.

ABOVE The Cat is back: Peter Criss keeping the beat during the 90s. **RIGHT** The cover of the promo-only release *First Kiss … Last Licks*.

OPPOSITE PAGE Bruce impersonates the main prop from the *Revenge* tour at a show in Bethlehem, Pennsylvania, October 1992.

RIGHT KISS's third drummer, Eric Singer, during the *Convention* tour.

BELOW Gene, Bruce, and Paul recreate some classic 70s-era choreography for 'Deuce.'

'Silver Spoon' … *eh*. Is that a Vini Poncia song? A great vocal by Paul, but that might have been one that I would skip over. 'Cadillac Dreams,' that is probably better suited for a Gene solo record than a KISS album.

I should mention, too, a lot of these songs … the Gene songs seem so much like Gene songs, with probably little contribution by Paul. I think it sounds like, *I'm doing my songs; you're doing your songs.* It doesn't seem like Gene and Paul would be joined together on each other's songs. 'King Of Hearts,' again, I wonder if Gene played bass on a lot of these songs, or did Paul play rhythm and Bruce play most of the guitars? It's hard to say. I don't really know. 'King Of Hearts' has a good chorus, but again, it would have been one that I would have been like … *It's OK.*

'The Street Giveth,' I thought that was a great song. A really good Gene song. And Tommy Thayer co-wrote that with Gene. Great chorus. Now, my guilty pleasure on the record is 'You Love Me To Hate You.' I bet nobody would say, 'Oh, that's a great song.' *I* think it's a great song, because there are two sections that sound *out*—the pre-chorus has, like, this really cool harmony. I don't know if Paul or Desmond came up with it, but Paul is singing really high. 'Somewhere Between Heaven And Hell' is another great chorus.

'Little Caesar,' that's a catchy song. I think Eric sang great. He sang great on the *Animalize* tour, when he was singing 'Young And Wasted.' I thought it was cool that he got to sing a song. Actually, I think 'Little Caesar' might have some presence in the [2018] KISS Kruise, to honor Eric. [Note: Bruce's band—featuring Brent on drums—did indeed perform the tune on the Kruise.] And then 'Boomerang,' although that's a Bruce co-write with Gene, I think it's a pretty long record, so 'Boomerang' probably gets lost, by the end of the record.

It seemed like as soon as Bruce joined the band, he was called upon as a songwriting collaborator for both Gene and Paul.
You've got to think that guitar is a songwriter's instrument—it goes along with melody. Guitar is the other melody instrument, so if you're the lead guitar player in a band, there is some credibility to writing music parts, too. And certainly, Bruce knows how to write great riffs and songs, and has ideas. And I've written many songs with Bruce over the years.

Gene and Paul are very strong and successful at bouncing ideas off of people. And it takes a little time to get a little comfortable with people—even though Bruce is a member of the band and playing live shows, songwriting is a different thing, and to connect with each other on melodies is different.

Let's discuss the sound of the album a bit more, as it was co-produced by Paul and Gene.

The drums, for me, are the one standout—like, this is very much a programmed sound of the 80s. Which I thought was unfortunate, because I thought *Asylum* was definitely *not* that. And there were *a lot* of songs ... not that it's a bad thing, but since there were a lot of songs, a few would get lost in the shuffle. It maybe reflected a little bit more of [how] the Gene songs were definitely him, and the Paul songs were definitely him, and not necessarily those guys connecting together. It's, like, everybody had their songs, and they were very separate.

But if I think back to things like *Unmasked*, maybe that was the case always—after a while, Gene did his songs, and Paul did his songs. *Asylum* seemed really *connected*, with the four guys playing on the record. Maybe *Hot In The Shade* seemed a little bit more ... pieced-together. And maybe [that's] a reflection of the 80s, and the timeframe of Gene [and] what he was doing then.

Hot In The Shade was Eric's last album with KISS. Let's discuss him as a drummer.

It's very cool that I actually got to meet him. I listened to a lot of those 80s-era KISS songs with Eric Carr, but I didn't get to necessarily jam them in a band or anything. I loved listening to them, but I would be in my basement as a kid, playing to those early KISS records. The 80s records, I was a fan, enjoying the music, but I didn't sit down and jam the songs. But now here I am, at forty-eight years old, revisiting all the 80s stuff, and finding a new appreciation for some of the cool Eric Carr songs. And they're actually really *a lot* of fun to play. I like emulating the Eric Carr era of KISS. Some of that stuff is out of my comfort zone, because I'm not a double-kick drummer, and we're going to step into some of that stuff, like 'King Of The Mountain,' where there is double-kick. I will say, though, that when *Revenge* came out—and I might be one of a bunch of KISS fans that will all agree—that band came out *swinging.* When *Revenge* came out, we were like, *Holy fuck ... look at this! There is a hint of the 80s era, but there is this cool throwback.* It definitely brought everything back in full circle—the way the band looked and sounded on *Revenge*. That definitely is one of my favorite KISS records.

Would you say *Hot In The Shade* did a good job of setting the stage for *Revenge*?
It was just a product of ... where were they going to go, from *Hot In The Shade*? If *Hot In The Shade* was self-produced, as it was Gene and Paul, to bring in Bob Ezrin ... and it was very unfortunate that Eric Carr got sick. That whole change was very shocking and disruptive, I'm sure. But I think bringing in Eric Singer toughened the sound up.

Because *Revenge* was *so* strong, *Hot In The Shade* will probably be pushed far back in the realm of great KISS records. But I think 'Forever' is still a standout of the best KISS songs. So, with all that going on in the *Hot In The Shade* era, 'Forever' is a very strong, shining light. And it's one of Bruce's best performances, and [one of the] great Paul Stanley vocals. Like I said, Paul was singing better than ever. But I think, on *Revenge*, Gene came back and went, '*Fuck you! Here I am.*' [*Laughs*] And just the sound of *Revenge*—oh my God. Great sound. There are so many layers of different things—push and pulls—on that record that you can't deny. Just the start, with the first track—it just brought you in. Like, *What's this?* And the videos were killer on *Revenge*, too.

Speaking of videos, let's also discuss KISS's look in the 80s. At the time, KISS's fashion sense didn't seem that odd, because many other metal bands were dressing similarly.
Here's the thing: KISS already had the 70s era. Bon Jovi, Poison, and those bands that were breaking, they were making their mark in the 80s. But KISS already had the legacy, and they already *owned* the 70s. To come into the 80s and fit in, that's not easy, because a lot of the bands from the 70s ... what else was big? I mean, look at David Lee Roth—he 80s'd himself, too, after the 70s era of Van Halen, with his *Eat 'Em & Smile* record and super-band and everything. Those guys were all wearing shiny jackets, too, and Dave was over-the-top. *Eat 'Em & Smile* looked just like *Asylum*—it was all interchangeable. It was still long hair and eyeliner, and it looked *Vegas*. It was this weird Vegas/MTV/hair band [hybrid].

You could say that Guns N' Roses brought it back to basics with much more of a street look and sound on *Appetite For Destruction* ... and, interestingly, you're currently in Slash's band ...

They killed it. Guns N' Roses came around in the era after '86 ... that's when you've got *Crazy Nights* and *Hot In The Shade* coming out. And Metallica is another band becoming the biggest band in the world in 1989. When you look at *Hot In The Shade*, which records came out then? *Appetite For Destruction* was such a raw, five-piece, dirty rock band. And then KISS was just *so* different. But Guns N' Roses was probably influenced by the 70s era of KISS in some way. I'm glad I lived through it, because I was very much wearing makeup and wearing spandex. We were emulating all our heroes back in the 80s, too. And we knew it was crazy. Guys looked like girls ... *it's just the way it was.* [*Laughs*]

HOT IN THE SHADE: THE TOUR WITH CURT GOOCH

On the strength of their first US Top 10 hit single in a decade, KISS hits the arenas once again—with a show reminiscent of some of their bigger 70s-era stage productions ...

When KISS initially tried to book a tour in 1989 to coincide with the release of *Hot In The Shade*, promoters simply weren't biting. After what had happened with *Crazy Nights*, they just didn't want to touch KISS—at least not on an arena level. They wanted them in theaters—and that was not going to work. So, KISS did something they had never really done before, which was to hold back the tour and see what happens. Well, lo and behold, *Dial MTV* was still a thing, and when the first single came out, 'Hide Your Heart,' it did nothing. But when the second single came out, 'Forever,' it was a game-changer.

All of a sudden, KISS had their first Top 10 hit since 'Beth.' They were high-profile, and they had a huge hit with 'Forever'—much bigger than 'Reason To Live' had been, or 'Tears Are Falling.' All of a sudden, a package tour was introduced, with Slaughter and Faster Pussycat. Both bands were successful enough at that point that putting them on the bill with KISS worked perfectly.

You had really good ticket sales throughout most of the shows on the tour, because the bill was so incredibly strong, for that moment.

The *Hot In The Shade* tour was absolutely the zenith of the non-makeup KISS years. This was Gene, Paul, Eric, and Bruce at the peak of their powers—with a setlist that looked like it must have been vetted over by a hundred diehard KISS fans. I don't know how any band could design a setlist as perfect as that one—especially coming from the disaster that was the *Crazy Nights* tour to this. It was unexpected, to say the least. And they did something on the *Hot In The Shade* tour that was so strong, where they opened with 'I Stole Your Love'—a throwback to the *Love Gun* and *Alive II* tours, when they did the same thing. And then they went into 'Deuce,' which had been their opening number from '73 through '76. Having 'I Stole Your Love' go into 'Deuce' was a hypnotic one-two punch … most KISS fans could have left the show after those two songs and been completely happy—everything else was a bonus. And the fact that they brought back 'Shout It Out Loud,' 'Calling Dr. Love,' 'Black Diamond,' and 'I Want You,' it was just absolutely *magical* to see that.

There is footage from the Tulsa, Oklahoma, show on YouTube. And if you look at one point of 'I Stole Your Love,' the camera zooms out, and you see the audience. I mean, people are *losing their minds* in the audience, watching 'I Stole Your Love' and 'Deuce.' You didn't see that at a *Crazy Nights* show, and you didn't see that at a *Revenge* show. It was just this absolutely ravenous fan base that was dying to be fed some scraps of what once was—and here you go, with 'I Stole Your Love' into 'Deuce.' It could not have been more perfect.

They also did something early on in the tour that was so unexpected and so out of left field, I certainly never would have guessed or anticipated this move. When they started the *Hot In The Shade* tour, they originally had 'Under The Gun' from *Animalize* in the setlist. That was a very strong song, and a great live song. And before we had what are now known as deep tracks, that was certainly a deep track that the fan base loved. For them to include that in the set completely validated the non-makeup years—especially after it having not appeared on any *Crazy Nights* setlists. For that to come back and be on the setlist—even though it only lasted about four to six weeks—to me was the one thing that completely validated 80s KISS. And here we were, with a beautiful blend of 70s and 80s KISS in 1990. It was just perfect. I went and saw six shows on the tour—I was so impressed. That was hard to do when you were still in high school, but I did it.

The KISS stage was basically a recreation of the album cover for *Hot In The Shade*, and they really did an elaborate production. The sphinx's mouth opened up, lasers were there, the band came through and broke through the lasers, ran down the stage, and kicked off with 'I Stole Your Love.' I haven't seen an opening that strong on a KISS tour since the *Dynasty* and *Unmasked* tours. It was a *very* strong opening. And, to this day, I will watch—almost on a weekly basis—some footage from the *Hot In The Shade* tour. Even if it's just the first five minutes—just to see that opening. It really was *that strong*.

And the one interesting thing about the production that I've never really seen any rock band do before or since is that they had—for some unknown reason—running water as part of the production onstage. They had this large, theatrical drain dripping this light stream of water into a bucket, where it was fed back through to the drain and just circled through. That was in the pit every night, with the water running. That was certainly unique.

Something else KISS did on that tour was expand from a seventy-five-minute set to a two-hour set. And it really was an almost flawless production. I say *almost* because the 'act III drama' they tried to create at the end of the show—the rising of the logo during 'I Want You'—was pretty much an epic fail. They basically had forgotten to do the logo. They were in Lubbock, Texas, and somebody had the *Stoned In Paris* bootleg LP in the lobby of the hotel, and Paul was walking through with the set designer, and he told the set designer, 'Here's what it needs to look like,' and showed the cover of *Stoned In Paris*. They designed it off the set designer's memory of what the *Stoned In Paris* KISS logo looked like! And the *K* was just an epic, epic fail. That should have been redesigned and fixed. I don't know why it wasn't, because that was just ridiculous. I still cringe when I think about that. Had that not been there, that would have been an absolutely flawless production.

Interestingly enough, when I was doing research for my first book, *KISS Alive Forever*, one of the hardest tours to find photographs from—other than *Lick It Up*—was *Hot In The Shade*, for some weird reason. We just had the hardest time finding onstage pictures of any real quality of the band from that tour. And if you look at magazines from that era, KISS were not really covered like they had been on *Animalize*, *Asylum*, and *Crazy Nights*. The industry was definitely on the downslope by that point—even though most of us weren't quite aware of it yet.

Hot In The Shade had been kind of a continuation of the *Crazy Nights* look, where they were trying to get a little more street, a little more leather. It worked for the time, but it's funny that you just don't see magazines or full-page pinups from the *Hot In The Shade* era. Even back then, you didn't really see them. The look worked for the time, and it looks OK now. But, visually speaking, it probably wasn't them at their best. There's nothing wrong with it—nothing embarrassing. It just looks a little contrived to me.

GIMME MORE: ERIC CARR REMEMBERED

After the tour in support of *Hot In The Shade* wrapped in late 1990, Eric Carr was diagnosed with heart cancer. Despite surgeries and chemotherapy treatments, the cancer returned, ultimately resulting in his death at the age of forty-one on November 24, 1991 (which was, as fate would have it, the same exact date that Queen's Freddie Mercury passed away). Here are select quotes from one of my earlier books, *The Eric Carr Story*, in which those close to Eric discuss how they'd like him to be remembered.

BRUCE KULICK Clearly, I think he was a huge part of a certain period of KISS that means a lot to a lot of fans. And I think the fans know that he really did care about them. He was more talented than they probably knew, but they certainly got enough of an idea of how great he was on the drums, how good a voice he had, and how much energy he had to play the role in the band. I think he was always the 'cute guy' in the band as well, and many of the girls really loved him. I take pleasure in knowing that I had the opportunity to work with a great, talented guy, and he is of course sorely missed by all.

CARRIE STEVENS [Eric's girlfriend, 1988–91; Playboy's 'Playmate Of The Month,' June 1997] From what I've been hearing from people, Eric did a really good job of setting his own legacy. I've been hanging around the rock scene a little bit again recently, and everyone knows who I am, because of him and *Playboy*. There's not a night that somebody doesn't come up to me, another guy in a band or a crew member, and tells me that Eric was one of the nicest people that they ever met, what a great drummer he was, and just what a down-to-earth, nicest person they ever met. I feel like people are extra nice to me and extra respectful of me because of him. So he's still supporting me. He's done a good job for himself, and I think he's being remembered exactly for what he earned. And he earned that reputation—no one can say an unkind word about the guy. I had to say, 'Only the good die young,' but believe me, I often thought, *Why him?* But I guess God probably needed him for something more important than what he was doing here. Maybe he's Gandhi somewhere else now, I don't know.

BILL AUCOIN [KISS manager, 1973–82] From my point of view, just as an incredible human being. I think of Eric as an incredible person, and a drummer second. Obviously, he was a great drummer, but I remember him as just an incredible human being. He was a sweetheart, willing to do anything for anyone. He was fantastic with fans. Fans would talk to him, and he would spend hours talking to them. He just wouldn't let it go. He couldn't have been a better person to have been with them during that time, when they were so disruptive and didn't know where they were going and weren't sure if KISS would survive. If anything, he helped them through it because of that personality he had, and that 'giving' emotion that he had. Not only to them, but to fans. I'm sure anyone who met him will never forget him.

CAROL KAYE [KISS publicist] Any time I spent with him, we always had a really nice time. He was funny, he was self-deprecating, he was just a very happy person. He had a great vibe and a great energy about him. I always looked forward to seeing Eric. He was just a very special person. He really was. He became like your family.

BOB EZRIN [producer, *Destroyer*, *(Music From) The Elder*, and *Revenge*] I remember him as a very talented musician, but more importantly, a very warm, generous, gentle, and happy person who was a joy to be around.

MICHAEL JAMES JACKSON [producer, *Creatures Of The Night* and *Lick It Up*] As somebody as a musician was defined as much by the passion that he had for being a player, and the pride that he had in being a member of KISS.

RON NEVISON Just as a sweet guy. He was just a quiet, sweet guy. Paul Caravello. I don't know how he got 'Eric' out of that. [*Laughs*] And where was he from, Brooklyn? So he was a nice Italian kid from Brooklyn, and a great drummer. That's how I would remember him.

CARMINE APPICE I think he should be remembered as the guy who replaced Peter, and he did it really well. He added to the band, and he was a kick-ass rock drummer. He showed it every night that he played with them. I thought Eric's style definitely fit in. Eric Singer plays more like Eric Carr than he does Peter Criss.

ROD MORGENSTEIN [drummer, Winger] I would like him to be remembered as one of the good ones. This is an industry where musician or label or booking agency and all the people involved—it's a rarity to meet someone who you just get a beautiful vibe about from the instant you meet them. He's one of the few people in my thirty-some-odd years of being a professional musician that I did get that feeling about. And it wasn't a growing feeling. It was something that I felt from the moment I met him. It's just a rare treat when you meet human beings like that. I think he should just be remembered as that special kind of all-around nice guy. He had no airs about him. In being in one of the biggest bands in the world, [he had] no pretension. He was just a sweet, nice guy. It might sound boring, but I think it's the highest compliment you can pay somebody.

A.J. PERO [drummer, Twisted Sister] He was one of the best people that I've met, being in this fucked up business. Eric was one of the best fucking people that I've met. As big as he was, I just never met anybody like him. God took him too soon. I wish he was alive today, I really do. Me and him became friends, but it was too short. My father died when I was twenty-five years old. It was too short—I didn't have the time that I had with my father. That's how I

153

felt about Eric. Right now, me and him should be hanging out. I feel cheated. I don't feel that I had enough time with the man to really become one of his best friends. The short time that I knew him was probably one of the best times that I've known anybody in my life, and I mean that from my heart. I miss him dearly, I really do. I never forget the times and the laughs.

BOB KULICK [brother of Bruce Kulick; uncredited guitarist on *Alive II*, *Killers*, and *Creatures*] One of the sweetest, nicest, most talented guys, and the worst thing that could happen, happened. To me, it's a sad story, because the ending was so bad. It's funny: the other day I was cleaning something up in the studio, and [I came across] one of the big tour books from back in the day. The thing's like three feet long! And Eric's in there. I'm looking at the pictures, and I'm just like, *Fuck ... look at his guy, man. A total star.* See, my brother was better at accepting his 'station.' That's what it is sometimes. I work with big artists, I produce big artists, but sometimes, they've said things to me that hurt my feelings. I had to accept that. You know why? Because I'm a big boy. I can dish it out, but I can take it. Unfortunately, he had a hard time taking it. That was the problem. Other than that, the guy was just an incredible human being.

MARK SLAUGHTER [singer, Slaughter, Vinnie Vincent Invasion] I'd like Eric to be remembered as the drummer who lived for drumming. The guy who had a great attitude, and, furthermore, he was a part of KISS for a lot longer than people perceive him to be. I think he, in a lot of ways, didn't really get the credit for what he had done. I mean, Peter Criss is an incredible drummer. Eric Singer is a great drummer. Understandably, any one of these guys that Gene and Paul have picked have always been stellar musicians. The reasons why they've been in KISS is because they deserve to be in KISS. And Eric—of all—deserved to be in KISS, to be *that person.* I'm very blessed to be a part of all that and see that, from behind the stage and behind his kit.

CARRIE STEVENS We had a ton of fun together. I mean, obviously, or we wouldn't have stayed together. I remember us being so goofy, being in Manhattan, and it would start to rain, and we'd be jumping in puddles and singing, and then ducking in restaurants, having Mexican coffee, and going out in the rain and jumping around again. I think he loved that young kind of spirit that I had, because he was very immature, too. [*Laughs*] He was really into watching movies. I know he said he wanted to grow up to be Paul McCartney when he was a kid. I used to call him and play Elvis songs on his answering machine ... and Winger songs. [*Laughs*] He liked old [movie] classics. I remember I'd be like, 'You like these *old* movies.' And he's like, 'Well, you're an actress. You should be watching movies.' But I wasn't as into it as him. We used to love the animated *Little Mermaid*. He loved that.

EDDIE TRUNK Just such a driving force in that band. I think they couldn't have found a better guy. His persona, his character, his warmth and love for the fans, and his talent I think were key. I question if KISS didn't hit a home run with bringing him in as the first replacement member, I don't know if KISS would have survived it. Because that's a sensitive, delicate thing, at a time when they were falling apart in every way. Then you go and endure a lineup change. If you don't bring the right guy in, and you brought in some schmuck or someone who didn't connect or didn't work, and a year later, you're bringing in another guy to take that spot and the revolving door starts, that really could have been the death blow for that band to totally not recover. But because of what he did persona-wise, musically, how relatable he was for fans, how much the fans pulled behind him, I really think that it gave the band a boost in a lot of different ways.

MARK WEISS [photographer] I'd like Eric to be remembered as someone who was happy at doing what he did, and he lived the dream. It sounds cliché, but [he was] probably one of the nicest guys in the business. He was kind of ahead of his [time], making a niche for heavy-metal drumming. He seemed really natural. It just seemed like KISS was the perfect band for him. I couldn't imagine him in any other band than KISS at that point. I think he did better without the makeup with them than with the makeup. He was more of himself.

MIKE PORTNOY [drummer, Dream Theater, 1985–2010] He was a genuine, kind soul. It's kind of sad that a lot of people, it takes them to pass away before people realize how sweet, gentle, and kind some people are. I saw the same thing recently when the Rev died, or Dimebag died, or Ronnie James Dio. It's sad. It takes somebody to pass away for people to appreciate how great they were. And Eric was one of those type of people. It wasn't until after he was gone that everybody came out of the closet saying, 'What a sweet guy he was.' It's just an example of you've [got] to appreciate people when they're here. And when you have a nice and genuine person like he was, you've got to appreciate people like that while they're still here on Earth with us.

CARRIE STEVENS [At the time this interview took place] I'm finally the age that Eric died. And when I turned forty-one this year, it really hit. And it is depressing to me—I'm still in love with a dead guy, and I'm still single. I would have jumped off a bridge if you told me, back then, 'Carrie, you're still going to be crying over him nineteen years later. You're never going to find a guy that was as good as he was to you.' It's so weird. I just went to the Rainbow … which Eric, Bruce, Christina, and I went to on his forty-first birthday, which turned out to be his last. I was there with my friend last Friday night, and when we were there, I told her that. And then as we were leaving, I was still talking about him. We turned on the radio, and his version of 'Beth' was playing. My jaw dropped. This stuff happens to me all the time. It's like he's there. He's like, *Hey, I'm watching you.*

REVENGE

Released May 19, 1992. Produced by Bob Ezrin.
US #6, UK #10. US certification: gold.

SIDE ONE

Unholy (Gene Simmons/Vinnie Vincent)

Take It Off (Paul Stanley/Bob Ezrin/Kane Roberts)

Tough Love (Stanley/Bruce Kulick/Ezrin)

Spit (Simmons/Stanley/Scott Van Zen)

God Gave Rock And Roll To You II (Russ Ballard/Simmons/Stanley/Ezrin)

Domino (Simmons)

SIDE TWO

Heart Of Chrome (Stanley/Vincent/Ezrin)

Thou Shalt Not (Simmons/Jesse Damon)

Every Time I Look At You (Stanley/Ezrin)

Paralyzed (Simmons/Ezrin)

I Just Wanna (Stanley/Vincent)

Carr Jam 1981 (Eric Carr)

SINGLES

God Gave Rock And Roll To You II (KISS) / Junior's Gone Wild

(King's X) / Shout It Out (Slaughter) (US did not chart, UK #4)

Unholy / God Gave Rock And Roll To You II (US did not chart, UK #26)

Domino / Carr Jam 1981 (US/UK did not chart)

I Just Wanna (Radio EQ) / I Just Wanna (promo only)

Every Time I Look At You / Partners In Crime (remix) (US/UK did not chart)

★

Despite the many ups and downs of the non-makeup era, you have to give Gene Simmons and Paul Stanley props. Although you could make the argument that KISS were keeping too close an eye on what other artists were doing, they *did* keep KISS relevant, and certainly toward the top of the hard-rock/heavy-metal heap (especially if we're using album sales, MTV exposure, and magazine coverage as a gauge). Which is all fine and dandy, but if you were to take such albums as, say, *Destroyer*, *Rock And Roll Over*, and *Creatures Of The Night* as the standards of what prime, filler-less KISS studio albums should be, few would say that such 80s efforts as *Asylum*, *Crazy Nights*, or *Hot In The Shade* came even close.

It just so happened that shortly after the dawn of the 90s, there was a new wave of rock/metal approaching—which was no bad thing, if you recall how predictable the two main metal subgenres (hair metal and thrash metal) had become. And while rock's heaviest hitters (Metallica and Guns N' Roses) continued to thrive, there was a whole new crop of heavy music that was about to abruptly turn the tides—as evidenced by the fast-rising popularity of such bands as Faith No More, Primus, Pantera, Alice In Chains, Nirvana, Soundgarden, Smashing Pumpkins, Sepultura, and more. In other words, a much more *real* sound and approach, both musically and visually.

Gene and Paul must have sensed the impending change, as their sixteenth studio effort overall, *Revenge*, was a clear return to the heavier/harder KISS sound, and certainly on par with their non-makeup triumphs. In fact, some fans would probably go as far as to say that *Revenge* serves as the quartet's last truly *great* (and certainly the most focused) studio offering.

Two important events occurred prior to the album that would determine the direction of the disc—the tragic death of Eric Carr, and the re-enlistment of Bob Ezrin as producer. KISS would not have to look far for Carr's replacement. The drummer from Paul's 1989 solo tour, Eric Singer (who had previously played with some of rock's biggest names, including Black Sabbath, Gary Moore, and Lita Ford) got the nod, and, in the process, became the first ever member of KISS to *not* sport jet-black hair.

Probably even more of a stylistic shape-shifter was the band's decision to hook up once more with one of the greatest rock producers of all-time, Mr. Ezrin. Besides overseeing (and, to various degrees, *masterminding*) the Alice

Cooper group's classic albums from *Love It To Death* through *Billion Dollar Babies*—as well as Lou Reed's *Berlin*, Pink Floyd's *The Wall*, and more—he also held the distinction of having produced what was largely considered KISS's greatest studio effort to date (*Destroyer*) *and* their worst (*Music From The Elder*).

Luckily, Ezrin was back on the right track in mind, spirit, and health (it's been well-documented that he was battling a cocaine problem during his previous KISS efforts, which may have played a part in *The Elder*), and, as a result, a one-for-all/all-for-one mentality carried over from the writing and recording of *Revenge* straight through to the end result. Wisely, instead of steering KISS into a more experimental direction (as he had on his two previous productions with the band, to varying degrees of success), he opted to make the album as stylistically and sonically cohesive as possible—with no need for his previous propensity for incorporating sound effects and between-track segments.

Another occurrence that should be noted (albeit one that's probably less significant than the two aforementioned) was that Vinnie Vincent was welcomed back into the fold as a songwriter. The end results would ultimately be a case of good news, bad news. Vincent helped co-pen some of the best tunes on *Revenge* (just as he had on the two previous albums that prominently list either Cusano or Vincent in the credits, *Creatures Of The Night* and *Lick It Up*)—'Unholy,' 'Heart Of Chrome,' and 'I Just Wanna.' But every time the speedy guitarist and KISS crossed paths, it would end in bad blood and supposedly burnt bridges. This time, it would lead to several lawsuits between Vincent and KISS, and the guitarist dropping out of public eye for many years (before returning in 2018).

It also turned out that *Revenge* arrived smack dab in the middle of the time when grunge was swiftly annihilating hair metal. And while KISS wouldn't suddenly start sportin' the flannels like some other bands did in an attempt to stay relevant (I'll give you a hint … it's a band whose name rhymes with *Motorbreath*), they most definitely did try to dress in a more serious 'n' heavy manner, with lots of leather and even Dr. Martens–style boots—a far cry from the neon glow of the *Asylum* era. It can also be said that Gene *finally* truly found a comfortable non-makeup era look in time for *Revenge*, highlighted by a Beelzebub-esque goatee that had him looking a bit like Tom Araya's not-so-distant cousin.

The *Revenge* album cover certainly suited KISS's newly discovered tough/hard/we-mean-business look—a black KISS logo on the side of steel sheets bolted together, with the album's title smeared in what could very well be blood. Which leads to the question: who exactly were KISS plotting 'revenge' against? *Others*, for not taking them seriously? *Themselves*, for getting further and further away from the heavy-duty *Creatures* sound as the 80s progressed? A definitive answer to this question has never been determined, but most fans could care less—they were just happy that their much-missed 'heavy KISS' had finally returned.

KISS wasted little time announcing their return. The album opens with the delightfully demonic rocker 'Unholy,' which features a breakdown section reminiscent of the bit at 2:48 of 'Only You' on *The Elder*, another killer Kulick solo, and lyrics that admittedly try a bit *too* hard—'*I am the incubus / I lay the egg in you / The worm that burrows through your brain.*' Regardless, 'Unholy' was easily the heaviest Gene-sung composition since probably 'I Love It Loud' … although 'Not For The Innocent' comes mighty close.

Also to be found on the album are such rockers as 'Take It Off' and 'Domino,' both of which have more in common—from a lyrical perspective—with the let's-party 80s than the let's-get-serious 90s. Other standouts include 'I Just Wanna' (whose verse melody bares quite a resemblance to 'Summertime Blues'—go ahead and compare them), and an anthem that first appeared on the soundtrack to *Bill & Ted's Bogus Journey*, 'God Gave Rock And Roll To You II' (originally recorded by Argent in the early 70s, although due to a lyrical overhaul the song's original writer, Russ Ballard, was now joined in the credits by Simmons, Stanley, and Ezrin).

As well as several more tunes that have subsequently become largely forgotten ('Tough Love,' 'Spit,' 'Heart Of Chrome,' 'Thou Shalt Not,' and 'Paralyzed'), the album includes a tribute to the late, great Eric Carr, 'Carr Jam 1981.' The song was supposedly first written around the time of *The Elder* but never released. However, eyebrows may be raised as to why Carr is listed as the song's sole writer on *Revenge*, when it appears as though the music was a collaboration between the drummer and Ace Frehley, since the song 'Breakout' from the self-titled Frehley's Comet album contains similar music, and lists Carr, Frehley, and original FC guitarist Richie Scarlet as the songwriters.

Although hair metal was all but dead and buried by the time *Revenge* was unleashed, a few power ballads that sounded distinctly 80s had slipped through the cracks and somehow managed to become sizable hits on the *Billboard* Hot 100 during grunge's peak years of '91–92, among them Mr. Big's 'To Be With You,' Saigon Kick's 'Love Is On The Way,' and FireHouse's 'When I Look Into Your Eyes.' With 'Every Time I Look At You,' it seemed like KISS had a tune on *Revenge* that could also storm the charts in a similarly gentle manner—and, with its acoustic guitar strum and tender lyrics, it seemed like the perfect follow-up to 'Forever.' Unfortunately, just as such previous seemingly can't-miss potential hits as 'Thrills In The Night' and 'Reason To Live' did not translate to chart success, neither did this one.

All in all, after spending much of the 80s either following trends or offering albums that were not entirely consistent from front to back, it seemed that KISS were once again truly ready to rock, with their most focused studio recording in years. And their fans seemed to agree—*Revenge* went on to become the second-highest-charting album of their entire career to date, its surprise #6 placement on the *Billboard* 200 beaten only by the #4 peak of *Love Gun* back in 1977, although these numbers would eventually be usurped by *Psycho Circus* (#3, 1998), *Sonic Boom* (#2, 2009), and *Monster* (#3, 2012).

KNOW THE SCORE: LONN FRIEND

The former editor of *RIP Magazine*—and one-time host of the 'Friend At Large' segment on MTV's *Headbangers Ball*—recalls his encounters with KISS during the *Revenge* era.

How did you first cross paths with KISS?

The first time I saw KISS was October 26, 1990 [at the Centrum, in Worcester, Massachusetts], in the midst of the *Hot In The Shade* tour. I wasn't a fan in the 70s, and I didn't really immerse myself in KISS and their music until I met Gene in '87, shortly after I took over *RIP Magazine*—by profession, we became involved with them. It wasn't just the *Revenge* record—that [provided] the most intimate of my experiences with them, and we'll get to that in a minute—but we were also involved with *Crazy Nights* and *Smashes, Thrashes & Hits*. My experience on that day at the Centrum—no makeup, Winger and Slaughter, and I flew in to just kind of get the experience. Those are three 'RIP bands.'

I never saw them in makeup, so the performance was like a really strong rock band—with no theater. But the fans were *so* nutty. I went into Mark Slaughter's dressing room after his set, and I said, 'Let's go watch KISS.' We went into the pit together, and Gene was flicking picks at us. It was so much fun, and I got it in that moment, from the fan perspective—what it was like to be at KISS show. Whether they had makeup on, or flames spitting out of guitars, or any of that bombast, it was just fun to be there—because the songs made you feel alive.

And I wrote about the story, where I was ready to fly home, and Gene hijacked me and said, 'You're going home with us on MGM Grand,' and I took a limo with him and Paul from New York, and I ended up interviewing both of them on the plane. That's where the relationship really started to evolve—seeing them, and having them talk so frankly about their love of The Beatles, and how they formed the band together. That was a great trip. Then I saw them again—and I don't remember the exact date—during the *Revenge* tour.

Didn't you get in hot water for playing a song off *Revenge* on the radio before its release?

As is the custom, as a magazine editor with what we called 'press lead,' you needed to get the music three months early, so your articles would hit at the time that the records were hitting the stores. I was in a unique position where I landed myself a syndicated radio show on the Westwood One Network—which was an offshoot of my MTV *Headbangers Ball* experience—[so] I was wearing the hat of magazine editor, and then that means I was getting the entire albums, the new releases, on a cassette, *three months* before they were hitting stores. It wasn't politically correct back then to play music before the record company serviced you with the single or the record. And that usually [would be] a couple of weeks prior to the store date.

I got the *Revenge* record, and I had my *Pirate Radio Saturday Night* show, and I decided that I was going to play … now, I didn't decide this on my own. I first asked for the blessings of Paul Stanley, if I could play 'I Just Wanna' on my radio show. And I said it might be politically incorrect, and he goes, 'No, *I want you to play it.*' So, when he gave me the go-ahead, I played it. And because I was in the Los Angeles market, and there were other rock stations in the LA market, they got pissed, because I had this music so early, and I was leaking it, through radio, for the fans.

Everything I've done in my career was for the artists and for the fans—I didn't care about the business so much, or the politics. In a way, I was sort of naïve about that, because I also did this with the Megadeth *Countdown To Extinction* record, too. I was giving fans what they would enjoy, without thinking of the repercussions.

Cheryl Valentine was the metal radio-promotion person at Mercury Records, and she immediately called me … as a matter of fact, she faxed me or called me—this was in the days before cellular technology. And she was upset. She wrote me a cease-and-desist to not play it again. So I took this as an opportunity to really stir up—and I knew this wouldn't bother KISS or their management at all—a real cause célèbre, by asking Paul on my show, and having him read the cease-and-desist letter on the air, live, and then I would play the song *again*. [*Laughs*]

And then that led to what we called the in-studio/on-air Paul Stanley bachelor party, when he married Pamela [Bowen, his first wife]. And Gene and Paul both came into the studio that day, and we took calls from fans—it was just a lot of fun. And then I ended up being invited to Paul's wedding— me and my then-wife, Joyce—at the Bel-Air Hotel. I felt like I [had this relationship] with several acts back then—that the trust of the magazine had gained and cultivated with these bands, made me almost like a family member. So I got invited to these things, and I took that as an act of friendship. What I did is try and cover the records as best as possible.

Let's discuss *Revenge.*
I loved the cover of 'God Gave Rock And Roll To You.' It's even more anthemic than the original—due in large part to Bob's sonic production. And 'Domino' and 'I Just Wanna.' 'Domino' is so archetypal Gene—*'That bitch bends over, and I forget my name.'* That's *so* classic, crotch-level Gene Simmons, that if there was a true return to form—as far as that 'God Of Thunder' / 'Dr. Love' zeitgeist—'Domino' had a great groove to it. 'I Just Wanna' is vintage Paul Stanley. It's a great play on words. Not being a student of the whole catalogue,

163

maybe they had always been informed, but perhaps, to the novice, *Revenge* was just a really good rock'n'roll record that sounded like a vintage KISS album— even though it came out in 1992. And 'Take It Off' is a great track.

KISS's image got grittier around this time, compared to the mid-to-late 80s.

KISS's image during the non-makeup years was: *We're not the best looking guys. We don't really care. We'll fluff up our hair and shit, but it's not theater to us anymore. We're going to realize more upon our performance chops and the quality of our songs.* Which led to an enormous hit with the ballad, 'Forever'—without makeup, practically unplugged, and it was almost as big as 'Beth.' And they got Michael Bolton to write with them, who understood a thing or two about how to have platinum ballads.

I always applaud Metallica, because they always took risks and chances. Well, that was essentially what KISS did when they took the makeup off and ventured into different musical stylings. They were taking risks—trusting that they could write songs that their generation of fans would still embrace and not abandon them. Until that day came—which, ultimately, it did—when they put the makeup back on.

Something to be said about these non-makeup records … they've always had strong players, but Bruce Kulick was as good a guitarist as any journeyman guitar player in rock'n'roll in the 90s. Bruce Kulick was *that guy*. He was strong. And Eric Carr was such a good drummer. I liked Eric—he was such a gentle soul. I only met him a couple of times. A hell of a drummer. And then then the other Eric comes in—Eric Singer—and he works with or without makeup. KISS realigned themselves more as songwriters and performers without the theater, and it brought out a different dimension of their musical capabilities. When you take the mask off, you're pretty naked. I mean, Gene's ego works with makeup or no makeup. Onstage, he's fairly confident.

And their videos were *so* hilarious in the 80s. It was, like, zero budget, but they wanted them to look like they were *gigantic*. That's part of the magic of KISS—they sort of get the joke themselves. And because they do, they know the fans get it, too. If you're on that same plane of understanding with your fans, you can reach as high as you want. And that's why they're so successful— because everyone is in on the same joke.

How popular were KISS with *RIP Magazine*'s readership at the time?

I would say the five most popular bands over my tenure—from '87 to '94—were Metallica, Mötley Crüe, Guns N' Roses, KISS, and Ozzy, just [based on] whatever I put on the cover and features, the most letters would come in, and fan reactions. And cultivating relationships with those bands was key to our success, because I got shoots that other people didn't get, and access that other magazines didn't get.

***RIP* put Gene and Paul on the cover in makeup (from the 'Rise To It' video shoot) for the June 1990 issue.**

The greatest story about that is how we fucked up the cover. My art director gets this exclusive photo—just for *RIP*—from that video, when they put the makeup back on. It was a no-brainer—it was going to be the feature story. And our logo was always on the left side.

So my art director, Greg Jones, he gets this photo, and it's not working. So he flips the photo—he flips the transparency, so the image is reversed, so the logo would fit nicely. It looked fantastic. Nobody on my staff that proofed it—throughout the process of putting the cover together—realized that, by flipping the photo, they put the star on Paul's *other eye*! And it wasn't until fans wrote letters—it went by *everybody*. But I had to write some sort of editorial apology for our faux pas. In hindsight, it's so funny.

It was impressive that *Revenge* scored so high on the charts in the midst of grunge and alt-rock mania.

That is when Nirvana, Soundgarden, and Pearl Jam were absolutely *dominating*. I mean, it's a cultural wave. Nobody is promoting the hair bands anymore—they're being relegated to the also-rans. It was a shift. You had to truly rise above. Where the winds were blowing in your favor just two years before, whether you were Def Leppard or KISS, you were at the top of the charts and releasing platinum records, it was an uphill battle to get any visibility on the mainstream media. *Especially MTV.* But I think that's why we should hold sacred as to why it's sad that magazines have disappeared—with the exception of places like the UK, where magazines are still such a powerful force. Here in the US, terrestrial publications have all but disappeared.

Is *Revenge* your favorite non-makeup era KISS recording?

Because of my intimate access to and being involved in the promotion and the marketing and editorial support of that record, I suppose it holds a special place for me. As a pure KISS effort, there were other really strong efforts of the non-makeup years. But I guess I could say, yeah, that's my favorite—for the reason of personal proximity to the project.

I saw KISS about four years ago in Las Vegas, and they didn't do any music from *Revenge*. I think I saw them do 'God Gave Rock And Roll To You,' but that was on the *Revenge* tour. If I was KISS, I'd be doing that song *every night*—I think that song is a great closer. And their version is *so* good—with or without makeup. When you have a catalogue that large ... I don't know how they do their setlist. It's almost like they should have fans give them suggestions—they should pull out different tracks.

But then, of course, they're well-rehearsed, and they have a lot of choreography in the show. So you can't stray that far from a template you're going to keep for the whole leg of the tour. I think it would be cool to hear 'Unholy' or 'I Just Wanna' live sometime—but I understand them relegating that to the 'non-live' tracks. I think, as an album, to put it on and hear how fresh those tracks sound, and how nasty Gene's vocals are on that record, and how sonically brilliant the album is ... I think the record holds up strongly, twenty-six years later.

KNOW THE SCORE: PAUL RACHMAN

The director of KISS's music videos for 'Unholy,' 'I Just Wanna,' and 'Domino' (as well as Alice In Chains' 'Man In The Box,' Temple Of The Dog's 'Hunger Strike,' and Pantera's 'Mouth For War') talks about what it was like working with the band circa *Revenge*.

How did you get involved in directing most of the videos for *Revenge*?

I was a music video director at this company called Propaganda Films, which was essentially David Fincher's company. There were about a dozen music video directors there. I had come in and went out to LA in late '88, and right before I worked with KISS, I had done the Alice In Chains 'Man In The Box' video, Temple Of The Dog ['Hunger Strike'], and Pantera ['Cowboys From Hell' and 'Mouth For War']. I was working a lot, and I was one of the directors who got on the list that they liked. Gene and Paul are very involved in every decision. They don't really let the record company decide for them—they actually looked at reels and decided on who was on this list.

I was sent the 'Unholy' track, which was the first single. I was actually very pleased to hear it, in the sense that it was a return to hard rock for them. In the late 80s, a lot of their music without the makeup on … it just wasn't the KISS that I knew when I was a little kid. They had moved away from that, and *Revenge*—and particularly, 'Unholy'—for me was like, *this is hard rock again.* I was into it. And the title of the song and the lyrics inspired an idea, which I came up with. It was really involving kids and the whole idea of evil kids, the devil—that whole iconography of *The Omen* and all those movies. I had this idea that was mainly visual, but I thought worked with their lyrics.

I remember they took meetings. I first wrote a three-page concept—a little script—of what my idea for the video was. They read them, and then they decided on what directors they were going to meet with. And I was one of them. I don't know how many directors they met with—there were a few— but I think they were doing them all in one day. I came in during the early afternoon, and I was ready.

The beginning of my pitch was the sonogram of a baby in a womb. I gave them the rest of my pitch, and they were silent. I was just *on* that day—I loved the song, I believed in my idea, I was able to describe it in a really strong way. It was a positive meeting. They had a few questions—not that many. I felt bold. And when we left, I think an hour later, I got a call from my agent from Propaganda Films, and she said, '*You've got the job.* They just canceled all the meetings with the other directors they were supposed to meet with.'

The *Revenge* videos seemed to be the complete opposite of their showy, glitzy videos of the 80s.
KISS were trendsetters when they started. When they started with the makeup on and really broke out as a concept band, they were trendsetters. I think they had a very keen understanding of how to ride the business. And I think that 80s era, that was when hair metal, big hair, ballads [were] riding big. And they

took that direction. I think they did need to change it up. I was a little younger then, and I was into the whole underground hardcore-punk movement at the time. But I think KISS, with the heavy makeup and big shows, had shifted—especially with punk rock. The big arena/big show thing was not what the kids wanted anymore. And then punk happened, and a new wave of heavy metal happened, and they rode that and took the makeup off.

This was Gene's song, so Gene was very involved. I went to meet with him at his house to talk about it. He wanted to talk about everything—he was very hands-on. I remember directing them was quite easy—they were very good listeners, and they liked what they saw. I do remember one moment on set—when you see them onstage a lot, they're separate, but they have a habit to come together and go shoulder-to-shoulder. When I was doing some full band shots, they kind of went into that move, and I was trying to get a very designed shot, where I placed them under certain lights, and I didn't want them to move around. I just wanted them to stand there. We did a couple of takes of that, and they were uncomfortable with it.

I remember Gene and Paul, they kind of huddled with the band, and they were like, *This doesn't feel like us. We move around a lot.* I understood that and respected it—and did some takes like that—but I really wanted the shot where they didn't move around. Where they just stood there—like they were pillars of rock, that didn't move around. I needed that shot. I wasn't able to convince them, and the record company was there, and I just said, 'Listen. You guys hired me for a reason. This is what I need you to do. *It's 1992 … it's not 1984.* I need you to do this—just trust me.' It just came out—I didn't think about it. When you're a director of a band, and you're trying to make your day, you just have to own the set.

They kind of huddled again, and I was like, *What the hell are they talking about?* I remember kind of creeping up, and I heard Gene or Paul saying, 'Well … maybe the kid's right. *Maybe we should listen.*' [*Laughs*] It was kind of charming, because it really gave me some confidence. When you're working with big stars—and I was in maybe my late twenties—you kind of need that confidence. And I wasn't snooping on them—we were losing time in the day, and I needed to shoot. We didn't have time to have these kinds of meetings in the middle of the day on set. So I think they respected me for that, because when I finished the video, they really hardly had any notes. I remember they really liked it, and I really liked it. I think it worked for them. In the end, them coming out so boldly with a hard-rock song on that record really set the path for them putting the makeup back on and going back to hard rock.

Gene and Paul have a very special relationship. They've kept it together for a long time—through good and bad. But Paul had a really good note about Gene's performance. There were a couple of takes I did of Gene alone, where he was just singing into the camera without his bass, and was using his hands. There was a moment in it that Paul caught, and said, 'Listen, lose that shot, because it's *Gene Simmons*—it's not *Ozzy Osbourne*.' [*Laughs*] And he was right! I took that one shot out. This was at a time when Ozzy was going big just as Ozzy Osbourne, and in his videos he was featured alone a lot without the band.

But it was a great experience, that particular shoot. When you get a great song and you have a great idea and you can execute it and everybody is with you, it's great. We shot late into the night—I had a lot of shots to get with these kids, and a lot of little cutaways and shots that didn't involve the band in them—and Gene stayed until the very, very last shot. He just wanted to see everything I was getting, to make sure I was doing my job. I respected that. And that set a relationship up for the whole year, for that whole album— where I basically did [most of] the videos for that album.

Fans point to this era as when Gene finally found his non-makeup image. Do you agree?
I think 'Unholy,' that song, [is when] Gene found his hard-rock roots again. And he was that kind of iconic, hard-rocking, 'Gene Simmons' again—even though he didn't have the makeup on. It was the Gene Simmons from the 70s, but without the makeup.

Let's discuss the set for the 'Unholy' video, and where it was shot.
On that video, we actually needed a really big stage, because there is a big corrugated metal wall that I built, that was probably, like … *fifty feet tall*. And I had three or four different sets—I had this woodsy/garden set for the kids, I had an overhead set where there was grass and we had a pentagram design that the kids were doing a 'Ring Around The Rosie' kind of thing. We needed these

all built in one giant space, so we could just move from set to set during the day.

But the big soundstages in Hollywood, a lot of them were booked. So we had to go to Long Beach—this giant soundstage where a lot of car commercials are shot. And that's where we built it. It was about an hour away, and that's where we shot it, because I needed the space. I know at one point, they were like, 'Why are we shooting in Long Beach? Why do we have to go there?' Well, that particular weekend we needed to shoot, that's where we could get the big space that I needed.

The KISS organization, they have their particular makeup people, stylists, and clothes. I remember the makeup people had to go to everybody's house early—they started to get into their 'KISS image' before they even got to the soundstage. So, they kind of show up as KISS already—and then they do additional makeup and stuff on set. But that was a really great experience.

You know, I'm coming out of hardcore punk, and I go to LA and I'm starting a career as a music-video director, and I really find my footing with MTV videos. And my recognition really came with grunge—with Alice In Chains and the Pearl Jam guys in Temple Of The Dog, and that Seattle sound. Which really connects back to punk—all those people listened to hardcore when they were little kids. So when I got the KISS record, the offer to write an idea for KISS, I was like, *Yeah, I remembered KISS with the makeup on, and I loved all those old songs.* But I was skeptical, because I was worried about, *What are they sending me? Some cheesy ballad that I'm going to have to do?* [*Laughs*] And when I heard 'Unholy,' I was like, *Yeah! This rocks! I'll do this!* I was psyched.

It was great, because when Gene and Paul went on MTV, and when they did the world premiere of the video, they were interviewed and they talked about me. They said, 'We worked with this new kid who just did all the Pantera videos. We really liked them, and we're going hard rock again.' It was all about the hard rock, the new image, and they were kind enough to credit me a little bit—so that was awesome.

I'd imagine that, for a major rock group like KISS, the video budgets would have been big.

They were good. They weren't the biggest, they weren't the smallest. They were good-sized. I can't remember exactly what it was, but it was fair. It was definitely in line with the amount of sales that they did. They come up with a marketing budget, and Gene and Paul are smart—they're not going to go cheap, and they're not going to overpriced. It was fair.

How does payment work with music videos? Do you still see money from them?

No. Music videos are all work for hire—it's owned by the record company. So, those videos … I don't know where the catalog is at now, but those were on Mercury Records at the time. I don't get anything from it. No music video directors ever got any points or anything. Occasionally, there was a small window to negotiate—like during the 'VHS home video days,' if you were doing a whole two-hour home video, there was sometimes some room to negotiate for a point or something. But it's not anything you'd ever see. But no, there were no royalties or anything like that involved for music video directors.

So you were just paid a flat fee and that was it, right?

Yeah. You basically get a percentage of the budget. So, the bigger the budget, the more money the director gets paid.

The next KISS video you did was for 'I Just Wanna.'

We had a great working relationship from 'Unholy.' I got to go to some shows, the record release party—all of that stuff. And KISS toured in Europe on that record, before they toured in the US. They were heading on tour and they wanted to get the follow-up video done before they got back to the US. They had a schedule of a release pattern. For 'I Just Wanna,' we shot it in London. They had one day off. This used to happen a lot with bands on tour—the record company would say, 'OK, we have a day off in London. Can you guys shoot in London? Come up with an idea and you can shoot it in a day.' That's what we did.

'I Just Wanna' was a Paul Stanley song, and it was a little more poppy. It wasn't the kind of dark, hard rock of a Gene Simmons song. It was the kind of brighter, poppy feeling of a Paul Stanley song. *Pop* may not be the right word, but just a different sound. I know Vinnie Vincent co-wrote some of these songs. And for 'I Just Wanna,' I listened to it and I needed an idea for one day in London. There wasn't a lot of time, so I wanted to find something simple, but I wanted them to *pop*. I wanted it to look more fun, a little brighter, a little poppier—and that's why I chose the 'white void' look.

That's not something that hadn't been done before, but it hadn't really been done with a band like KISS. It wasn't a look you would expect from KISS. So I thought that would work. And being able to shoot them on a white void, it really helped the editing, because you could really *pop* the edits—from wide shots to close-ups—and have a lot of fun with that. And Paul Stanley moves a lot—he looks more flexible and twisty. I think that would work well over the white background.

So we flew to London, and I remember we went to Wembley Arena, to see the show. We got there, like, a week before the shoot, because I had to find a British crew, British location, a soundstage. We shot at a movie soundstage—Samuelson [aka the Production Village, in operation from 1979 to 2000], which is a famous soundstage just out of London. So I found my crew and had my idea. We had a whole prep day, but we were in London, so we went to the show.

I remember it was funny, because KISS keeps these sets in different countries for their tours. They have storage spaces. And they toured with the set from one of their previous tours—it was the whole Egyptian motif [from the *Hot In The Shade* tour]. So, here was the tour for *Revenge*, but they're still using this set from a previous tour from the hair metal days! [*Laughs*] I was like, *Wait a minute … they don't have a new look?* I felt like they should have just got gone with lights, black curtains, and their logo—instead of pulling out the whole Egyptian thing. But it was a great show. They had the fire, the flames … it was KISS. I was backstage, and it was great.

I remember we had another day off—it may have been the day before the show—and I remember walking around London. We ended up on Portobello Road or one of those roads where there's a lot of shops. And we ran into them! I remember walking around with Gene, and he would go to these little stores and would point out all this KISS stuff that was bootlegged. He'd go, 'That's illegal … that's a bootleg … all this stuff. We're just getting ripped off.' I don't know if he ever did anything about it—he probably did. He was like, 'It's *millions of dollars* that we're being ripped off.' They were fun to hang out with.

So that was a one-day shoot again, and was very quick. I remember doing lunch and talking with Gene about Europe, and he would complain about these countries—how bad the food is in certain countries, and how some of these countries still don't have good air-conditioning. He was like, '*World War II is over! Get good air-conditioning, damnit!*' It was a very *American* criticism—it was a laugh, it was great to hear this stuff.

We shot that in London, and I think we brought everything back to LA and edited it in LA. On that one, we had to get some tapes to them on the road—the cuts. It was very smooth and very easy. They liked the video. That video actually broke out—it had a longer run. The song was a little poppier, so it might have done better on radio—other than rock radio. But that video broke out a bit. My taste personally leans towards 'Unholy,' but 'I Just Wanna' was the successful single for them—at least music video–wise.

What do you recall about the 'Domino' video?

When I got the song, I was a little less excited about it. I didn't fall in love with that song like I fell in love with 'Unholy.' Creatively and conceptually, it was a little more challenging for me. Here, you have a story about a woman or something—the lyrics told a little more of a story, from what I remember. We were going to shoot in LA. We didn't want to be in a soundstage again, but I did shoot a performance part for the video at SIR, where they used to rehearse. That was set up a little bit like a rehearsal. And then I shot Gene in this big Cadillac up in Ventura Boulevard.

You know, that video didn't gel as well creatively, for me. And I think it kind of surprised them, too. Listen—*it's hard*. Making a film is hard, making a music video is hard. You work with a band over and over and over again—not every single video is going to be the perfect hit. Just like not every single song is going to be the perfect hit. I knew when I was finishing the edit that this song and this concept and this video wasn't gelling like the previous two. It was a disappointment. If I remember correctly, I think the song was sent to radio a little earlier than the video. It wasn't in sync. And that's always a big challenge—where pressure is coming on the release of a video. I don't know if that song took off on radio.

And a lot of these records, you get to the third single, and you're starting to wane. The first single is big, the second single you keep going. If you have a more successful or as successful third single, you're already in the realm of that being rarer. It's hard. So I think that was the case with the choice of the song. I think it wasn't taking off on radio. And then there was a lot of hope that the video would save it—but that never really works. That was a little bit of a disappointment. And I remember I think Gene said, 'We were going two for two, but we can't say we're three for three.' And I knew that. He was right.

And it's not a terrible video. It just wasn't as shaped, conceptually. It didn't really communicate, it wasn't in your face, it wasn't really jumping off the screen. It just wasn't *there*. And I don't know if the song was there. I mean, I always believe it's hard to make a bad video for a great song. But it's *really* hard to make a great video for a not-great song. You really need both things to work in conjunction. I really tried to toe the line with this one, but I think I was a little off. We were all a little off, creatively. And that was that—that was the *Revenge* album. [But] I was still on good terms with them. They didn't throw me off the boat. [*Laughs*]

I remember, during *Revenge*—while we were in London, even—they were already talking about putting the makeup back on. That was starting to become the plan. That was in motion already—in terms of the future. A few years later, Gene and Paul called me up, because they were putting the makeup back on, and they needed a little promotional video to communicate that. They really wanted to use all their old footage to create what would now be known as a 'sizzle reel'—to announce they were putting the makeup back on.

What was pretty cool was, I started to meet with them again. I went to Gene's house again—we hung out at a cottage area away from his house that's his office. Doc McGhee had come in to start managing them now. He wasn't managing them when I did *Revenge*. Doc McGhee was going to be their manager when they put the makeup back on. I met with them and got set up in an edit room—with all their old footage. But, this is *old* footage. We're in the 1990s, and I'm dealing with footage from the 1970s—which, nostalgically, is cool, but doesn't quite work in terms of the *sizzle*. If it's going to be *KISS is back with the makeup*, it really needed a new look. And they hadn't put the makeup on yet, they didn't have the production, they didn't have anything. So there was nothing to shoot yet.

I remember being with them to talk about this at SIR once—they were re-making all the costumes, because the old costumes were all in storage bins and were relics. They were fragile. So these boot-makers and clothing-makers were coming by, taking measurements, and literally re-made all the old costumes. And I remember sitting around with them on the phone about that, and them explaining it to me. That was pretty cool to see.

So, anyhow, I gave it a shot at trying to make a sizzle reel for them putting the makeup back on, but it was clear that the old footage wasn't really going to carry it for five minutes. It would be good to have thirty seconds of it and then, *bang*—you'd need something new. They didn't really have that. So we kind of stopped that edit, and they ended up going with animation. I wasn't an animator or a director of animation, but there was this promo video for them putting the makeup back on—because I saw it—and they hired these animators, who basically did a Claymation of KISS with the makeup on. And that worked great. That's kind of the last time I worked with them.

I have run into Gene and Paul independently. I go to LA a lot, and I'll run into Paul at a Starbucks or something. And they're always nice—'How are you doing? Good to see you!' I ran into Gene years ago, and I remember he said, 'You're still a very handsome young man.' [*Laughs*] I got a gold record from them, and I enjoyed working with them. I'm very proud to be a part of KISS history.

How would you describe the four band members at the time of *Revenge*?

You can tell that Paul and Gene have worked together for a very long time. They definitely know each other. Like I said, when Paul Stanley called me about a really good note about Gene, that was a little bit of a lifting [of] the veil: *OK, these guys work together, and are willing to challenge each other like that*. I don't know how easy it's been for them to keep this band alive like this, but they've kept it together. They definitely have a great working relationship. They're very different personalities. I remember they have a healthy back-and-forth, and they know each other, so it works.

Bruce Kulick and Eric Singer very much knew they were working for Paul and Gene—they're doing whatever Paul and Gene tell them to do. I remember talking to Eric about something—I forget what it was—but I remember him saying, 'As long as it's OK with Gene, I'm fine with it.' [*Laughs*] They were all really nice. Very professional. It's a well-oiled machine. It's pro. And Bruce was a super-nice guy. And Gene and Paul respected them—I think there was a lot of professional respect, a kind of family/professional respect. But Gene and Paul make the decisions, and when they put the makeup back on, that didn't include Eric Singer or Bruce Kulick. Eric came back in later, with the makeup, but when they first went out, it was the original band. But that didn't last long, I guess. [*Laughs*]

How would you compare working with KISS to the other bands you worked with at the time?

KISS were more *mature* rock stars. I don't mean that they were older—they had deeper experience in the music business. You could tell right away that the younger bands I would work with, they were much more emotionally connected to being a rock star. I think, with younger bands, their personal lives and their rock star or music business lives are blurred. But with KISS, it was very distinct. When Paul was touring and we shot in London, he had his fiancé with him [Pamela Bowen]—who became his wife. And Gene had a family. I would go to his house, but I wouldn't go to his home—I would go to his office at his house. So they were just more experienced, and [had] been through it. They had established themselves. Working with KISS is like, *We're making another record, we're going out on tour again, we've been doing this for years, we've found the separation of our lives and the business.* Whereas with the younger bands, these are not bands with families. That was very apparent.

REVENGE: THE TOUR WITH CURT GOOCH

Realizing that fans got a kick out of the larger than life *Hot In The Shade* stage, KISS go *big* again with the *Revenge* tour setup ... while digging out deep cuts that had not been played live in well over a decade ...

The *Revenge* tour started off in clubs in April of 1992. This was Eric Singer's live debut in KISS. The problem with doing a club tour is that many people believed KISS were now only big enough to play clubs. They didn't understand this was a promotional tie-in. They thought, *Oh, wow ... KISS is playing clubs now? God, that's horrible!* And so that kind of created a negative image—coupled with the fact that the alternative underground had risen to prominence in the months preceding *Revenge*.

KISS did a short UK stint, too. That whole period of time, I had already kind of grown disinterested to a point, but I was still there. I had seen two of the club shows. And then, we got to the arena shows in North America. I went to a rehearsal in Bethlehem, and when I walked into the rehearsal, the Statue of Liberty on the stage had already blown up, and you could see the skull face was visible.

And I literally sat there, looking at Eric Singer—who had escorted me in—and looking back at the stage, looking back at Eric, and looking back at the Statue of Liberty, and thinking, *Is this an elaborate practical joke?* The skull reminded me *so much* of the Spinal Tap skull. And I just thought the *Revenge* stage looked like the most cliché heavy-metal bullshit.

Revenge, on the arena tour, was a real eye-opener—just as to what happened to the band. For example, Bethlehem, because it was the first show [October 1, 1992, at the Stabler Arena] and they were close enough to New York, it was a very small arena—maybe eight-to-ten thousand—but it was close to sold out. It looked fine. But the next series of shows I saw were in Florida. The first one was in Daytona Beach [October 29, at the Ocean Center]. And when I walked into the venue, the first thing I noticed … I literally stopped in my tracks and just stood there, because we were five minutes away from the lights going out for KISS, and there was *nobody* in the venue. There couldn't have been a thousand or two thousand people in the venue. My friend said, 'Is this the *Creatures* tour?' It hadn't yet dawned on us—the same difference.

And they went out with the two weakest opening acts for that period of time—Faster Pussycat and Trixter. *Especially* Trixter. I mean, I don't think Trixter sold one single ticket, and Faster Pussycat were a club band by that point—they literally lost their record deal in the middle of the tour! At that point, 'retro' had just kicked in—we weren't quite there yet. And KISS was just considered uncool.

I'll never forget being in the lobby of the Phoenix Biltmore, the day before the last show of the arena tour, and the hotel manager was talking with some employees at the hotel, and they said, 'What's going on over there? Why are those people asking those other people for autographs?' And the guy said,

'That's the KISS Army. They're here to meet KISS.' And the girl was like, 'KISS?! Oh my God … *how uncool can you get?*' At that moment, people did not want anything to do with hard rock or heavy metal for some reason. And KISS were branded that forever, and there was no getting around that.

For *Revenge*, they definitely continued the trend they started on *Hot In The Shade*—with the longer, two-hour shows, and including different deep cuts. Eric Singer—in particular—had been a big fan of the first three albums, and, in particular, *Hotter Than Hell*, and I think it was he that got 'Watchin' You' into the set. They definitely added new 70s deep cuts that hadn't been there during the *Hot In The Shade* period. But by that point, as great as that was, it just wasn't enough to save that tour. The whole world had changed. All of a sudden, we were in *90210* Land, and KISS just wasn't on that radar—and they weren't going to be, no matter what.

In 1992, grunge and alternative music had certainly come into their own, and KISS's look became almost comically dirty—trying to have some sort of crossover appeal, Gene grew a goatee, they were wearing, like, a bootleg comic book company's shirt … to look 'underground' and 'street.' It was just laughable how these multimillionaires are pretending that they're these guys with dirt underneath their fingernails, living out of a breadbox somewhere. It lacked credibility in my opinion.

And even though musically—with Eric Singer there—they were tight, the whole thing … I don't know, it was just the wrong band for the wrong time. It was probably the last rock-arena tour to go. Because, in late '92, everything was pretty much over and done by that point.

GIMME MORE: SOLO

While KISS were issuing studio albums and touring on a regular basis during their non-makeup era, all of their former members (and even current members) remained busy with work outside the band.

ACE FREHLEY

I'm prepared to go out on a limb to say that, out of all the KISS members past and present to embark on solo careers, Ace Frehley's has been the best—in terms of the quality of the material he has issued over the years and remaining true to the style of hard rock that you'd expect. It seemed like almost immediately after it became public knowledge that Ace was out of KISS in 1983, rumors began circulating about him launching a solo career, under the name Frehley's Comet. However, other than a one-off appearance on the Gene Simmons–produced 1984 Wendy O. Williams album *WOW* (on the track 'Bump And Grind'), fans would have to wait until 1987 to finally hear the Comet. (A doomed relationship with Bronze Records—which went out of business before an album could be issued—prolonged the process.)

In the end, Frehley's Comet was rarely utilized as an actual band name, but it was the title of Ace's solo debut in '87. Joining Ace on *Frehley's Comet* were guitarist/singer Tod Howarth (who replaced original Frehley's Comet guitarist Richie Scarlet), bassist John Regan, and drummer Anton Fig (who had previously played on Ace's classic '78 solo debut, and served as the long-time drummer for David Letterman's TV shows). The result was the second best solo effort of Ace's career (behind only his aforementioned '78 effort). Although the production—courtesy of Eddie Kramer—is a bit too glossy at times, the album spawned at least one stone-cold Ace classic, 'Rock Soldiers' (as well as the song 'Into The Night,' whose music video received some significant MTV play at the time), and remains one of his most consistent solo efforts.

From there, fans were treated to a pair of releases in 1988: a live EP with one studio track (*Live +1*) and another full-length studio effort (*Second Sighting*), the latter of which was a bit more pop-sounding when compared to its predecessor (and the only album to be actually credited to Frehley's Comet). The following year came *Live+4*, a concert video of a show at London's Hammersmith Odeon, packaged with several music videos.

By 1989's *Trouble Walkin'*, Howarth was replaced by Scarlet, and Kramer was back behind the recording console, resulting in a more rockin' effort … albeit with material not as strong/memorable as the '87 effort (although it did amusingly contain Ace's version of 'Hide Your Heart'). And then … *nothing*— Ace would not issue a single full-length solo album during the 90s, although he did continue to play shows, and offered up the song 'Cherokee Boogie' for the 1996 compilation *Smell The Fuzz: Guitars That Rule The World 2*.

PETER CRISS

If an award could be given to the ex-KISS member who was part of the most projects that most of the public never heard a single note of during 1983–96, Peter Criss would be a deserving winner. After issuing a pair of forgettable solo efforts after his first departure from KISS—1980's *Out Of Control* and 1982's *Let Me Rock You* (and recording a Budweiser jingle that remained unheard until years later!)—Criss's name was linked to such projects as The Criss Penridge Alliance (formed with Stan Penridge, who co-wrote 'Beth' and other assorted solo Peter tunes), Balls Of Fire (best remembered as being the only Criss-related group to be fronted by a woman, Jane Booke), and The Keep (which included none other than Mark St. John on guitar).

Peter managed to squeeze out only a single solo disc between 1983 and 2006—*Cat #1*. Out of all of his solo efforts, the album is probably his most rocking (and showcases his underrated lead vocal capabilities)—no doubt thanks to the gentleman supplying lead guitar on the tracks 'Bad Attitude,' 'Walk The Line,' and 'Blue Moon Over Brooklyn' ... Mr. Ace Frehley. Peter could also be briefly heard via guest vocal appearances on recordings by Black N' Blue (the song 'Best In The West,' from the 1986 Gene Simmons–produced LP *Nasty Nasty*) and Ace (the title track, '2 Young 2 Die,' and 'Back To School' from 1989's *Trouble Walkin*').

VINNIE VINCENT

While there were certainly unmistakable hints during his tenure with KISS that Vinnie Vincent was a shredder, no one could possibly have predicted the warp-speed soloing he would unleash as a member of The Vinnie Vincent Invasion. Just two years after exiting KISS, VV reappeared in 1986 with the self-titled debut by his new group, which also included singer Robert Fleischman, bassist Dana Strum, and drummer Bobby Rock. Listening to the disc today, *everything* about it is over-the-top—Fleischman's high-pitched vocals, the nonstop shredding, the hair-metal lyrical clichés ('Boyz Are Gonna Rock,' 'Shoot U Full Of Love,' 'I Wanna Be Your Victim,' et cetera). And that's just the music—once you take a gander at what the band *looked* like, you discover they were arguably the most glammed-out of all the glam bands of the era (and that's saying something, given the pretty stiff competition they had from the likes of Poison, Pretty Boy Floyd, Nitro, et cetera). But after hearing what is the album's most reasonable tune, the mid-paced 'Back On The Streets,' you can't help but wonder what could have been if VV kept things a bit more restrained—and, also, if *he* would have pulled double duty and also assumed lead vocal responsibilities (it turns out he has a very good singing voice, that's much less grating than Fleischman's).

Shortly after the album's arrival, Fleischman was excused from the band (for reasons that have never truly been explained), and replaced by a then-unknown Mark Slaughter. Perhaps the switcheroo was due to image—the mullet hairdo'd Fleischman's non-glam look stuck out like a sore thumb in the photos included with the album, whereas the younger and more attractive Slaughter would fit in much better. And while their debut didn't exactly storm the charts, it *did* create a bit of a buzz around the band (especially after they landed some plum opening spots on high-profile tours, including Alice Cooper and Iron Maiden)—which led one to believe that VVI's sophomore effort would put them over the top.

Although both sound and look were wisely dialed down a bit in time for 1988's *All Systems Go*, the album slipped through the cracks in the post–*Appetite For Destruction* era—despite including several tunes that were as good as just about any of the hair-metal tunes that radio and MTV were peddling at the time (especially the power ballad 'That Time Of Year'). Strangely, the album peaked at the exact same chart placing as the band's debut on the *Billboard* 200: #64.

Not long after that, however, the VVI were kaput, following a mutiny within the ranks that resulted in Slaughter and Strum co-forming Slaughter (who would open for KISS on the *Hot In The Shade* tour, and score a double platinum hit with their debut, *Stick It To Ya*), and Rock rocking with a variety of rockers over the years, including Nelson and Lita Ford, among others. Nearly ten years would pass before VV issued another recording—1996's four-track EP *Euphoria*, which marked his reunion with Fleischman. And despite grunge and alt-rock having rendered hair metal obsolete by this point, you have to give VV credit for sticking to his guns—stylistically and sonically, these four tracks could have easily been tacked onto (and would fit snugly on) VVI's debut.

Throughout the 80s, Vincent offered his songwriting talents to others (sometimes also appearing on the tracks to boot), including such hit acts as John Waite (the song 'Tears' from 1984's *No Brakes* ..., which had previously been recorded by Peter Criss on 1982's *Let Me Rock You*) and The Bangles ('Make A Play For Her Now,' from 1988's *Everything*). Additionally, Vincent appeared on the aforementioned Simmons-produced Wendy O. Williams album, *WOW*, in 1984, co-writing the song 'Ain't None of Your Business' with Gene and Eric Carr, and also playing guitar on it. And, of course, VV was welcomed back into the KISS fold as a songwriter for their 1992 album, *Revenge*, resulting in co-writing credits on 'Unholy,' 'Heart Of Chrome,' and 'I Just Wanna.'

MARK ST. JOHN

The year 1986 saw the release of not just one album by a former KISS member (The Vinnie Vincent Invasion's self-titled debut) but *two*, as White Tiger, featuring Mark St. John, issued their self-titled debut that year, as well. Rounding out this short-lived band were singer David Donato (whose claim to fame was very briefly being a member of Black Sabbath in the 80s, but never appearing on any of their albums), bassist Michael Norton (Mark's brother), and drummer Brian James Fox (later a member of Silent Rage, who recorded an album for Simmons Records).

Interestingly, there are quite a lot of parallels between White Tiger and VVI—both leave lots of room for their former KISS six-string stars to shred, and both succumb to hair-metal clichés. A case in point comes when they exclaim their desire to stand tall and rock ('Rock Warriors'), as well as showing their tender/melodic side ('Love/Hate'). Both bands also opted to unabashedly embrace the mile-high-hair look of quite a few metal acts at the time.

What separated these two similarly styled/attired acts, however, was that the VVI's material was slightly more memorable, and had major-label backing (VVI were on Chrysalis Records, whereas WT were on the indie EMC imprint). Demos were recorded for a proposed second White Tiger album (and eventually leaked within trading circles, sometimes under the title *Raw*), but the band was finished by 1988 ... right around the same time that the VVI were splintering as well.

From there, St. John had brief musical affiliations with actor-turned-singer David Hasselhoff (appearing in the music video for the track 'Is Everybody

Happy') and Christian rocker Ken Tamplin (supplying lead guitar on the track 'Livin' For My Lord' on Tamplin's 1990 album, *Axe To Grind*). And, as mentioned earlier, St. John joined forces for a spell with Peter Criss in the band The Keep, although this resulted in no officially released music. In fact, little was heard from St. John for much of the 90s, although a self-titled limited-edition EP with a focus on melodic rock, credited to the Mark St. John Project, was issued in 1999 (with singer Phil Naro, bassist Stan Mizcek, and drummer Roger Banks also lending a hand).

Despite being considered one of the shreddiest shredders of the era, it was not until 2003 that St. John finally got around to issuing an all-instrumental recording that showcased his soloing skills (something he probably should have started doing way back in the 80s, when guitarists such as Joe Satriani were first creating a buzz), entitled *Magic Bullet Theory*. Sadly, this would be the final recording issued during St. John's lifetime, as he would pass away on April 5, 2007, at the age of fifty-one. (According to the Orange County Coroner, the cause of death was a brain hemorrhage bought on by an accidental overdose of methamphetamines.)

ERIC CARR

Although no solo recordings were issued during Eric Carr's lifetime, he did demo quite a lot of original material during the 80s—songs to be considered for KISS albums, for other artists, and also for a proposed animated television series, *Rockheads*. Years after his passing in 1991, two compilations of this material were officially released: 1999's *Rockology* and 2011's *Unfinished Business*. And some of this material was as good as—and sometimes even better than—the songs that eventually comprised such albums as *Asylum*, *Crazy Nights*, and *Hot In The Shade*. For example, a track such as 'Eyes Of Love,' which certainly surpasses any filler track on any of those albums. This, again, can be classified as a missed opportunity.

But what was *not* a missed opportunity was that Eric was able to get some of his songs placed on other artist's recordings, including Bryan Adams ('Don't Leave Me Lonely,' from 1983's *Cuts Like A Knife*, co-written by Eric, Adams, and Jim Vallance), his old friend Ace Frehley ('Breakout,' from *Frehley's Comet*, co-penned by Eric, Ace, and Richie Scarlet), and Wendy O. Williams (co-writing 'Ain't None Of Your Business' with Gene and Vinnie, and playing drums on 'Legends Never Die,' both of which are on *WOW*).

BRUCE KULICK

Bruce Kulick did not issue any solo recordings during his tenure with KISS, but once his time was up with the band in 1996, he gradually made up for lost time. He issued three solo efforts (2001's *Audio Dog*, 2003's *Transformer*, and 2010's *BK3*) and co-formed a pair of groups: Union with ex-Mötley Crüe singer John Corabi (with whom he recorded a self-titled debut in 1998, followed by 1999's *Live At The Galaxy* and 2000's *The Blue Room*), and ESP with his ex-KISS bandmate Eric Singer (1998's *Lost & Spaced*, 1999's self-titled, and 2006's *Live In Japan*).

Kulick did sometimes guest on other artists' recordings during his KISS career, however, including select songs on albums by his ex-Blackjack bandmate Michael Bolton (1985's *Everybody's Crazy* and 1987's *The Hunger*), plus albums by Ronnie Spector (1987's *Unfinished Business*), and Don Johnson (1989's *Let It Roll*), among others. After exiting KISS in 1996, Kulick remained busy by steadily guesting on other artists' recordings (including albums by Graham Bonnet, Lordi, and Lita Ford) and tribute albums, as well as playing live shows with Grand Funk Railroad since 2000.

Kulick's KISS connection remained strong even post-'96, as evidenced by his appearances on solo efforts by both Gene and Paul (2004's *Asshole* and 2006's *Live To Win*, respectively), as well as playing on KISS's supposed 'reunion' album with the original lineup, 1998's *Psycho Circus* (and even earning a co-writing credit, with Paul, on the tune 'Dreamin''). In 1999, Kulick produced and played guitar on a posthumously released collection of Eric Carr demos originally recorded during the 80s, *Rockology*.

ERIC SINGER

Although his true solo project—Eric Singer Project (ESP)—came after the closure of the 1983–96 window, Eric had kept the beat for several renowned rockers prior to joining KISS, including Lita Ford (although he did not appear on any recordings), Black Sabbath (1986's *Seventh Star* and 1987's *The Eternal Idol*), Gary Moore (1987's *Wild Frontier Tour: Live At Isstadion Stockholm* home video), and Badlands (1989's self-titled debut). He also played on Paul Stanley's solo tour, and on Alice Cooper's tour in support of his 1989 album *Trash*. He even served as a hired gun in music videos, ranging from hit clips (Alice Cooper's 'Poison') to obscurities (Olivia Newton-John's 'Culture Shock').

PAUL STANLEY

While Paul Stanley did not issue any solo albums during the non-makeup era (his first solo release after his '78 self-titled offering was 2006's *Live To Win*), he lent his songwriting talents to a variety of artists, mostly within the realm of hard rock and metal. For starters, two 80s-era tracks that have already been discussed in this book, 'Sword And Stone' and 'Hide Your Heart,' were covered by a variety of artists, while a Simmons/Stanley composition, 'It's My Life,' was recorded by artists including Wendy O. Williams (on 1984's *WOW*) and King Kobra (on 1988's *III*).

In addition to co-writing songs together that ended up on KISS albums in the 80s, Stanley worked with Jean Beauvoir on several of the latter's other projects, including Voodoo X (the quite *Miami Vice*–sounding 'A Lover Like You' from 1989's *The Awakening*) and Crown Of Thorns (the quite hair metal–esque 'Winterland' and 'Dirty Walk, Dirty Talk' from 1991's six-track self-titled EP). And during the non-makeup era, you could have also detected Paul's name under the songwriting credits for countless releases by obscure artists, including War Babies ('Hang Me Up' and 'Cry Yourself To Sleep,' from 1993's self-titled release), Jeff Paris ('Jump The Gun,' from 1993's *Lucky This Time*), Lenita Erickson ('You're Gonna Be The One,' from 1996's self-titled release), and more.

Paul launched a solo tour in 1989 and appeared on a few other artist's albums, including providing guitar on the aforementioned *WOW* by Wendy O. Williams (on the track 'Ready To Rock') and backing vocals on the 1992 House Of Lords album *Demons Down* (on the song 'Johnny's Got A Mind Of His Own'). But probably his most intriguing extra-KISS recording from the non-makeup era was the song 'Shocker,' credited to The Dudes Of Wrath and included on *Shocker: The Music*, the soundtrack to the 1989 Wes Craven film.

Although not written by Paul (Desmond Child, Jean Beauvoir, and Guy Mann-Dude are credited as the song's authors), his unmistakable vocals are featured throughout The Dudes Of Wrath track. And just who were the 'dudes'? They included quite a few well-known names within the realm of rock/metal—Guy Mann-Dude and Vivian Campbell (guitars), Rudy Sarzo (bass), and Tommy Lee (drums). But it's in the song's vocal department that things get really interesting—Paul shares the lead vocals with Desmond, while the backing vocalists included several other recognizable names, the most notable being Desmond, ex–Alice Cooper guitarist Kane Roberts, and … Van Halen's Michael Anthony!

Meanwhile, as drummer Charlie Benante explains elsewhere in this book, Anthrax have recorded their share of KISS covers over the years. And since they were friendly with Gene and Paul … why not invite the duo to pitch in with some backing vocals? Both men obliged, resulting in renditions of 'Love Her All I Can' (included on the 'Black Lodge' CD single) and 'She' (from the *Kiss My Ass* tribute disc).

It also seemed as if Paul was serious for a spell during the 80s about branching out into the field of producing other artists. It has been reported over the years that he was in talks to work with Guns N' Roses (on the album that eventually became *Appetite For Destruction*) and Poison (on the album that eventually became *Open Up And Say … Ahh!*). Both of these could be considered major missed opportunities, as these records went on to huge chart success, with *Appetite* selling a staggering *eighteen million copies* in the USA alone since its 1987 release.

GENE SIMMONS

Like Paul Stanley, Gene Simmons did not release any solo albums during the non-makeup era (his first solo release after his '78 self-titled offering was 2004's *Asshole*), but he certainly kept himself busy managing, producing, and writing songs for other artists. While we have already had Ron Keel guide us through the majority of Gene's production credits during this period, he helped pen songs for a lot of the albums he produced as well—Wendy O. Williams's *WOW*, Keel's *The Right To Rock*, Black N' Blue's *Nasty Nasty*, and Doro's self-titled release all feature tunes either penned or co-penned by Gene.

On *WOW*, Gene even supplied bass, under the alias Reginald Van Helsing. And, as mentioned above, he lent his vocal talents to a pair of Anthrax covers of KISS classics in the 90s. He even briefly managed the recording career of Liza Minnelli, and signed bands to his on-again/off-again label, Simmons Records (including House Of Lords, Silent Rage, and Gypsy Rose), during the late 80s and early 90s.

It appears that Gene sought to manage rock artists as well. In an interview for my book *A Devil On One Shoulder And An Angel On The Other: The Story Of Shannon Hoon And Blind Melon*, the band's drummer, Glen Graham, recalled a meeting that would have occurred sometime in the early 90s. 'I remember David [Rudick, Blind Melon's subsequent lawyer] sitting us down very carefully, and saying in no uncertain terms, [Gene] wants to start a management company. He understands the tides are turning. The shape of the hard-rock scene is moving from LA/glam to a Nirvana thing. He understands that you guys are next up, so he wants to get in on this.'

According to Graham, Gene invited the band to his home, to talk business. 'We're sitting up in the second story of his guest house, which is like a KISS shrine, and over the fireplace is a circle of twenty-two overlapping platinum KISS albums framed in this gigantic shadowbox frame. And then Paul Stanley came in, and that was weird. I think he had been egged on by Gene: *You've got to come see these guys.* And Paul sat there with his little white espadrilles on, legs crossed, jangling his gigantic ring of keys. Basically looking off into space, while Gene told us about the topsy-turvy world of heavy rock. It's just a business.'

Ultimately, Gene did not end up managing Blind Melon, but this episode proved once more his keen sense for seeing potential in artists before others seem to—as evidenced by his discovery of Van Halen and Cinderella, years before their big breaks.

ALIVE III

Released May 18, 1993. Produced by KISS and Eddie Kramer. US #9, UK #24. US certification: gold.

SIDE ONE

Creatures Of The Night (Paul Stanley/Adam Mitchell)

Deuce (Gene Simmons)

I Just Wanna (Stanley/Vinnie Vincent)

Unholy (Simmons/Vincent)

Heaven's On Fire (Stanley/Desmond Child)

SIDE TWO

Watchin' You (Simmons)

Domino (Simmons)

I Was Made For Lovin' You (Stanley/Child/Vini Poncia)

I Still Love You (Stanley/Vincent)

SIDE THREE

Rock And Roll All Nite (Simmons/Stanley)

Lick It Up (Stanley/Vincent)

Forever (Stanley/Michael Bolton)

Take It Off [bonus track] (Stanley/Bob Ezrin/Kane Roberts)

SIDE FOUR

I Love It Loud (Simmons/Vincent)

Detroit Rock City (Stanley/Ezrin)

God Gave Rock And Roll To You II (Russ Ballard/Simmons/Stanley/Ezrin)

The Star-Spangled Banner (Francis Scott Key)

SINGLE

I Love It Loud (live) / Unholy (live) (US/UK did not chart)

★

Back in the 70s, it was a concert recording that shot KISS's career into the stratosphere. Of course, I'm talking about 1975's *Alive!*, a recording that gave us the definitive version of 'Rock And Roll All Nite' and is widely/rightfully considered to be one of the greatest live rock albums of all-time. Two years later, a not-too-shabby follow-up was offered, *Alive II*. Metal mathematicians may have predicted that, going forward, KISS would issue a live album every two years, or when they had at least three studio albums to pull tracks from. But neither theory proved to be accurate—aside from the *Animalize: Live Uncensored* VHS release in 1985, there was maddeningly *no* live KISS album in the 80s. Which is a shame, as Eric Carr sure could pound those skins in a live setting. In 1993, however, fans finally got their wish with the arrival of *Alive III*, culled from performances during the *Revenge* tour in Cleveland, Detroit, and Indianapolis. And, as on *Revenge*, KISS once again hooked up with a producer from their past: Eddie Kramer, the same chap who produced both *Alive!* and *Alive II*.

As KISS have stated honestly in the past, quite a bit of post-recording doctoring was done in the studio on their first two concert offerings. (In their defense, KISS are not alone in this—countless other artists of the era used the same sly scheme on their live recordings.) Judging by what you hear on *Alive III*, there were quite a few add-ons and fix-ups done to the initial concert recordings here as well. While it's not as laughable as, say, the moments on *Alive II* where you hear several Paul Stanley voices singing choruses together, one trick that they use again on *Alive III* is the obvious insertion of loud crowd roars. A case in point is 'Watchin' You.' As much as I and many fellow diehard 70s KISS fans adore this track, it's hard to swallow the idea that an arena-sized crowd would react so raucously to this *Hotter Than Hell* obscurity … as if they were witnessing Queen performing 'We Will Rock You / We Are The Champions' at Live Aid.

From a tracklisting standpoint, though, *Alive III* certainly doesn't disappoint, as it does a respectable job of balancing the best of the 80s (the set-opening 'Creatures Of The Night,' plus 'Heaven's On Fire,' 'Lick It Up,' 'I Love It Loud,' and 'Forever'), the early 90s ('Unholy,' 'I Just Wanna,' 'God Gave Rock And Roll To You II,' 'Domino,' and the bonus track 'Take It Off'), and even the 70s ('Deuce,' 'Watchin' You,' 'Rock And Roll All Nite,' and 'Detroit Rock City'). It even includes a set-closing rendition of 'The Star Spangled Banner,' on which it sounds like Bruce Kulick channeling both Jimi Hendrix (the Woodstock-like opening) *and* Brian May (when the double-tracked harmony lines kick in).

Something else KISS get right here is making a point of including the slow-burning ballad 'I Still Love You,' which is certainly one of Paul Stanley's top vocal showcases (and displays how he is one of most underrated rock singers of all time), as well as 'I Was Made For Lovin' You,' which until now had never appeared on a live recording. But what they *don't* get right is not including a single track from *Asylum* or *Crazy Nights*—particularly notable by their absence are the songs 'Tears Are Falling' and 'Crazy Crazy Nights' (crowd-pleasers that have been included in quite a few setlists over the years). A deep cut or two from the 80s (let's say 'Fits Like A Glove,' 'Under The Gun,' or 'Hide Your Heart') would have been nice, too.

But again, the main complaint about *Alive III* is just how 'alive' it truly is. Something I could never fathom—and I'm sure other rock music listeners feel the same way—is why bands think their fans would rather have a doctored recording than a *true* live representation, warts and all. The whole point of seeing a band play in concert is to see if they can pull it off live, and if there is a flub or two, *who cares* … we're all human, right? As a result, if you want to hear a *real* live KISS recording from the non-makeup era, hunt down one of the better soundboard recordings that are available on YouTube or in fan trading circles (Nashville '84, Houston '85, and Cleveland '92 should satisfy your needs). Otherwise, if you want to hear a not-so-live live recording—but one that presents KISS the way that Simmons and Stanley *want* fans to hear them live—then, by all means, give *Alive III* an inspection.

KNOW THE SCORE: BRUCE KULICK

Bruce looks back on the *Alive III* era.

Just how 'live' is *Alive III*?

The biggest problem with *Alive III* was sometimes the drums didn't sound right, and I'm pretty sure that Eric's drums could have been mic'd a little bit better. But there were ways around that. We also found that the crowd sounds were not recorded full enough, either. It's not that unusual for bands to 'supplement' the reaction. [*Laughs*] For my parts, I did fix one or two things—they were for very minor things, but since we had the opportunity to do it, I was able to seamlessly touch it up, and I did. And I will admit that. I don't remember how much Gene or Paul did, because I wasn't necessarily always there. But I can promise you *Alive III* was much less micro-tuned in the studio than *Alive!* and *Alive II*. Now, I wasn't there for *Alive!* and *Alive II*, but from what I hear, I'm pretty confident in saying that. I'm not trying to brag about *Alive III*, I just know that we didn't have to do major surgery in any way. And I have tapes of all the nights [from which] we chose the actual versions that were released, and the playing was quite high quality. I do think we used a little more [of] one night than any of the others. And there were a couple of songs that we wanted to include that weren't in the set, so we did them at soundcheck [one being 'I Was Made For Lovin' You']. I thought that was crazy, but it's something we did.

How do you think *Alive III* compares to *Alive!* and *Alive II*?
It's a completely different band. Different era. I think *Alive III* is a great record. Many times when I've toured—especially internationally—if I want to do a general overview of my career, I use that as a basis. Because I do like the way I play 'Love Gun' or 'Detroit Rock City'—even though it's not my era. Obviously, for the KISS Kruise, it made more sense for me to play only [songs from] my era. And maybe, in moving forward, that's all I'll do—I don't know. But certainly, *Alive III* I felt like the songs that were vintage were done very respectfully, but also in their own kind of animal. We were never trying to overly imitate the original versions, or even the original live versions, if you get what I mean—the pre-makeup-years versions. And, of course, all the new stuff that we were promoting—things like 'Unholy' and 'I Just Wanna.' I thought it had great performances, great playing, great vocals, terrific song list. I'm very proud of that record.

Some of the people interviewed for this book praised the *Hot In The Shade* tour, as far as the setlist was concerned. How do you think the *Revenge* tour compared?
Well, we went a little longer maybe with the setlist on *Hot In The Shade*. It was the first time we were including more older tunes—in combination with

new ones. I can't remember one tour being more effective, in the sense of the setlist, but I do think that we were in a good place, which is why it's really tragic that it all ended.

How was the band's playing at that point, on Eric Singer's first tour?
Eric came in at a really difficult time, and I think he absolutely did the right job, playing with a lot of passion and fire. He always knew his place—that's why he's done so well with them—he knows how to work with Gene and Paul very well. He's a total pro. I explained a lot to him before we got started, because I wanted him to know what the dynamics of the band were. And he was, shall I say, a good listener. He just fit right in—in a tough time. The breaking in of somebody new can be a real nightmare, and you never know. But I think he did a terrific job.

Do you wish there had been a live album back in the day that featured the lineup with you and Eric Carr, as well?
Yeah, that would have been nice. But I was really happy that at least *Animalize Live Uncensored* got out there. We know there are lots of YouTube videos that are out there and stuff, and we all know that *Asylum* was the one that had the least documentation, unfortunately. But *Animalize Live Uncensored* says a lot—even though we played the songs so fast. *It was insane.*

KNOW THE SCORE: DEREK SHERINIAN

Though he is best known for playing keyboards with Alice Cooper, Dream Theater, Billy Idol, Black Country Communion, and Sons Of Apollo, one of Derek's first gigs was touring with KISS in support of *Revenge*—and appearing on *Alive III*.

How did you get the KISS gig?
Eric Singer and I played together in the Alice Cooper band, and then Eric got the KISS gig. Then there was an opening for the keyboard slot, so Eric recommended me. I went in, played the intro riff to 'Love Gun,' and I got the job. That was it!

What do you recall about the tryout? Was it in front of the full band?

They were in preproduction. We were at Mates [Rehearsal] Studios in North Hollywood. I walk in, and the first thing that Gene said to me is that I *looked like the love child of Cher and Paul Stanley*. They were cool, and the first thing they had me do when I got behind the keyboard was play the 'Love Gun' riff. Which I did, and then Gene just reached his hand out, shook my hand, and that was it. It was that simple.

What do you recall about rehearsals with the band for that tour?

I just remember it was a month of preproduction rehearsals at Mates, and I remember it being very surreal—because I was a KISS fan as a kid. Not totally crazy, but I got the *Alive II* record, and I was definitely into them, so to be in a room, looking up and seeing Gene Simmons holding the bass, and then looking to the left and seeing Paul Stanley with his guitar, it was very surreal and very cool.

Since KISS were going in a heavier direction at the time, were you told to not make the keyboards sound too pop or 80s-sounding?

No. Before me, they had Gary Corbett playing keys, and they had a specific formula of what they were having the keyboards play. It was doubling Paul with a root fifth. And the sound was like a brass analogue sound. That sound—mixed in with the guitars—makes it sound fuller. So I was doing a lot of that, and I was singing background vocals as well.

How would you describe the band's personalities?

I would say there was humor going on every day. Both Gene and Paul are very sharp-witted and sarcastic. Paul is *extremely* sharp-witted, but Gene is always goofy, always looking to laugh and have a good time. There was a good energy.

How would you rate KISS as musicians?

Are they virtuosos? No. But I think Gene Simmons is a really good bass player. I hear some traits of Paul McCartney in his bass lines, and I think he is probably the better musician, between him and Paul.

Let's discuss the stage setup for the *Revenge* tour.

I remember the centerpiece of the stage was a big Statue of Liberty, and I would trigger the sample for the crumbling of it. And then it would turn into a skull, and instead of the torch, it was a big *fuck-you* finger. [*Laughs*] That was the big prop. But I remember there were lots of ego ramps and lights, and there were lasers. It was a good show.

You were not onstage but rather performed offstage …

It was the first—and only—time. That's not what I would want to do, but in certain situations—like KISS or Van Halen, or bands like that. I don't know if I would do it now, but at that time, I felt it was a great opportunity, and it was going to be a lot of fun. I wanted to learn from Gene and Paul. They're business-savvy—they're very smart, business-wise, with how they run the band. And I figured it would be an invaluable experience, to be exposed to those guys. So I looked at it as a really positive experience—despite not being on the stage.

How consistent were KISS live, on that tour?

I think Eric Singer really was crucial in making that band solid. Because if the drums are solid, that's a huge thing. If you have a shitty drummer and mediocre musicians around the drummer, that's a problem. But if you have a really solid drummer, that's going to get you to the promised land. And Bruce played pretty solidly, also. So, no matter how Gene and Paul played on a given night, between those two guys, they would sound solid.

What were your favorite songs to perform live?

I liked playing 'Detroit Rock City.' And 'Parasite' was a really cool song.

As a whole, how was the tour?

I thought the crowds were receptive, but from my point of view, KISS was a victim of the times. I think *Revenge* was a very strong record, sonically. And visually, I think Gene finally found a cool place outside of the makeup—where he looks really comfortable in his skin. I thought there were some really strong songs on that record. But at that time, all the Seattle shit was going on.

We were playing some arenas ... I remember ARCO Arena in Sacramento—there may have been less than two thousand people. Some of the arenas just looked really bleak. And I don't think that has any blame on KISS. I think they put out a great record and put their best foot forward. It was just the times were fucked for everyone. And they knew it. It was a horrible time for that kind of music.

Interestingly, though, that was when Dream Theater—a band you later played with—became popular.
Thank God, because I was out of work at that point, and I was basically sat out all of '93. And then I got the gig for Dream Theater in '94, while basically everyone else was out of work—all my friends. Fortunately, I had some chops, and I was able to step into that band and make it work.

Something else that was strange is that, at the time, KISS toughened up their image and put out a heavy album, yet they brought out bands that were more aligned to pop-metal, like Great White, Faster Pussycat, and Trixter. Whereas perhaps bringing out bands such as Pantera, White Zombie, or Stone Temple Pilots—who were all KISS fans—would have made more sense stylistically, and helped boost ticket sales.
I think it would have been more strategic. You have to double down on what you're doing, and by bringing out one of those other kind of bands ... I don't know. You can 'Monday morning quarterback' it, but at the time, it didn't seem like the move to them, I guess.

At what point during the tour was it brought to your attention that they were going to make *Alive III*?
I found out about it only a couple of weeks before it was recorded. It was kind of a surprise.

The album was recorded in three locations—Cleveland, Detroit, and Indianapolis. Does anything stick out about those dates?
No. I just remember that the recording trucks were there at those three shows.

195

Did you get to meet the producer, Eddie Kramer?

Yes, I did. He was a nice guy—I liked him. When you work with iconic guys like that, it's cool. The only memory that I have of him was that when we were in the studio, doing some fixes, he would keep a 'fart chart' up on the wall. Any time he would fart or someone else would fart, he made a hash-tag on this chart. I'd walk in the studio, and there were all these hash-tags of these farts he'd been documenting. I had never seen that before! That's what I remember about Eddie Kramer. It's absolutely true.

Since you owned *Alive II* when you were younger, I'd imagine that playing on *Alive III* must have been quite an honor.

It was very cool. I don't think that album is held with the esteem that the *Alive II* album is held, but I'm still honored to be on it.

I can't recall if you were properly credited on *Alive III*, or if it came to light later that you'd played on it.

I think I'm credited underneath *the caterer*. [*Laughs*] It was a secret—they didn't want people to know they had a keyboardist. They didn't deny it, but it just wasn't talked about. And I didn't. I kind of honored it—it was what it was.

Here's a funny story—I was endorsed by a synth company at the time, and when I got the KISS gig, my keyboard company wanted to exploit that. So I asked Gene if it was OK if I can use the KISS name in this keyboard ad. He goes, 'Derek, let me tell you something. There's two things that rock fans hate: *sidemen and keyboard players*.' [*Laughs*] So he said no.

After the *Revenge* tour wrapped up, did you play with KISS ever again?

The only other time I played with KISS after that was on the Ramones tribute record [2003's *We're A Happy Family: A Tribute To Ramones*], 'Do You Remember Rock 'n' Roll Radio?' I was brought in to A&M Studios, and I played piano on that track. It was cool—Eric called me up, and I had just got the gig with Billy Idol that day. I finished rehearsal, shot down to A&M Studios that night, and recorded on the KISS song. That was an action-packed day.

After KISS, you joined Dream Theater. Were they aware of your previous work with KISS, and did it help land you the gig?

They saw that I had played with Alice Cooper and KISS—I wasn't just some guy with a dream, trying to break in. They saw that I had some seasoning. So I'm sure that worked in my favor.

Are you still in touch with KISS?

I don't call them, but I have open communication with them. Whenever I run into them in town, they're always very nice. I think Gene and Paul are cool, and I respect them—what they've achieved. I'm honored to have been part of KISStory.

GIMME MORE: A NON-MAKEUP-ERA GUITAR GUIDE WITH BRUCE KULICK

Since there was no tour in support of *Alive III*, let's take this opportunity to have Bruce discuss the instruments that KISS's guitarists were most associated with during the non-makeup era.

BRUCE'S GUITARS

Clearly, the band wanted the Floyd Rose kind of guitars. It was *that era*, you know? And, fortunately, I had a Charvel guitar set up that way. It certainly wasn't necessarily something to go tour with, but I used it on that ghost track for *Animalize*. I never thought at the time that I would be the guitarist of KISS, but I realized, 'Everyone's got to have the right tools for the job.' So, I went to Sam Ash [in New York City], and there was a used blue Charvel Strat in the window, and that came home with me. I don't remember how I got the BC Rich off-hand, but I always loved the BC Riches—the black BC Rich Eagle. And then we took one more to Europe—because we needed a backup—and I remember getting the gold Charvel.

It was an interesting period for Charvel, actually—those models are not that common, I found out years later. But those were the three guitars that came with me on tour for *Animalize*. I then helped design a Jackson guitar [a white guitar with a zebra print design on part of it], and you've got to remember that Jackson *was* Charvel then—it was very common for musicians of that era to reach out to Grover Jackson personally, and that's how that relationship started. So, it was a custom paint-job.

I think ESP really started in '85. They were always more of a 'Strat parts' company from Japan, and then they started to offer models that were … I guess you could call them metal versions of Fenders—one pick-up, Floyd Rose. And I liked their necks even better than Charvel—Charvel always had a very flat profile. The roundness or more Fender-ish version that ESP were making back then were really comfortable for me. So I started a good, healthy relationship with them. And them having a New York connection—which is where I lived—worked really well.

The Multi-Swirl ESP, I gave it that name—just like I gave the yellow ESP from *Crazy Nights* a name, the Banana guitar. Which is really funny, because this morning, my wife and I saw a Kramer—Kramer was actually ESP parts for quite a while in the 80s, and of course, Eddie Van Halen was affiliated with some Kramer guitars back then, and so was Richie Sambora—but they offered a color, and they called it the 'Yellow Banana.' And that's modern—they were offering it like that! Not that calling a yellow guitar 'Banana' is radical or anything … *I'm just saying.*

So, the Multi-Swirl, I have the prototype, and I am making guitars to offer some of the fans, and I just released minis of those. That finish [sometimes referred to as Kulick Graphics by guitarists] was very unusual. That was for *Asylum*, and was something that Paul helped me with—he had an idea for something that would be colorful and interesting. Which was what *Asylum* was like—we were wearing pretty crazy clothing. [Living Colour's] Vernon Reid did a different color scheme on his ESPs, and Japan jumped into it and they liked it. At times, I saw it referred to as the 'New York finish.' But, anyway, I did want to experiment with fun things on the guitars—why not?

The Banana guitar was just parts, really. I chose a yellow body—I didn't know if it was going to be an amazing-sounding one—and I chose the neck. I also did the same thing with a white one—which appeared a little later in a lot of pictures, which became evident on *Hot In The Shade* and *Revenge*. Those bolt-on guitars just happened to sound tremendous. Fortunately, I still own the Banana and the white one. Some of the lesser ones I got rid of many years ago, and most of them are at Hard Rock Cafes, which is nice—I prefer them at Hard Rocks, rather than someone's closet or someone's home. But they're *amazing* guitars—there was just something about those that really defined a lot of my go-to guitars of that era. For recording, as well—which is unusual, because sometimes your live guitars are not the same.

But ESP kept evolving—they introduced the Horizon, which I started to play. I had a red one and a sunburst one. And then, later on, I asked them to make me Explorer shapes—which they did. And now they're their own, and they don't copy guitars anymore, because they got away with that then. I still have a great relationship with them, actually. Certainly, they were one of the big guitar companies of that era.

There are actually two 'radioactive' guitars—one is originally the red BC Rich Gunslinger, which I decided to put the radioactive symbols on, to kind of match my outfit [as seen in the 'Crazy Crazy Nights' video]. And then, later on, for the 'Turn On The Night' video, my tech guy put decals of those radioactive symbols on my black ESP Horizon. I had that on the KISS Kruise—they had a little museum, and they asked me if I would have a couple of guitars involved. So I did it.

But it's funny, the radioactive connections—it's kind of cool. It was just some clothing thing that the costume designer suggested. It was something that became a little connected to my era, and there's nothing wrong with that. Happily, I still own the two guitars. I like the ESP better as a playing guitar than the BC Rich, but they're both very iconic for their own reasons.

The Les Paul Junior I used for *Alive III*—meaning the *Revenge* tour. What was interesting was, at one point, I had an injury with a collarbone, and heavy guitars were not going to be a good thing for me. So I was looking for cool guitars that were under eight pounds. I did find that some of the older Les Paul Juniors are light—they can be under eight pounds, easily. Because there's not a maple top on them.

That one was almost an embarrassment for the store to sell it to me—because it was *so* beat up. The sales person actually didn't even take money at first, he just said, 'Take it home and see if you like it.' I gave it the nickname Frankenstein, because I think the neck was repaired and replaced, and there were a lot of things about it that were really abused. But it's just an amazing-sounding guitar. This company, Rock 'n' Roll Relics, did a limited release of a copy of it, too. They weren't cheap—because they were US-made, and [making a replica of] a guitar is expensive—but they did a really great job of copying it. And that Junior did appear on *Revenge*, but more *Carnival Of Souls*, really.

The only regret I have, I guess, with my KISS years and my guitars is that since I loved so many different kinds of guitars—from Gibson Les Pauls to a Les Paul Custom to a Junior to a BC Rich to all the ESP models—I'm not *defined*, like how Slash is defined by a Les Paul, or Eddie Van Halen you think of one or two guitars, like his Frankenstein. But that was my passion—*I loved guitars*. I always had three, four, or five for each tour, and I kept swapping them out. I had fun with that, but I don't have a definitive *what do you think of when you think of Bruce?*

PAUL'S GUITARS

In some ways, Paul was defined by the [Ibanez] PS10. But he played *so many* guitars through my era—one year he was big on the Les Pauls, one year he was playing the Steinbergers … he also was experimenting and fooling around with different models all the time. But we both had an affection for BC Rich. I loved that Paul had that connection with BC Rich too. They started to change a lot during the mid-to-late 80s, and they started to do bolt-on designs and stuff like that.

Paul would use heavier strings, because he's not playing solos. I would on occasion, though, mention to the roadie, 'This one really plays well,' because Paul was always about the performing—not necessarily, *OK, what is the best tuning guitar?* I always found that interesting. But it was always fun to introduce to each other the new guitars in the store … it's just like guys that are into cars and motorcycles—you can't help it, right? I show sometimes people my guitar collection, and if they're not a guitarist, they don't get it. And if they're a guitar player, they totally get it! Paul and I certainly had fun with the guitars.

Around *Revenge*, he went back to using the Ibanez PS10 … then he got involved with Washburn and other companies … then he went back to Ibanez. He's always been really passionate about whatever company would follow his vision and do it the way he would want. And he's still into the vintage stuff, from what I understand. He's a guitar nut, like all of us. Gene, not so much. Although Gene is opinionated about what he played. If it was too complicated—meaning too many knobs—Gene didn't want to know about it.

GENE'S BASSES

I thought those custom Pedullas were great. I was shocked when he offered them in the auction. Again, he's not attached to anything like that. And then he developed kind of his own version, and he's got good ones. I mean, he has some *killer* Punishers—even toward the end of my era with them. But I think those Pedullas were really cool—especially the dragon one. And we would record with those, too. On occasion, I would play bass in the studio, and I would have played one of his instruments. Good stuff. I don't remember the Jackson Axe too much, but I found that the Axes were hard to manage or hold. That's an odd shape to be dealing with, in my opinion.

VINNIE'S GUITARS

Those Double Vs are most associated with Vinnie—although that was after KISS. I felt his thing was the Double V version of a Randy Rhoads guitar [by Jackson]—with an added flair. It's like taking that and adding another wing to it in the back. For that era, that was probably very appropriate—knowing that Vinnie was always trying to be flamboyant, it was a perfect guitar for him. He clearly was always attracted to that look—instead of a traditional Flying V from Gibson, he went with the Randy Rhoads. And, back then, that was a pretty amazing time in the metal guitar world—because of the Jacksons and Charvels. It's sadly a lost era, it seems.

MARK'S GUITARS

I barely remembered the instrument that he used when we were out on the *Animalize* tour. But he liked Kahler tremolos, which are a different tremolo system. I'm not a fan of the Kahlers—*at all*. You can offer me the most incredible deal on a vintage BC Rich, and if it has a Kahler on it, I'd go, 'Nah, I can't do it.'

Mark played a Jackson with KISS, and I remember it was Grover Jackson who got him on the shortlist for KISS, because Paul actually asked for players. We all have something in common in a way, but we were also using the proper tools of the trade for that era.

GIMME MORE: MICHAEL ANGELO BATIO DISCUSSES *ALL* OF KISS'S GUITARISTS!

The 80s were full of over-the-top shredder guitarists, but the speed demon king was Michael Angelo Batio, best known for his work with the hair-metal band Nitro, and for being ambidextrous enough to be able to play the two halves of a double-neck guitar simultaneously, and also to navigate a quad guitar. So … who better to dissect and analyze the playing style of KISS's guitarists?

PAUL STANLEY

In the early 80s, I was signed to Shrapnel Records—that's Mike Varney's label, with Tony MacAlpine, Yngwie Malmsteen, Paul Gilbert. I was a handsome young guy, and I had a really good promo shot. So I actually auditioned for KISS. And I was *so* scared—it changed my life. And I'm going to say—in all fairness to them—I was this unknown Midwestern kid named Mike Batio. I dressed like a Geico insurance salesman, I had just gotten out of college, I did not have any clue about what the image in LA was like at that time. Because it was 1982.

And this is how I'm going to answer your question about Paul Stanley as a rhythm guitarist—when they flew me to LA, we auditioned on Sunset and Gower, at SIR. We played 'Dr. Love,' 'Sunshine Of Your Love,' and a couple of other songs. I actually sang 'Dr. Love,' and Gene Simmons was laughing, because I didn't know the right words, because I hadn't bought the songbook at the time—I just got them off the record.

Here's what I can tell you. I had been playing since I was ten years old, but I had never really played with famous musicians before. I was just a Midwestern kid. *I never heard power emanating from a stage in my life like I heard KISS.* And I'm telling you right now, it was big league, balls-to-the-walls. I was just blown away. So, what do I think of Paul Stanley? I jammed with him, and I thought, *Man, he's got the sound.* You can say what you want—there's a lot of guitar players who can maybe out-riff him, but when it comes to just plugging that thing in and rocking, God, *it was unbelievable*. It was so powerful and professional. I had never heard anything like it.

GENE SIMMONS

I'd be lying if I said he was Jaco Pastorius … or Victor Wooten, or Stanley Clarke. But I think that—especially on some of the early KISS songs—he wrote memorable bass lines, and he had an aggressive bass sound. I think it fit KISS perfectly. I don't think he's a virtuoso player, but I think he played the right part for the song. And he had a good sound—that aggressive, growly, old-school bass sound. Just little things, like [the bass motif that comes after every verse line in 'Detroit Rock City']. If you play the song, you *have to* play that bass line. But just that little part in the verse is very *signature* to the song, and it's a bass line. So, credit where credit's due.

I think he's a product of the times. The non-makeup era was really the 80s and part of the 90s, and the production back then [involved] very simplistic drums. Like, the 70s and grunge opened drums back up to ghost notes on snares, and just a more fluid, free-form style of drumming. Like, John Bonham, and you listen to Pearl Jam and all those bands with piccolo snares— it opened up the drums to a natural sound.

And the 80s were *not* like that. The 80s had gated snares—you know, Def Leppard, Heart. Everything was very simple, beat-wise, on drums and rock. Not Whitesnake, but think about Def Leppard and Heart in the 80s. And I think the bass lines reflected that. I mean, a lot of guitar parts were just eighth-note rhythms—like 'Lick It Up.' I think [the simpler bass lines of the non-makeup era] was a product of the musical sound of the times. I'm sure if it had been the 90s, when it was more open, and there was more open guitar chords and free-flowing drums, it might have been a little different.

VINNIE VINCENT

I liked the Vinnie Vincent Invasion records, and I know he did *Lick It Up*. I also played with Bobby Rock in Nitro—he played in the Vinnie Vincent Invasion. I know that Vinnie was not the easiest guy to deal with—he was real temperamental. But here's what I think about Vinnie Vincent—aside from that really fast playing on those two records, I'm not really sure that was all real. I'm not sure the tape wasn't sped up. I don't know. I mean, the way it was, it was *so* vicious. And I'm super-fast, so I never really believed that was actually him—I thought it was a little 'studio magic.'

But saying that, *everybody* uses magic, and I think his songwriting was what made KISS's taking off their makeup happen. He was a great songwriter. 'Lick It Up,' I mean, that alone, right there. When they took off their makeup, I think a lot of it was due to Vinnie Vincent's songwriting. He was a great songwriter at that time. He was the perfect guy for the transition from the makeup to the non-makeup, musically.

MARK ST. JOHN

I knew him personally. He was a bizarre guy. We were both friends with Wayne Charvel. Wayne and I were real close, and Wayne built some of my really famous guitars, like the quad guitar—the one in Nitro's 'Freight Train' video—and he built my rocket guitar. Wayne was a genius, and Wayne knew Mark St. John. We actually did a promo for Gibson guitars together—Mark and me.

I don't mean to sound weird, but I never cared for Mark, personally. I'm a people person … he just made me uneasy. Not in a weird way, but his attitude—it was like a guy I didn't like to hang out with too much. As a guitar player, I thought he was really good. Was he KISS's best choice as a guitarist? That I can't answer. I think a lot of people could have done what he did. I think they liked his look, because he had that bushy, curly hair. He had the look that they were looking for at that time, and he was a good enough guitarist.

BRUCE KULICK

I like Bruce a lot. I thought, again, he had that look that fit the band, because KISS has always been image conscious. I played with Bruce in Vancouver in the late 90s—we broke the *Guinness Book Of World Records* for playing with over 1,500 guitarists, 'Rock And Roll All Nite.' It was the longest version of one song played with the most guitarists. I thought Bruce was great—they knew how to pick musicians to fit what they were doing. I thought Bruce was perfect for that. And he was a nice guy—we hit it off really well. The record has since been broken many times, but it was cool to play that with him. I just enjoyed it, and I thought he was great with KISS.

And, while we're at it, why not ask Michael about Ace and Tommy?

ACE FREHLEY

I had several life-changing experiences, career-wise, with KISS. I was in a band called Episode. We were a really popular cover band, and I was eighteen years old, and the whole band was the same age. We auditioned, and it was us and one of our friend's bands that opened up for KISS. We're talking 1974—this is before they were big. And they were all dressed in makeup. They played in the Maine West High School Fieldhouse [in Des Plaines, Illinois, on November 2, 1974]—packed to the rafters. But the word was out on this band—they were ready to explode.

And I remember, I met them without their makeup, and then I saw them onstage with their makeup. And I always thought Ace, back then … I never saw a guy look like that. He looked like this space angel onstage. The image was so striking, all of them—but Ace, back then, his features and his really straight hair, it just was mind-blowing. And I thought his guitar parts perfectly fit the music. It's that thick, mid-range, Les Paul-ish sound. I mean, that's what I like to use—even today.

I thought he played exactly what he was supposed to play. Kind of like C.C. DeVille in Poison—are you going to say he's the first chair in a symphony orchestra? No. But Richie Kotzen—as great as he is—could not take C.C.'s place. C.C. fit Poison like Mick Mars fit Mötley Crüe, like Ace Frehley fit KISS. He was the best guitarist possible for that band.

TOMMY THAYER

A lot of people give him grief. I don't. I remember seeing Black N' Blue, and he had kind of a striking stage image. I saw them play a bunch of times, especially at the Country Club in Reseda—all of us used to play here, a beautiful venue. I just never thought much, either way, of his guitar playing. And I think, right now, all he has to do is play KISS faithfully—which he does. He looks the part. I think he fits the part real good. Anybody who criticizes him, my take is, *You do it! You're awesome? You look like him, you play like him, and you tour like him.* He fit the role. I think he was a really good choice to be *Ace The Second.*

Lastly, Michael recounts the time Gene Simmons gave him valuable career advice ...

I can't say I'm super-close to Gene Simmons, but I have been to his house. He gave me advice. I know he's a really tough businessman—I've heard it from a lot of people—but hey, he's got the leverage to do it. *He's Gene Simmons.* And he's not the easiest person to deal with—he's always looking for his side, which is great. And I respect that. But I'll tell you, when it comes to musicians, he said some stuff to me that was life-changing. For example, they never knew—and maybe they'll find out now—that I was this Midwestern kid that auditioned for KISS, because I didn't get the job—Vinnie Vincent did.

One of the reasons I didn't get it was I was awestruck. I mean, if *Wayne's World* had been out then, I would have been on my hands and knees, going, 'I'm not worthy!' I was a fan. It really made me realize fan-boy versus peer. I didn't look at them like a peer—I looked at them like, *I'm a fan, and it's an honor to play with you.* Which it was. And I changed that. Ever since that time—from Eddie Van Halen on down—I just treat them like normal people. Even if I were to meet Paul McCartney, I wouldn't go up to him and go, 'OH MY GOD! PAUL!' I'd be like, 'Hey, man, *how are you doing?*' I'd be as natural as I can. I'd be nervous, because it's McCartney—but I sense that even when people come up to me. Either people treat me like a peer or they're fans.

But one of the coolest things that I had happen to me was, I was in a band called Michael Angelo. I had lived in LA for three or four years—I looked like a total rock star. I understood LA, and we were headlining all the clubs—packing all the places. And I got in touch with Gene Simmons, and he said, 'Well, send me your music.' I sent him three songs, and one of them was written by this rhythm guitarist named Guy Mann-Dude, who went on to become pretty famous himself in guitar circles. And he was a great drummer—he played with Oingo Boingo, Jon Anderson. A world-class musician.

And Simmons calls me up, and goes, 'What are you doing? What is this song, "I'm Too Young To Cry Forever"? What are you talking about? You're not twenty-one years old—you're not too young to cry forever! This song is crap! You look good, you've got the shag haircut, you're a handsome guy—you're light years ahead of other guitar players. But that song is not you. That song sucks!' He didn't know I didn't write it. [*Laughs*] And he goes, 'I want you to come down to the studio … *now.*'

KISS was recording—I can't remember what album—but I think it was at Cherokee Studios. I went down there, I talked to him, and he goes, 'Listen, KISS was KISS *before* we had a record deal. Madonna was Madonna. No label made our image. If you don't know who you are, no one will know who you are. That song is not you. And that song was written in third person. Do you know what KISS songs are? *"I* wanna rock and roll all nite," "They call *me* Dr. Love." The only guy that can write in third person is Tom Petty—if you can write like Tom Petty, *great*. But I didn't hear it.' Again, he didn't know I didn't write that song that he hated so much, and I kicked Guy out of the band, and he got real pissed—he hasn't talked to me since.

But Gene thought I was good enough, and he cared enough to give me *The World According To Gene*, and I used that in workshops and motivational speaking. 'If you don't know who you are, *nobody* will know who you are.' And I've been to Gene's house, too. When I got together with Nitro, he had Simmons Records. I sent him a tape, and he said, 'I love the name Nitro. Your singer [Jim Gillette] is the most obnoxious singer I've ever heard in my life … *I like it.*' He was interested in signing us to Simmons Records. He goes, 'This could be bigger than KISS … it might not. I don't know—you guys are *so* outrageous.' But he liked me and he thought we were taking a real stand on things. And he admired that.

He's always been nice to me. Gene Simmons never yelled at me or was weird. He gave me advice that he really thought would help. What can you say? I've jammed with him, I've opened up for him, he wanted to sign me to his record company. But with Nitro, we were already signed to Rhino Records—and Rhino alone was worth a quarter of a billion dollars, so it's not like we needed somebody to get us a record deal. And even after Nitro was signed, I would hang out with him at NAMM. It was really cool.

The thing that defines both the makeup *and* the non-makeup eras of KISS are the songs. Paul Stanley in the studio sounds great. And I think the non-makeup era … when you look at those old videos, Paul looked cool, and Gene Simmons looked cool. I remember when I met him back then, I always thought a lot of the Hollywood stars that I met looked better in person than on the screen.

I'll give you an example—I'd never met Arnold Schwarzenegger, but you know like when you saw him in those early movies, like *The Terminator*? His skin looked so smooth and tight on his face—it really was a striking look. And I remember when I first met Gene Simmons, he had that kind of complexion. His skin was not wrinkly—it was really tight and really smooth. It was something that just struck me, that this guy is really cool-looking in person. When they took off their makeup, I thought they looked cool. They dressed cool.

But it wasn't just taking off their makeup—*it was their songs*. It was 'Lick It Up.' That song alone was so good. They had so many good songs without their makeup … I really truly believe it's not just that they didn't wear makeup. Forget the looks—they had good music, they had good songs. *That's the secret.* Even in the early days of KISS, they had good songs, and Ace wrote good guitar parts. But it's purely the songs that made KISS without makeup. They looked good, but the look was secondary—they were able to come out with that song at the right time, put out the right video, and they kept doing it over and over. *Just like the Stones and The Beatles.*

KISS MY ASS: CLASSIC KISS REGROOVED

Released June 21, 1994. Produced by Lenny Kravitz, Alan Reynolds, Gene Simmons, Paul Stanley, Clif Norrell, Gin Blossoms, Gavin MacKillop, Billy Gould, J. Mascis, Nuno Bettencourt, The Lemonheads, Tom Hamilton, Matt Hyde, The Mighty Mighty Bosstones, Yoshiki. US #19. US certification: gold.

SIDE ONE

Deuce (Gene Simmons) **Lenny Kravitz & Stevie Wonder**
Hard Luck Woman (Paul Stanley) **Garth Brooks & KISS**
She (Simmons/Stephen Coronel) **Anthrax**
Christine Sixteen (Simmons) **Gin Blossoms**
Rock And Roll All Nite (Simmons/Stanley) **Toad The Wet Sprocket**
Calling Dr. Love (Simmons) **Shandi's Addiction**

SIDE TWO

Goin' Blind (Simmons/Coronel) **Dinosaur Jr.**
Strutter (Simmons/Stanley) **Extreme**
Plaster Caster (Simmons) **The Lemonheads**
Detroit Rock City (Stanley/Bob Ezrin) **The Mighty Mighty Bosstones**
Black Diamond (Stanley) **Yoshiki**
Unholy (German Version) [bonus track] (Simmons/Vinnie Vincent) **Die Ärzte**

SINGLE

Detroit Rock City (The Mighty Mighty Bosstones) /
Detroit Rock City (KISS) (US/UK did not chart)

★

In the mid-90s, it seemed like every bloody veteran musical act under the sun was getting the tribute treatment—that is, an album of various artists covering their favorite tunes by said band or singer. In 1994, it was KISS's turn, with the arrival of *Kiss My Ass: Classic Kiss Regrooved*. Most of these sorts of tribute albums seemed to be instigated/assembled by a record company, but in KISS's case, it was the band themselves who supervised their own tribute release, which admittedly is a bit odd, and funny—some would say it's self-serving, and defeats the purpose of a tribute album in the first place. But, that said, by assembling the artists and songs themselves, KISS could at least exercise some quality control, as the album was comprised of artists that they preferred, rather than someone else *supposing* who would serve the songs best.

Interestingly, *Kiss My Ass* was not the first KISS tribute album to hit the record-store shelves. The first one went by the name of *Hard To Believe: A KISS Covers Compilation*, and was issued by the indie label C/Z Records in 1990. Unlike *KMA*, this first album did not collect musicians from a wide variety of genres, but rather homed in on punk, grunge, and alt-rock acts. And while the majority of the artists were obscure then and remain obscure now (gee, I wonder what Smelly Tongues are up to today?), several renowned bands featured on it, including the Melvins (covering 'Goin' Blind') and some itty-bitty band called Nirvana ('Do You Love Me?').

But getting back to *KMA*, it is impressive that such a wide range of artists have mentioned KISS as a major influence over the years—and in fact, from about the late 80s onward, just about *every* major new rock recording artist seemed to list KISS as an influence. And this was a golden opportunity to drive this point home, once and for all. From that standpoint, *KMA* was a major success, in that it offered representatives of such styles as R&B/soul (Lenny Kravitz with Stevie Wonder), country (Garth Brooks with KISS), alt-rock (Shandi's Addiction), jangle-pop (Gin Blossoms), grunge (Dinosaur Jr.), ska (The Mighty Mighty Bosstones), hard rock (Extreme), heavy metal (Anthrax), classical (Yoshiki), and industrial (Die Ärzte).

But now, if we can all be honest for a second … how many times do music fans actually play these tribute albums, after the first few curio-listens? I'd bet that the number is frighteningly low for many. But to KISS's credit, *Kiss*

My Ass is unquestionably one of the best tribute albums ever assembled. The reason? Many among the wide variety of artists who contributed opted to put their own unmistakable stamp on a KISS klassic, rather than offering up a straight re-reading of the original.

For example, although I cannot say I am the biggest fan of Toad The Wet Sprocket, their reimagining of 'Rock And Roll All Nite' as a sad country/folk number works surprisingly well. And the same can be said for Extreme's take on 'Strutter,' which sees the pop/funk-metal band slow down the tempo and wittingly incorporate elements of 'God Of Thunder' into the guitar solo, as well as bits of 'Shout It Out Loud' and 'Love Gun' at the end.

If I were to cast my vote for the best track of the entire set, however, I would have to go with 'Calling Dr. Love' by Shandi's Addiction. It's understandable if this band's name doesn't ring any bells, as this was their only recording *ever*. So, why was this seemingly unknown band allowed to contribute to such a star-studded event? Well, let me explain who Shandi's Addiction were: Tool singer Maynard James Keenan, Rage Against The Machine guitarist Tom Morello and drummer Brad Wilk, and Faith No More bassist Bill Gould.

Now, of course, I may be a tad bit biased, since FNM are one of my all-time fave rock bands (heck, I even wrote *The Faith No More & Mr. Bungle Companion*), but what makes the tune stand out so much is that it is a 'reworking' that still manages to retain the essential elements of the original (most notably the guitar riff). And in case you were wondering, yes, the band's name is a play on one of the leading alt-rock bands of the late 80s and early 90s, Jane's Addiction (with the name of KISS's 1980 pop hit 'Shandi' added in for a chuckle).

Another standout of the set is Anthrax—a band who have never been ashamed to advertise their appreciation of KISS—taking on 'She.' Heck, they've covered so many KISS songs over the years—'Parasite,' 'Love Her All I Can,' 'Watchin' You,' and even the '78 KISS dolls commercial theme song—that, with a few additions, they could assemble *their own* KISS tribute album!

Other pleasant surprises included Lenny Kravitz giving 'Deuce' a more soulful flair (with Stevie Wonder supplying harmonica) and X Japan's

Yoshiki offering up a great symphonic, all-instrumental version of 'Black Diamond.' But undoubtedly the strongest tune on the collection from a commercial standpoint was an exceptional cover of 'Hard Luck Woman' by country giant Garth Brooks, who is backed on the track by none other than … KISS.

Admittedly, not all of the selections here are winners, especially The Lemonheads' blah take of 'Plaster Caster.' The biggest fumble, though, was the choice of one of the set's weakest selections—The Mighty Mighty Bosstones sleepwalking through 'Detroit Rock City'—*as a single*. The obvious single choice would have been Garth Brooks, whose 'Hard Luck Woman' had 'crossover hit single' written all over it. (Perhaps *Mr. Brooks himself* stipulated that the song not be released as a single? Anything's possible in this crazy music biz.) Lenny Kravitz would have been a sensible second single choice, and heck, even Shandi's Addiction's 'Calling Dr. Love' would have made more sense than the Bosstones' 'Detroit Rock City' as a single—at least it would have been played more on alt-rock radio at the time!

While *Kiss My Ass* would prove to be a worthwhile listen for KISS fans, it's hard not to think what *could* have been, as it has been noted that some of the other artists who were asked to participate—but ultimately did not—include Nine Inch Nails (taking on 'Love Gun'), Soundgarden (tackling 'War Machine'), and Madonna (putting her stamp on 'I Was Made For Lovin' You'). A phone call was even placed to Nirvana, to gauge their interest in recording another KISS cover while they were making what was to be their final studio album, *In Utero*, but that did not come to pass either.

Regardless, as stated earlier, *KISS My Ass: Classic KISS Regrooved* remains one of the best tribute albums ever assembled. And let's give credit where credit's due—we can largely thank Gene and Paul for that.

KNOW THE SCORE: BILL GOULD

Faith No More's bassist discusses his brief affiliation with Shandi's Addiction, and memories of appearing on *Kiss My Ass*.

How did you get involved in covering 'Calling Dr. Love' with members of Tool and Rage Against the Machine?

Somebody in KISS—probably Gene—had contacted our manager, to see if anyone in Faith No More was willing to do it. And I was a KISS fan growing up. Our manager at the time was also managing Rage Against The Machine. I think Tom Morello was also into the idea, so we hooked up together that way. And he suggested Maynard [James Keenan]. So that's kind of how it came together.

Were you friends with any of them previously?

I didn't know Maynard at all, but I knew Tom a little bit. I just thought it would be an interesting thing to do—to play with guys I'd never played with before.

Who came up with the name Shandi's Addiction?

That was Maynard.

What do you recall about rehearsing and recording the song?

We decided, when we were going to do it, that we were going to do it a little differently. So, Brad, Tom, and I met at a rehearsal space, and just kind of banged out the musical part. I hadn't met Maynard yet. We came to a little arrangement, and we went and recorded it, I think, probably the next day. It was done at a studio in the Topanga Canyon—I don't remember the name of it. I remember that the owner freaked out, because he didn't think he was going to get paid—and he shut down the project! There was a lot of very strange drama going on.

Maynard came in and did the vocals later, in San Francisco, at this studio called Poolside. It was actually a very interesting experience, because I picked up Maynard at the airport, and I didn't know him. It's sometimes not easy to read his humor if you don't know him. I said, 'So, are you looking forward to doing this KISS thing?' And he's like, 'They should be paying me to do this.'

I was like, 'Well … that's a nice way to start the project!' So I said, 'Do you like KISS?' And he says, 'You don't understand … I was *the biggest* KISS fan in my school. I was the guy that paraded KISS around.' And when they did *The Elder*, he lost all the respect from his peers—he was very traumatized by that. So he had misgivings about getting involved in the project!

But it was really amazing—we got to the studio, turned on the tape, played the song, he heard it once, he sang a take from the beginning to the end, said, 'That was good,' said, 'I want to do one more to double it,' sang that, and he was finished. It was done in, like, ten minutes! And his voice … he doubled himself the first time, *exactly*. I've never seen that in my life since then. Ever.

You just brought up *The Elder*—what are your thoughts on it?
I kind of dropped off after *Alive II*. But I actually have *The Elder*—I actually have the record, but I don't play it very often. Oh, boy … it's an *iconic* piece. That's all I can say! My opinion means absolutely nothing—it will stand the test of time, no doubt about it.

I kind of look at that record as an Andy Kaufman–esque work.
Absolutely! 100 percent.

Was 'Calling Dr. Love' ever performed live by Shandi's Addiction?
No, never. That was it. We had to videotape the entire recording session—that was part of the condition. So there was always videotape going while we were recording. I don't think we recorded Maynard singing … I can't remember. But Gene actually was *very* involved. He wanted to know when we had the rough mix done, and when we had Maynard come in. He would listen to everything and call me on the phone and comment on it. Very respectful, but also, he definitely had opinions. He actually had really good feedback. Gene was great on the phone.

I think we recorded it in the summertime, and then, around December, I get this package at my house … it was a fruit basket from KISS, and they all signed a Christmas card! I've got to say, I've never seen a band do anything like that. It was cool. They were very, very professional in that way—I hate to use the word *professional*, but they were so hands-on and so focused on that project. I hadn't seen anything like that before.

I remember you wore a Gene Simmons T-shirt when Faith No More played *The Tonight Show* in 1993.
I don't even remember that, but I'm sure I did. That's something I would do.

I also remember reading in the book *Faith No More: The Real Story* that Gene once told Mike Patton that he had thought Faith No More covering The Commodores' 'Easy' was a risk. Do you have any memory of this?
He came backstage and was very cool and polite. He said something to Mike like, 'Why do you do that song?' And he goes, 'I don't know … it's a joke.' And he goes, 'So, you're telling the audience they're stupid, right?' And he's like, 'I don't know … I guess, if you put it that way!' He just could not figure out why you would play a song that would torture the audience. He couldn't understand it—which I thought was pretty funny, actually. I mean, KISS, they come from a different mentality than I think where we come from. I like them, but the humor part of our band—he didn't quite get that.

What did you think of *Kiss My Ass* overall?
I think that was a good record. I liked that record. What is interesting is it was done around the same time that we did the *Judgment Night Soundtrack*. To me, that *KISS My Ass* record was sort of like *Judgment Night*—there were a lot of really odd pairings of people working with a different genre of music. It seemed like around that time, it was kind of the thing to do. I think that was really healthy.

Interestingly, it seems like KISS influenced quite a few alt-rock bands of the early 90s. Why do you think this is?
I have no idea. I know why *I* liked them. In a way, it wasn't 'intellectual' music. They just had a lot of hooks—kind of like in the way the Ramones are hooky. To me, KISS is kind of hooky. You couldn't really take them that seriously, but there was something charming about them. At least that was my take.

It's interesting that you just made the comparison between KISS and the Ramones, because early KISS and early punk don't sound that far apart.

Both of them go back to The New York Dolls. You can see one went one direction, and one went the other. But the roads are kind of similar.

KNOW THE SCORE: CHARLIE BENANTE

Anthrax's drummer returns to chat about not only *Kiss My Ass* but also the other times his band have covered KISS.

Before covering 'She' on *Kiss My Ass*, Anthrax covered several other KISS songs, including 'Parasite,' 'Love Her All I Can,' and even the song from the KISS dolls commercial ...

Cover songs were the fun aspect of recording. After you painstakingly recorded *your* songs, and made sure they were all great, *now we can have a little fun ...* and the KISS doll commercial song was always a song we would goof on. We loved it ... but we also thought it was cheesy, at the same time. But we wanted to do it. To make a long story short, we couldn't get the rights to do it, so we couldn't put it out. But we had a ball doing it. And then, every other KISS song we've done, we did it with 100 percent heart—so much went into it, to make sure it was up to their standards. The first one we did was 'Parasite,' then we did 'Love Her All I Can,' 'Watchin' You,' and then 'She' for the *Kiss My Ass* album—*with* Gene and Paul. Gene and Paul sang on 'She,' and they produced it.

I wasn't even aware that Anthrax had covered 'Watchin' You.'

Yeah, it's from the *Stomp 442* sessions. It was a B-side to 'Fueled.'

What do you recall about getting invited to appear on *Kiss My Ass*?

We were contacted about it, and we immediately said we wanted to do 'She'— the live version, because it has that awesome 'Let Me Know' section at the end. Gene and Paul produced it. It was two or three days in the studio with those guys, and it was a complete joy. I can't tell you how much I loved it. Being with them, and just listening to their critiques.

216

I remember those two were so happy when I first laid down the basic track, I remember Paul saying, 'You've really got the feel for this whole song down.' At that point, I was in my late twenties, early thirties, and I remember telling him, 'Well … I've only been practicing for this moment *all these years!*'

How was it to see Paul and Gene lay down vocal harmonies in the studio?
It sounded so good when they did it. It's like, 'Well … *there it is!*'

There was an abundance of tribute albums at the time of *Kiss My Ass*, but I can't think of a band more deserving of one than KISS, judging by the wide variety of artists they've influenced and inspired over the years.
Oh, absolutely. Then again, I always say that the reason why I think KISS appealed to me so much was they had the thing that I was into the most: *music and horror*. The look of them, even if you didn't know what they sounded like, you couldn't help but go, *What the fuck?! What is this?* Just that cover of *Alive!*—being that I'd never seen this band in concert, I was always wondering, *What's going on during this song? Are bombs going off?* But this was different now. Everything was lit up. It was like performing with the lights on. But when you see KISS performing for real, it has a definite mood to it—a vibe.

You can go down the list of different musical styles that KISS influenced— glam metal, thrash metal, alt-rock …
They influenced everything you just said, and they also influenced the showmen in people, too. Because it's the one thing that Paul always said—he *hated* bands that would just get up there and look like slobs and just play their instruments. He thought that was 50 percent, and the other 50 percent was putting on a big show. *Look the part.* And that's the thing about Paul Stanley— when you see him, you can just smell *rock star*. He just has this vibe to him. He's awesome.

I feel he's one of the most underrated rock singers, too.
I was pissed off when people were passing around that video of him with his voice [in reference to an audience member's clip of 'Love Gun,' filmed at a

KISS performance in Barcelona on July 7, 2018]. I was like, *Give the guy some respect.* People are like, *End it. Call it a day.* Look, I can't say enough about people wanting to do something because they love to do it. If they can't do it to the best of their abilities, does it mean that they have to give it up?

I know myself, when I have problems and injuries, I can't do it to the best of my abilities, and I need to take a little bit of a break to heal up a bit, then I'm recharged, and *bam*, there I go again. Maybe that's something Paul should do. Maybe he shouldn't do such long extensive tours. Maybe take it down a bit, so that he is able to be healthy. Everybody is getting up there in age—it doesn't get easier. Especially for those guys—they're walking around in seven-inch heels, and they're moving around. I would say, let them have their farewell tour, and go see it as the fan that you are.

Although people focus on the visual aspect of KISS, it seems like they are never given proper credit for their songwriting. One of the most *anti-visual* musical movements, grunge, had bands that listed KISS as an influence—Melvins and Nirvana covered KISS songs, and members of Soundgarden, Pearl Jam, and Alice In Chains have said they were an influence, too.
If you're in our age group, there is no way you could have missed KISS. They had to have *some* impact on you. Either you fucking hated them, or you were a complete freak about them.

That's another thing—nowadays, they seem to be universally respected, or at least credited, for their accomplishments and influence. But in the late 70s and early 80s, there was a clear love/hate thing with KISS.
Oh, dude, when I was growing up, there were kids in my neighborhood that fucking *despised* KISS. Just assholes. You couldn't wear a KISS shirt or anything. And that's just the way it was.

What did you think of the *Kiss My Ass* album as a whole?
I thought it was awesome. I thought Garth Brooks did a great job. I loved the Lenny Kravitz song. I thought it was a really good collection of people. I can't believe they got these artists from different parts of the music world to do it.

KISS CONVENTION TOUR WITH CURT GOOCH

Although KISS performed sporadic live shows during this period, there was no tour in support of *Kiss My Ass*. By now, however, the popularity of KISS conventions had risen so dramatically that KISS decided to launch one of their own in 1995, with an acoustic performance and Q&A by the band at each date …

By late '93, there was the Foundations Forum in Burbank, California, on September 11—a weird little one-off show, with all deep cuts and a setlist that was promised to only be from the first six records. They did do a few one-off shows in San Antonio, Chicago, Phoenix, and Nashville in 1994, but nothing of any note happened—except for the fact that in Chicago, Eric Singer was allowed to sing 'Black Diamond' for the first time. And at the Phoenix show, they brought back the US *Animalize* stage set—minus the logo, of course. And they did a brief tour of South America—their first since 1983. A lot of fans seemed to care about that, and I know they were doing weird things—like opening with '100,000 Years,' and Paul would play with his hair back in a ponytail one night. Just weird stuff that doesn't make any sense at all.

Then, in 1995, KISS got very creative and did the KISS Convention tour. I attended two of the conventions, and it was insane in the sense that, literally, I was haggling with *Gene* via email over the price of my table—as a dealer there! And the entire convention netted the band around one million dollars. They produced the ads, wrote the ads, cut the ads, designed everything themselves. They did a lot of work that went into that, and asking a hundred dollars a ticket was *a lot*. In a way, that was kind of the precursor to the reunion tour.

But here KISS were, playing hotel ballrooms for a few hundred people each night, and then, in New York, I think it was one year to the day later, was the first of four nights at Madison Square Garden—*sold out*. I've never seen a more dramatic turnaround in my life. [Note: KISS played at the Roseland Ballroom as part of the Convention tour on July 30, 1995, and then played Madison Square Garden from July 25–28, 1996.] I mean, who goes from playing to five hundred people at a hotel ballroom to selling out the Garden in twelve months? It was a stunning accomplishment, to say the least.

The KISS Convention tour actually started in Australia. It had been fifteen years since KISS were in Australia, and they finally returned to the

219

land where KISS had been bigger than any other band at any other point. Forget about America in '78—Australia in '80 was KISS at the peak of their powers. But going back to Australia, there was certainly a big desire for that fan base to see them out of makeup, and part of that was that they started doing the convention tour over there. They were literally letting fans videotape the shows—which was certainly the opposite of everything you've been told before—and KISS were doing two-hour acoustic or semi-acoustic shows in these hotel ballrooms that were so informal that fans could come up onstage and sing with the band, or their kid would come and fill in on drums for a song! It was just ridiculous, what happened. It couldn't get much more informal than that.

They were including things like 'Comin' Home,' 'Plaster Caster,' and 'Mr. Speed' in the setlist every night. Every single night, they would attempt 'Let Me Know,' 'Acrobat / Love Theme From KISS' … 'When You Wish Upon A Star,' I think, was even at one of the shows. They would go as deep and as crazy as you could get them to. It was certainly an interesting period of time.

KISS are *so* lucky—more so than any other band—in the sense that by the late 70s, their fan base had changed from the teenagers of the early and mid-70s to eight-to-twelve-year-olds being the dominant force in the audience by *Dynasty*. KISS are so lucky that happened, because those eight to twelve-year-olds grew up to be teenagers, and a majority of them stayed with the band through thick and thin, because KISS reminded them of their childhood. That was their happy place, their happy time—and KISS was a cherished part of that.

There's not another fan base on earth that I can think of where you have the original fan base, and then a second generation of fans that got the band through the non-makeup years—to the point of where they could get back to do the reunion tour. Most of the people that were in the audience—I have been a KISS fan since age five, and there I was in the *Asylum* crowd at twelve, and going to *Crazy Nights* shows when I'm fourteen and fifteen. That wouldn't have happened, had I not grown up with the bubblegum cards and *Kiss Meets The Phantom Of The Park* and the Colorforms. That might have been a negative for them in '79, but ultimately, that second-generation fan base served them very, very well throughout the non-makeup years.

GIMME MORE: KISS VIDEO GUIDE WITH BRUCE KULICK

Even after taking off the makeup, KISS remained quite a visual rock act—embracing the home video medium, as well as getting support from the very powerful (at the time) MTV. Here, Bruce offers his thoughts on all of KISS's home video releases *and* promotional music videos from the non-makeup era—even ones he was not a part of!

HOME VIDEOS: ANIMALIZE: LIVE UNCENSORED (APRIL 19, 1985)

A document of KISS's entire performance at Detroit's Cobo Hall (the same venue Alive! was recorded at) on December 8, 1984.

It's funny, just yesterday I scanned an advert for it. For me, it was just another gig, but obviously there were cameras there. You should also know that, in that era, putting out a VHS was a *big* deal—it was new. The technology suddenly became available in everyone's homes. And there were equal amounts of Betamax probably and VHS back then. That advert that I'm looking at right now shows Beta first, and then VHS underneath it.

It was exciting—Detroit has always been good to KISS. I'm definitely proud of it, although it took me a long time to look at it, because the tempos were so incredibly fast. *Untamed. Uncut. Unleashed.* That's what the advert said.

It was always my intention to fit in—in a respectful way. To be me, but at the same time not totally rewrite what was done so well [before]. And I will say that I didn't understand what Vinnie was doing. It wasn't my band to tell him to not do it. I don't really remember [Paul's stage raps], but … I've heard some people do some funny things with them, edit them together. He'd always be having an over-the-top kind of front-man vibe. And I will admit it was unique, and, in retrospect, kind of comical, to a degree. But it's what you do when you're at that age, with that crowd and everything. He was always such a unique performer, and the energy level he would put out—even when he was just going to introduce the song—was always off the map.

EXPOSED (May 18, 1987)

Part spoof, part documentary of KISS's career according to Gene and Paul, with most of their promo videos up to this point, plus makeup-era live clips.

Is that the one where there's a house, and you're visiting KISS in a house and everything? It was mostly embarrassing to me, in retrospect. Now, I understand them [only] giving me two lines, because I'd only been in the band a year … but Eric was in the band a lot longer than that, and they basically stuck us with the monkey! So, what can I say? I think [Gene & Paul] were really so excited that making a VHS tape in a way was like making a film of the band. And they both wanted to be the stars of the film, which I can't completely blame them for. But then, if there are four guys that they are talking about in the band, then, is the balance at all reasonable? I got it—they were very competitive with each other, so what chance did *I* have?

CRAZY NIGHTS (June 6, 1988)

A video EP of all three promotional videos from Crazy Nights.
I enjoyed those videos. Most of them were kind of live, or a combination. They were good videos—they were colorful and entertaining. Good songs.

X-TREME CLOSE-UP (August 18, 1992)

Another documentary of the band's history, once again featuring a mixture of interviews (more serious this time than on Exposed), promotional videos, and performance clips from throughout KISS's career.
I never took offense to them delving into the past, so I can't say I had any issues with it. And anything that was put out that I was involved in, I was happy to get any good screen time, for sure. But nothing really stands out about it to me.

KISS KONFIDENTIAL (August 16, 1993)

Mostly a live document of the Revenge tour (edited together from performances taped November 27–29, 1992, at Auburn Hills, Michigan; Indianapolis, Indiana; and Cleveland, Ohio) plus interviews and a few vintage clips.
It was a good thing for the band to put out. A lot of the video stuff I wasn't that involved with, so that's why I didn't have a big attachment with it. I have some friends that are big fans that help me with some things, and they have their connection to these releases that you're talking about. And I have much less of a connection. [*Laughs*]

Kiss My Ass: The Video (August 23, 1994)

Modern-day interviews mixed with only makeup-era performance footage.

I don't remember too much about that. It's obviously related to the tribute album. I'm sure I have it in my collection, but I'd have to sit down and spend time with it to tell you what I thought.

Kiss Unplugged (March 12, 1996)

The now-famous acoustic performance (filmed on August 9, 1995, at Sony Studios in New York City) that ultimately led to the reunion of the original KISS lineup.

Obviously I loved that. I thought the performance was amazing. I loved the sentiment of the whole thing—bringing out the original guys, and then us all playing together. That was just well done, by a very strong company—meaning the people who provided content for MTV.

The guy involved with it, Alex Coletti, is a big KISS fan, and you noticed that when you looked at it, you see Eric Singer, you see me—you know what I mean? The experience of being there is *equal*—unlike a lot of the other product, where it can be, like, 80 percent Gene and Paul, and then the rest is whoever else is in the band. *Unplugged* was not filmed that way. But forgetting anything to do about the production, the performances I thought were amazing. And the playing and the song list—it's definitely one of my highlights.

PROMOTIONAL MUSIC VIDEO CLIPS: 'LICK IT UP' (1983)

The first time many people saw the faces of Gene, Paul, Vinnie, and Eric sans makeup.

I liked that the band was not going to be in makeup anymore, so I thought that was unique. For a non-makeup look, I thought they were saying, *We're still cool and we're tough*. So, yes, I did like it.

'ALL HELL'S BREAKIN' LOOSE' (1984)

Similar in look/vibe to the 'Lick It Up' clip (sorta like Escape From New York).

I will say one word—*macho*. I really liked it—I thought it was cool.

'HEAVEN'S ON FIRE' (1984)

Mark St. John's one and only video with KISS, which proved to be quite popular on MTV.

It was just like a fun *here they are, looking like stars, with girls and everything, and being silly.* It was appropriate for the time. And, obviously, that was Mark's first introduction to the KISS world, and I thought he looked good in it. I thought everybody looked really cool.

'THRILLS IN THE NIGHT' (1985)

Shot on December 14 and 15, 1984, in Cleveland and Louisville, along with extra clips added in from Animalize Live Uncensored. An unreleased version had all four members in various 'roles' that were filmed but later scrapped.

I don't remember too much about it, other than we grabbed it in Louisville, Kentucky, or something like that. I have a photo or two that some people had of us in character—it was very funny. I don't think [the character roles] would have been a bad idea, but obviously, when they looked at it, they thought it looked ridiculous—so they just went to plan B.

'TEARS ARE FALLING' (1985)

In which Bruce plays the solo in what appears to be a rainstorm.

I have to admit, I really thought that was good. I loved that I had a very clever way of being featured, and I really felt like much more of a real member of the band, by that happening. So, I liked it.

'UH! ALL NIGHT' (1985)

It could only have happened in the 80s (part I).

All of the *Asylum* videos I enjoyed, and I thought they were well done. I think we went to England for that one. I liked it. I thought no matter how flamboyant the band might have been, we were cool. They were definitely representative of the *Asylum* era, and I thought they were colorful and entertaining—totally.

224

'WHO WANTS TO BE LONELY' (1986)

It could only have happened in the 80s (part II).

I don't know why they kept sticking me in the water!

'ROCK AND ROLL ALL NITE' (LIVE, 1987)

Comprised of a variety of clips edited together from Exposed, and probably the most played KISS clip back in the days of VH1 Classic.

If I was included in anything that they also wanted to show that was vintage as well, I enjoyed it. Well, that was a big hit—so that made sense. It is kind of ironic, but I'll take whatever screen time I can get. [*Laughs*]

'CRAZY CRAZY NIGHTS (1987)

KISS mime and strut their stuff ... before Paul walks on hands.

That was exciting. I had my 'radioactive' BC Rich. We were introducing a new stage.

'REASON TO LIVE' (1987)

In which Bruce can be spotted playing keyboards, and Paul's female friend seeks revenge.

Another good live video—US-made, though, as opposed to the British ones we were talking about. We wanted to make it a little more credible—like the way Van Halen did 'Jump.'

'TURN ON THE NIGHT' (1988)

An attractive blonde enjoys a KISS gig during the Crazy Nights tour.

It was entertaining. We were doing a gig, we were able to just ... the crowd is there, so we may as well use them, right?

'LET'S PUT THE X IN SEX' (1988)

It could only have happened in the 80s (part III).

'X In Sex' was interesting—with all the models and using a building down in the Wall Street area that, architecturally, had an X in it. I will say that the person that did it probably was *too much* of a fashion video director for my taste—but that's what Paul was looking for.

'(YOU MAKE ME) ROCK HARD' (1989)

It could only have happened in the 80s (part IV).

It was like a circus thing or something!

'HIDE YOUR HEART' (1989)

A love triangle gone south.

It had the storyline and the rooftop in LA. I thought it was entertaining.

'FOREVER' (1990)

One of KISS's most tasteful clips of the non-makeup era.

I'm not in it enough, but I do really like it. *OK, the camera can turn around one more time over here … hey, it's me playing the solo. Hello!* I think the vibe that it puts you in was very pleasant. That song is still super-important.

'RISE TO IT' (1990)

Featuring Gene and Paul back in makeup at the start, and with just the back of Bruce and Eric's noggins shown.

They realized that it was too awkward to do anything other than have Eric and me as *we're there, but we're not in any kind of character or doing anything*. It was up to them to do their thing. I know Larry Mazer was involved in choosing that. I don't know if it was the right thing to do or not, but that was what they were thinking.

'GOD GAVE ROCK AND ROLL TO YOU II' (1991)

Eric Carr's final music video with KISS.

I certainly was glad that Eric did that, and that he was included. It really meant a lot to him. He had more energy than me—quite honestly. I think the video is good—stomping around on the wet floor. What a terrific song. And maybe even more could have been done, but it's a great track. I don't think you can ruin it in any way—no matter what you do.

'UNHOLY' (1992)

SPOOKY! SCARY! SATANIC!

Very creative, I thought—to set the mood for something dark and crazy. It's a good video. I look real intense in there, and I'm really a *puddycat*. [*Laughs*] I guess that's movie magic right there.

'I JUST WANNA' (1992)

To borrow a line from Cream, 'In the white room …'

I like the white background—I thought it was cool.

'DOMINO' (1992)

Gene goes cruising in his convertible.

Maybe a little odd, because you've got Paul playing bass a little bit, and Gene driving a car. Some of that was a little weird. But such a great song—I didn't care.

'EVERY TIME I LOOK AT YOU' (1992)

Paul sports some Don Johnson–esque facial hair in this rarely aired clip.

I like that one. I just looked at it online, recently. Another one with a mood to it—kind of like 'Forever.' A little different mood, but I liked it.

'I LOVE IT LOUD' (live, 1993)

KISS rocking arenas in '93, baby!

That was kind of promotion for *Alive III*. I don't remember much about it, to be honest. But the footage for *Alive III* was exciting.

'ROCK AND ROLL ALL NITE' (UNPLUGGED, 1996)

A seated/acoustic rendition of KISS's top arena anthem.

Really, one of the last things I did with the band, if you think about it. I was very happy with it.

KISS
UNPLUGGED

Released March 12, 1996. Produced by Alex Coletti.
US #15, UK #74. US certification: gold.

SIDE ONE

Comin' Home (Ace Frehley/Paul Stanley)
Plaster Caster (Gene Simmons)
Goin' Blind (Simmons/Stephen Coronel)
Do You Love Me (Stanley/Bob Ezrin/Kim Fowley)

SIDE TWO

Domino (Simmons)
Sure Know Something (Stanley/Vini Poncia)
A World Without Heroes (Simmons/Stanley/Bob Ezrin/Lou Reed)
Rock Bottom (Frehley/Stanley)

SIDE THREE

See You Tonight (Simmons)
I Still Love You (Stanley/Vinnie Vincent)
Every Time I Look At You (Stanley/Ezrin)
2,000 Man (Mick Jagger/Keith Richards)

SIDE FOUR

Beth (Peter Criss/Bob Ezrin/Stan Penridge)
Nothin' To Lose (Simmons)
Rock And Roll All Nite (Simmons/Stanley)
Got To Choose [vinyl bonus track] (Stanley)

SINGLE

Every Time I Look At You / Rock And Roll All Nite (US/UK did not chart)

★

If it seemed like every veteran musical act was getting the tribute-album treatment in the 90s, a close second to that would the unplugged phenomenon. For the unenlightened, this particular craze started with the popularity of *MTV Unplugged*, which saw some of rock and pop's biggest names perform stripped-down, acoustic (make that *amplified* acoustic) versions of their songs, with quite a few episodes also released as albums and/or home videos. And although the show had its share of outstanding performances (Neil Young, Pearl Jam, and Nirvana among them), it also spawned its share of stinkers (Poison, Ratt, Hootie & The Blowfish, and so on).

I'm sure many fellow KISS fans will agree with me when I say that their entry into the *Unplugged* canon is undoubtedly one of the better performances by a rock band on the program—both performance-wise *and* in terms of historical importance. By now, the Stanley/Simmons/Kulick/Singer lineup was a well-oiled machine, especially when it came to performing acoustically. The KISS Convention shows were entirely acoustic-based, so recording an *Unplugged* show made perfect sense—with a setlist that just about any diehard KISS fan would approve of.

Undoubtedly, the most significant thing to come out of KISS's *MTV Unplugged* performance, however, was that it saw a reunion of the original lineup—the first time since 1979 that all four original members played together in front of an audience. KISS fans worldwide can thank the *Unplugged* folks for inadvertently putting the reunion tour of 1996 in motion.

Instead of focusing mainly on their best-known tracks, quite a few deep cuts were dusted off, in particular the obscure-yet-delightful one-two-three punch that kicks off the set: 'Comin' Home,' 'Plaster Caster,' and 'Goin' Blind.' And it didn't stop there, as such overlooked tunes as 'Sure Know Something' (how this tune wasn't a mega-hit in '79 remains one of life's great mysteries), 'A World Without Heroes' (*The Elder*'s tender ballad), and 'See You Tonight' (from Gene's '78 solo album) got some well-deserved love. You also can't go wrong with 'Do You Love Me?' (which would soon— deservedly—become a concert regular once again) and 'I Still Love You' (which, as stated previously, does a remarkable job of showcasing the vocal abilities of Señor Stanley).

It turned out that there was even room for the non-makeup era at

Unplugged, too, with the inclusion of both 'Domino' and 'Every Time I Look At You' from *Revenge*. (It would have been a real corker if, say, 'A Million To One,' 'Thrills In The Night,' or 'Reason To Live' had been included, too, but beggars can't be choosers.) It should also be noted that quite a few tunes that were performed did not make the final cut, but can be viewed or heard on the unedited versions that have made the rounds in fan trading circles for years (and on YouTube)—including 'Hard Luck Woman' (sung by Paul), 'C'mon And Love Me,' 'Heaven's On Fire,' 'Spit,' and a hysterical country reworking of 'God Of Thunder.'

But the real story of *Unplugged* occurred toward the end of the set, when Bruce and Eric momentarily exited, and Ace and Peter reunited onstage with Gene and Paul once more. The reunion itself had seemed completely improbable just a short while earlier, since Gene and Paul were not exactly *complimentary* about their former bandmates in the press circa *Revenge* and *Alive III*. But all seemed to be forgiven on August 9, 1995, at Sony Studios in New York City. Kicking off the mini-reunion was a rollicking and fun version of '2,000 Man' with Ace on lead vocals, followed by an acoustic-guitar reworking of 'Beth' with Peter singing. Then the whole merry six-man gang congregated onstage for 'Nothin' To Lose' and a set-closing 'Rock And Roll All Nite' (the latter of which saw Ace and Peter sing a few lead lines each).

Listening back to *Kiss Unplugged* today, what has allowed it to hold up so well over the years is that, unlike the three *Alive* albums, it does not sound like an excessive amount of fix-ups were done in the recording studio afterward (and, most importantly, there's none of the annoying added-in crowd noise that plagues *Alive II* and *Alive III*). For a band known primarily for blowing up stages and cranking up their amps, *Kiss Unplugged* also proved that the lads were quite adept on their acoustics. And it also confirmed once and for all what KISS fans had been trying to convince their detractors of for years: that underneath all the extravagant stages and gimmicks was a band whose quality of songwriting, singing, and playing was every bit as good as that of other rock artists—something that could no longer be denied after hearing them perform in this nowhere-to-hide acoustic setting.

KNOW THE SCORE: ACE FREHLEY

KISS's original Spaceman looks back on their classic *Unplugged* performance and his return to the band.

What are your thoughts on *Unplugged* when you look back on it today?

Well, I wasn't sober at the time, so I wasn't looking my best, and I wasn't playing at the top of my game. But it still had a major impact on our fans, and necessitated the reunion tour. I remember the fans in the studio going crazy when the four of us played together as a unit, because that was the first time we had performed together in God knows how many years.

Was it a challenge to play those KISS songs acoustically, with KISS thought of first and foremost as an electric-guitar-based band?

Not really. I'm pretty proficient on the acoustic guitar, as well as the electric. And I play bass on most of my songs. Actually, the two songs that Gene and I wrote for [Ace's 2018 solo effort] *Spaceman*, 'Without You I'm Nothing' and 'Your Wish Is My Command'—we started off playing them on acoustics.

'2000 Man' was an interesting tune to tackle for *Unplugged*.

Yeah, well, it always went over well in concert, and people always say to me [that they] really like the twist we put on '2000 Man,' because if you listen to the Stones' original version, on *Their Satanic Majesties Request*, it's a lot different. I have a thing I say—I *Ace-ified* it. [*Laughs*]

Do you remember if 'New York Groove' was considered for *Unplugged*?

I don't think so. I mean, to be honest with you, I didn't even want to record that song originally, when I was recording that '78 solo album. Eddie Kramer's assistant had brought it to Eddie's attention, and then he played it for me, and I didn't really think it was a good song for me. But he persevered, and every few days he'd bring it up, and go, 'We *really* should try that song.' So, finally, he talked me into it. And then, once I got started working on it, I started to like it more and more, and it just turned into what it is today. It turned out to be my biggest hit.

How was it to be playing with the band again at the taping of *Unplugged*? You hadn't played live with them in almost fifteen years.

It was great. I remember walking into SIR to do rehearsals, and we all hugged. It was like old times. I feel really comfortable about those guys—they're my rock'n'roll brothers. We've all said negative things about each other over the years from time to time, but it's like two brothers quarreling. And the press really amplifies the negative stuff that we say about each other, and minimizes anything that's positive. I guess it makes better copy.

I can remember Gene and Paul were taking swipes at you in the press ...

Well, I think they were a little pissed at me that I quit the band. And what really aggravated me a lot of times was, I've seen interviews where they say they've *fired* me. Or, what they would do—in kind of a slick way—they would say, 'When we fired Peter *and* Ace.' Peter was fired, but I was never fired. Both times I decided to leave the band, they wanted me to stay. Even with my problems, I always came through in concert. I just wanted to clear that up, because some people think I was fired. *I was never fired.*

What do you remember about the audience's reaction, when you and Peter came out onstage?

It was mayhem. There were only about two hundred people in the studio audience. I remember getting a lot of calls from people that were pissed off, because I didn't invite them. It was a really limited guest list! Some of my friends were really upset that they didn't get an invitation, but there were limitations on how many people we could invite to the event.

Have you listened to the other songs on the album, with Bruce and Eric Singer?

God, I haven't listened to that record *in years*. To me, it was just something that turned out to be a magical event, and it was the catalyst that kicked off the reunion tour. But I never really paid much attention to that record.

Would you ever consider playing another all-acoustic set again—be it with KISS or solo?

I think it's possible. Obviously, when we played electrified, it's much more

232

exciting. But I wouldn't rule it out. I'm always the guy who says *never say never*. Paul started using that recently. [*Laughs*] He's using my line. People are asking him, 'Is Ace going to be on the last tour?' And he said, 'I wouldn't rule it out,' and he also said, 'I'll never say never.' Who knows what the future will lead to.

KNOW THE SCORE: JULIAN GILL

The author of various KISS books, including *Danger Zone: An Exploration Of KISS's Crazy Nights* and *KISS On Tour: 1973–2017*, among others, weighs in on KISS's *Unplugged* appearance (and beyond).

Do you agree that the KISS Convention tour set the stage perfectly for *Unplugged*?

Absolutely. During 1995, they had started doing these 'unplugged' shows. And by the time they went in to do the actual *Unplugged* session for MTV, I think they had done ninety-three songs throughout the year—but some obviously not all the way through. So they had a very good idea about which songs from their catalogue worked, and, during that tour, they distilled it down to a set of core songs. They weren't afraid to try some different songs out for purely comedic value, but it was pretty clear that they stayed away from some.

What were some of the more obscure songs KISS performed during their Convention tour?

Some of the obscure ones that they pulled out briefly—or didn't make it all the way through—were mainly *The Elder* songs. They took a few stabs at 'I' and 'The Oath,' and they also went into things that other singers or former members of the band would be singing—stuff like 'Shock Me' on one occasion, and 'Rocket Ride' I think one time, as well. They tried some really weird stuff, like 'Torpedo Girl,' 'She's So European' ... 'Uh! All Night' was even attempted.

There are some there that leave you shaking your head and cringing that they would even attempt them, but it's pretty clear that they would take a stab at them or play a riff—to make people smile. I think that's more where those obscure or uncomfortable songs come into play—if they just played a few notes, they'd make people in the audience happy, and then they could move on and never have to think about them again.

Do you think the *Unplugged* taping was Gene and Paul's way of feeling out Ace and Peter, to see if they would be able to work together again?
I think that plays a part on the periphery. My opinion about the *MTV Unplugged* thing is more that it was about Gene and Paul wanting to have KISS be respected, in the same manner that so many other bands that had been a part of that series had been. I mean, Aerosmith had done one by that point. It was a franchise, and they believed KISS needed to be represented— regardless of the lineup, regardless of Peter and Ace coming back into the picture. But that added value. That was obviously a major selling point for getting MTV interested in KISS—which they hadn't been for many years.

How do you think KISS's performance compares to other artists' *Unplugged* sets?
Well, commercially, not so much—even with the reunion and looking back in hindsight, I think KISS being measured by a different set of criteria to so many of the other acts makes it very difficult to compare apples and oranges. For KISS fans, it's very positive—it kind of kept the party line that KISS songs were written on acoustic guitars, and should sound good unplugged. So in that sense, like the other bands that had done *Unplugged* sessions, the material worked.

But look at Clapton's—he sold twenty-six million copies and won Grammys for his *Unplugged*. Page and Plant, they came in and did a half-reunion of Led Zeppelin, performed four new songs, and reworked a lot of their catalogue into a completely different format. Aerosmith managed to strike a balance between their pre- and post-MTV eras, and did some bluesy covers and did somewhat obscure songs. And then, of course, Nirvana, who for me are my personal favorite *Unplugged* session—because they went in there, they did an insane set that very much didn't focus on the most popular set, put the Meat Puppets up onstage, recorded it in one take, and walked off, basically. So, how does KISS compare? KISS is compared by being represented. You don't compare KISS—*KISS is KISS.*

Which songs from *Kiss Unplugged* were your favorites?

I'm a bit of a Paul Stanley fan, so this won't come as too much of a surprise— 'Sure Know Something,' 'I Still Love You,' and 'Every Time I Look At You.' Those are the three songs—particularly the latter two—that just blew me away, with Paul's absolutely stunning vocals. This is the tail end of what was his real powerhouse period as a vocalist—'94 through the end of '95. They had just been on fire.

Paul's voice was powerful, and the emotion and passion that he put into those songs was absolutely stunning. I can still get shivers whenever I listen to those versions. But let's not take away from Gene—Gene is rock solid on bass on those particular songs, as well. Eric Singer's harmonies are perfection. These songs were taken to the next level, but Paul still had that power to inject, and maybe a little frustration in his mind that the songs had never been given their due back in the day with the public.

Are there any songs that you think should have been included but were not?

'Let Me Know' is a personal favorite that I think tells a story—it was a missed opportunity to tell that story of Gene and Paul meeting for the first time, and that being an introduction for the song, to say how he came to Stephen Coronel's house, and met Gene for the first time, was asked if he wrote music, and played the song, [which] was then known as 'Sunday Driver.' That would have been a great intro and a great acoustic song to play. 'Forever' was a big hit but was not on there. And for me, again, my personal tastes, 'Love Her All I Can'—just a really kind of happy pop song, translated onto the guitar, is one I sit around playing on my acoustic all the time.

Watching the raw footage of the taping, there were a lot of restarts and do-overs. Is this normal for *MTV Unplugged* tapings?

Yes and no. There is no 'normal' for *Unplugged* tapings, from what I've seen. There are bands that just go in there and go through it one take, are happy to leave in a guitar flub or a lyric error. A band like Nirvana, as I mentioned, did their set in one take. Oasis went in and did theirs *without their singer!* There is no right or wrong. What I think is the key thing to keep in mind for KISS is that they simply did what they felt was right for them, the songs that they were performing. And I'm not surprised they did multiple takes for theirs, because, in some ways, they've always had to prove more about the validity of their music than other acts have—just because of the ball and chain that is the makeup era.

In your estimation, how important was *Unplugged* to the eventual reunion of the original lineup?

Very—in that they pulled it off. They were able to pull both Peter and Ace into rehearsals prior to the actual taping. I know they did several days—Gene, Paul, Eric, and Bruce brought in Ace and Peter, just to work on those songs. So they did a lot of work. It was maybe that first taste of a reunion, to judge what the reaction would be. It was also just to see if they could make it through rehearsing three songs or so, and see if they would be able to get through there was a new challenge.

There had been acoustic sets done for radio and little songs here and there prior—Peter and Ace had done an acoustic section during their tour [1995's Bad Boys Tour, which saw Ace and Peter hit the road together with their solo bands]. But to see if it could all work was a very important thing—to see if the personalities could be in the same room, and under duress. But as far as the reunion, this is all just about it being a bandwagon thing that was the culmination of the band was touring that year.

Do you think that KISS's *Unplugged* proved once and for all that their material could stand on its own, and that they didn't necessarily need an extravagant stage show?

Yeah. It was a passive-aggressive middle finger to a certain extent, because it was them going back and playing the music simply and saying, *There is no show here. There is no electric. There is no smoke bombs.* Admittedly, it wasn't *totally* unplugged, and it did have orchestral support. But hopefully it did surprise some with how well the songs did work acoustically. In some ways, it's confused—'Every Time I Look At You' is lush with orchestra and almost precious, while 'Plaster Caster' and 'Goin' Blind' are quirky with irreverence. But forget the critics—ultimately, the way I judge this album is [the] guaranteed smile I have on my face every time I listen to it or watch it.

Were you disappointed when it was announced that the Kulick/Singer lineup was ending, so that the reunion could happen?

I was *disgusted*. I thought it was the death knell for the band. I thought a reunion would be a great idea if they had just left it to one tour, and essentially tell Bruce and Eric to go off and do their thing for a year, then put in a highly focused tour—like they did with the first leg, that went from June '96 through July '97. That would have been great for me. That would have been enough … and after that, just let it go. Because I thought it would kill the band's creativity. I thought it would kill the band's forward momentum, and it would always then be about the past, and that they would never get out of the makeup again. *And that's kind of what's happened.*

GIMME MORE: ON-CAMERA INTERVIEWS

There was no tour in support of *Kiss Unplugged*, so, in its place, how about a guide to some of KISS's standout on-camera interviews from the non-makeup era? While it's darn near impossible to chronicle all of them (it seems like every so often, another rarely seen vintage interview is discovered and uploaded to YouTube), here is a list of some of the better ones that aired in the US, and what you can expect from each. (And kindly note, KISS's 'unmasking' on MTV is discussed at length earlier in the book.)

FRIDAY NIGHT VIDEOS (NBC, 1983) featuring Gene Simmons and Paul Stanley

A standard Q&A about taking off the makeup interspersed with makeup-era footage and the 'Lick It Up' video clip … complete with both interviewees displaying their hairy chests. Paul offers the memorable quote, 'All KISS is trying to say is, *You're only going to live once, so you'd better make the most of it.*'

NIGHT FLIGHT (USA, 1984) featuring Gene Simmons

The most memorable bit here is when Gene offers to challenge any rock band to a 'battle of the bands' with KISS. When veteran journalist Lisa Robinson pronounces Van Halen as being the biggest band at the moment, Gene boldly declares, 'Anytime, boys!' Now *that* would have been quite a double bill, folks.

RAW FOOTAGE FROM NIGHT FLIGHT (USA, 1984) featuring Paul Stanley

Paul describes the meaning behind the *Animalize* album title, the things the band knows the most about (spoiler alert: 'living well and women'), and how KISS 'sweat their butts off trying to do the best show we can'—and even acts like a total pro when the goofy camera people have to restart the interview after a few minutes, due to a technical flub. While the mistake is being ironed out, Paul tells the interviewer, 'I'm going to listen to Billy's album on the way out.' This leads one to wonder, which Billy is he referring to? Joel? Idol? Squier? Crystal?

MTV INTERVIEW (MTV, 1985) featuring Paul Stanley

Here, Paul is interviewed by one of the original MTV VJs, Martha Quinn, to promote the just-released *Asylum*, during a stop-in one afternoon. Topics discussed include the new album, the song 'Uh! All Night,' and the fact that the 'Tears Are Falling' video features what was then cutting-edge technology, having been filmed in black-and-white, with color added in afterward.

NIGHT FLIGHT (USA, 1985) featuring Gene Simmons

Gene chats again with Lisa Robinson and explains that KISS started doing what they do for two reasons ('fun' and 'girls'), and discusses why they decided to take off the makeup, as well as dating Cher and Diana Ross. He also states that he doesn't think he will ever settle down or have children—don't tell Shannon, Nick, or Sophie!

ENTERTAINMENT TONIGHT (CBS, 1985)
featuring Gene Simmons and Paul Stanley

In this news report on the *Asylum* tour's opening night, which features one of the only bits of pro-shot concert footage that exists from the period (a snippet of 'Detroit Rock City'), Paul jokingly says that the reason for their flamboyant costumes is to stop confusion between KISS and Willie Nelson and Waylon Jennings, while Gene says 'caring' is the main thing that keeps KISS current.

THE DR. RUTH SHOW (Lifetime, 1985) featuring Gene Simmons

Since Gene has bragged about having had sexual relations with nearly five thousand women over the years (the number tends to fluctuate), his appearance on *The Dr. Ruth Show*, hosted by diminutive German-American sex therapist Ruth Westheimer, certainly makes sense. Surprisingly, Gene comes off as quite down-to-earth, and even likable, discussing KISS, the upcoming film *Never Too Young To Die*, and, of course, groupies. He also states once more that he will probably never get married, and doubts whether he will ever have children. And, truth be told, of all the wigs that Gene sported post-1983, the one he wears here is one of the better-looking of them, since it looks most similar to his hair during the 70s.

RADIO 1990 (USA, 1985) featuring Eric Carr

Possibly the first time Eric got to be interviewed on US TV all by himself was during a weeklong stint co-hosting *Radio 1990* with the show's usual VJ, Kathryn Kinley. Unlike Gene and Paul, who seemed to put on a bit of an act during their interviews from the era, Eric comes off as a quite matter-of-fact chap. He recounts how he joined the band and lists some of his favorite heavy-metal bands at the time, which, if you don't mind the surprise being spoiled, include Led Zeppelin—'my favorite band, period'—as well as Scorpions, Helix, AC/DC, Hanoi Rocks, and Accept.

HEAVY METAL MANIA (MTV, 1985) featuring Paul Stanley

The short-lived *Heavy Metal Mania* was a precursor to *Headbangers Ball* that aired monthly (rather than weekly) and was usually hosted by Twisted Sister's Dee Snider. For this episode, however, Paul Stanley served as host instead, and the results were not far off from the vibe of the later *Exposed* home video: a party atmosphere inside what is supposedly Paul's home, with lots of females and a few stabs at comedy sketches (including one bit that Mitch Weissman recounts elsewhere in this book).

Guest VJ (MTV, 1985) featuring Paul Stanley

Here, Paul dons a Santa jacket and shows off some snazzy gift ideas for the holiday season (including a cutting-edge 'waterproof Walkman') with the help of 'Santa's helpers,' Sharon and Lydia. Intriguingly, besides KISS, not much in the way of hard rock or metal videos were shown, with the focus instead on acts like Power Station, Art Of Noise, and Marillion.

RADIO 1990 (USA, 1986) featuring Gene Simmons

In another discussion with Lisa Robinson, taking place this time in what appears to be a recording studio, Gene talks about his roles in *Runaway* (which he admits is not a very good movie, but adds that he is 'OK' in it) and the upcoming *Never Too Young To Die*. He even offers a bit of a dis on poor Dudley Moore—'I would probably not do a Dudley Moore-ish [role], you know, *The little wimp with the world against him*, it just doesn't appeal to me'—before the music video for 'Uh! All Night' is shown.

GOOD MORNING AMERICA (ABC, 1986) featuring Gene Simmons

Gene appears via satellite to discuss the film *Trick Or Treat*. During the chat, he explains why he chose to take the role of Nuke The DJ (we learn that he was originally offered the role of rock star Sammi Curr but turned it down), and talks about the rebelliousness and positive influence of rock'n'roll.

NIGHTLIFE (syndicated, 1987) featuring Gene Simmons

Gene models a decidedly 80s look (shorter hair, blazer, black leather pants, snakeskin cowboy boots) for this interview by the comedian David Brenner on his short-lived talk show. Highlights include a discussion of what Gene would have looked like if he had become a rabbi, (once again) why KISS took the makeup off, and replicating the look that supposedly scored him the role of Dr. Charles Luther in *Runaway*. There's also a preview of Gene as Malak Al Rahim in *Wanted: Dead Or Alive*. And, at the end, Brenner even admits to Gene, 'I've always enjoyed you.'

GUEST VJ (MTV, 1987) featuring Gene Simmons and Paul Stanley

Despite not having any new releases to promote, Gene and Paul pop up here (along with some female friends) for a nighttime guest-VJ gig on what appears to be Paul's birthday. They play several sneak-preview clips from the *Exposed* VHS release, which at the time was still several months away from hitting the shops.

Unlike the last time Paul served as a guest VJ, this time quite a few rockin' videos are shown (besides KISS), including clips by David Lee Roth, Van Hagar, and Bon Jovi. Then, after a Heart vid is shown, it is announced, possibly for the first time, that Ron Nevison would be producing the next KISS studio album.

RAW FOOTAGE FROM THE 'CRAZY CRAZY NIGHTS' VIDEO SHOOT (1987)
featuring Gene Simmons and Paul Stanley

If memory serves correctly, this footage first aired during an MTV News piece, or possibly on *Entertainment Tonight*. Regardless, while there's nothing too out of the ordinary in this chat with Gene and Paul, what *does* make this clip a must-see is the two-minute segment of interviews with members of the audience outside the venue at the video shoot. Were it a little longer, this segment could have served as a worthy follow-up to the cult classic *Heavy Metal Parking Lot*.

TOP OF THE POPS (CBS, 1987) featuring Gene Simmons, Paul Stanley,
Bruce Kulick, and Eric Carr

For the short-lived US version of *Top Of The Pops* (not to be confused with the long-running show of the same name over in England), pop and rock artists performed their latest single, with singer/actress Nia Peeples serving as the show's host. On this particular episode, not only do KISS perform 'Crazy Crazy Nights' (perhaps 'perform' isn't very accurate, as it sounds as if they are miming to the studio recording, while Paul's vocals are either live or re-recorded to make it *sound* live), they also appear in a show-opening skit in which Paul keeps opening up the wrong dressing-room door.

GERALDO (CBS, 1988) featuring Gene Simmons and Paul Stanley

This episode of *Geraldo*—the long-running talk show hosted by the heavily-mustachioed Geraldo Rivera—is entitled 'Sex On The Road,' and Gene and Paul are joined for a chat on the subject by none other than … Willie Nelson! Standout bits include Gene declaring, 'Women seem to be attracted more to guys onstage who wear more makeup than they do,' which certainly seemed true in the glam-metal era; Paul pulling a prank by saying he brought along a photo from Gene's infamous 'Polaroid collection,' only to then pull out a cutout of a dog; and Gene paying tribute to Geraldo by putting on a faux-mustache.

Other highlights include an audience member saying that Gene and Paul aren't very good-looking, and Geraldo at one point offering the suggestion that KISS should put out 'KISS condoms' … something that they would in fact eventually do. Unlike most other interviews that feature both Gene and Paul, Gene speaks far more than Paul this time around. (Most of the times the duo would appear on talk shows, they would split the chat time about 50/50 … mirroring their songwriting credit ratio on most KISS albums during the non-makeup era!)

THE OPRAH WINFREY SHOW (CBS, 1988)
featuring Gene Simmons and Paul Stanley

Here, Gene and Paul are joined on the show by renowned groupie Pamela Des Barres and author Jackie Collins to discuss the expected topics of rock'n'roll, sex, and groupies. While Paul looks as expected for the era, Gene has a different short-yet-shaggy hairstyle and a black leather trench coat, and whoever applied his makeup went *way* overboard with the rouge on his cheeks.

One highlight is Gene stating that the idea of marriage is out of the question when spending the night with a groupie—but that it is a chance to 'scale the heights of Mount Olympus'—to which Des Barres retorts that she *did* actually seek marriage when having relationships with rockers. Gene also discusses his Polaroid collection, mentioning that he has slept with over two thousand women, which draws gasps from the audience. Then, after an audience member explains the difference between 'women' and 'sluts,' Paul satisfies a fan's request for a simple 'peck on the cheek and a handshake' (although it appears as though the handshake is replaced with a hug). As an added bonus, it's an absolute hoot viewing all the vintage 80s hairdos (or *hairdon'ts*) in the audience.

THE DECLINE OF WESTERN CIVILIZATION PART II: THE METAL YEARS
(New Line Cinema, 1988) featuring Gene Simmons and Paul Stanley

The first *Decline Of Western Civilization* film, which chronicled the LA punk scene of the late 70s and early 80s, was outstanding and realistic. *Part II?* Not so much. Focusing on the metal scene of the mid-to-late 80s, it contains plenty of Spinal Tap–like moments—tops being W.A.S.P. guitarist Chris Holmes's notorious interview in a pool, while guzzling vodka (truth be told, he doesn't really *guzzle* it but rather pours it all over his face) in the presence of his mother.

Scattered throughout the film are interview bits with Gene (inside a lingerie store) and Paul (laying down on a bed, surrounded by scantily-clad females). Since both of the chaps' interviews are more about image than substance, not much new is to be learned here, I'm afraid. Also featured are interviews with fellow rockers including Ozzy Osbourne, Alice Cooper, Steven Tyler and Joe Perry, Lemmy Kilmister, and Dave Mustaine, among others.

THE LATE SHOW (Fox, 1988) featuring Gene Simmons and Paul Stanley

After the failure of *The Late Show Starring Joan Rivers*, whose host left the show in 1987, the Fox Network opted to keep *The Late Show* going with several different hosts, the best-known of them probably being Arsenio Hall, who went on to host his own popular show, *The Arsenio Hall Show*, for another network. But the show was also hosted for a spell by a bloke by the name of Ross Shafer, who welcomed Gene and Paul for an appearance.

Instead of appearing together, Gene comes out first on his own (with former Major League Baseball umpire Ron Luciano also on the couch), and Shafer for some strange reason makes the claim that Gene rarely makes TV appearances. (The fact that we are already several pages deep into this section makes that claim an utter fallacy.) When Paul finally appears (with his hair slicked back and in a ponytail), the interview resumes, the main topic being the thing that every single KISS-related interview seemed to focus on during this era: carnal knowledge. So it makes perfect sense when, halfway through, sex therapist Dr. Joyce Brothers joins the discussion!

However, the most interesting part of the interview comes when Ross fields some questions from the audience, including one from a fan who inquires about how they create their concert setlists, and suggests they consider adding more tunes from *Dynasty* and *The Elder*. I wholeheartedly agree, good sir!

MOUTH TO MOUTH (MTV, 1988) featuring Gene Simmons

Mouth To Mouth was a short-lived, live nighttime talk show on MTV (back in the era when it was actually *not common* for there to be non-music content on the channel), hosted by Steve Skrovan, a standup comic who would go on to write for such popular TV comedy shows as *Seinfeld* and *Everybody Loves Raymond*. During the interview segment, Skrovan points out that Gene's ex-girlfriend, Cher, was on the show the night before, and that in a recent *Playboy* interview she described Gene as 'square and very Jewish, which doesn't seem to jive with your stage persona.'

Another standout moment comes when Gene is asked to name all of KISS's albums up to that point in chronological order, and almost pulls it off … but skips over *Destroyer* (the audience applauds afterward as if he has actually pulled off this feat successfully). To Gene's credit, although he has been criticized by some for his lyrical depiction of women in certain songs and his bragging about the number of women he has slept with, he does state in this interview, after an image of a slightly overweight female is shown, 'I think women of all sizes, all shapes are wonderful, and I will worship at their feet—because I think all women deserve it.'

Interestingly, he also mentions that 'in maybe January or February, I'll sit down and start writing my memoirs—whatever I can remember.' In the end, Gene's memoir, *KISS And Make-Up*, would not actually hit bookstores until December 2001.

MOUTH TO MOUTH (MTV, 1988) featuring Paul Stanley

Just a month after Gene's appearance on the show, Paul followed suit in December of '88, to promote the *Smashes, Thrashes & Hits* compilation. He explains that the meaning of 'Let's Put The X In Sex'—whose video had its 'world premiere' on this program—is that 'we should keep the mystery in sex,' and that '(You Make Me) Rock Hard' is about 'aerobic exercise.' Echoing Gene's pro-female sentiment a month earlier, he then states, while discussing the 'X In Sex' clip, 'We respect women—we like them to be seen, also.'

Other standouts include Paul applying his famous Starchild makeup design on the host's face, discussion of a recent unpleasant experience at a Four Seasons Hotel in Vancouver, and some not too flattering thoughts about new metal music ('I think it's real great to hear bands where I can play the songs when I don't even know them … I think it's great to hear bands that are *familiar*'). But the undoubted highlight of the entire episode comes when Paul straps on a Steinberger guitar and does a one-man rendition of 'Rock And Roll All Nite' (a song usually sung by Gene).

HARD 'N' HEAVY VOLUME 3 (Picture Music International, 1989)
featuring Gene Simmons

Hard 'N' Heavy was a VHS series that compiled metal videos, interviews, and animation, and Gene is featured in its third volume. The lighting of the interview is noteworthy, since it is unlike the look of most other interviews at the time: a single light shines on Gene's face in an otherwise darkened room. And since there is no threat of being censored, Gene gets to fully speak his mind, offering quite a humdinger of a quote concerning why he strapped on a guitar in the first place: 'I physically wanted to fuck myself to death.' One interesting observation concerning KISS interviews from the 80s compared to, say, the early twenty-first century, is that the topic of sex is almost always discussed in the earlier era, whereas merchandising and money are almost always discussed in the later era.

HIT PARADER'S HEAVY METAL MELTDOWN (WWOR, 1989)
featuring Gene Simmons

A TV version of the then-thriving metal magazine *Hit Parader* was akin to *Headbangers Ball* and *Hard 'N' Heavy*: a mix of interviews, videos, performances, and more (hosted by a gent named Erik Palladino). In the show's first episode, Gene takes us on a guided tour of his 'LA digs'—really, just one room (seemingly his game room), which includes multiple gold and platinum records hanging on the walls, a fan-made belt comprised of various skulls, and a vintage KISS pinball machine. The first signings to Simmons Records, Silent Rage, are spotted playing pool.

GUEST HOST (MTV, 1989) featuring Eric Carr and Paul Stanley

Instead of the usual 'guest VJ' stint (where an artist spins videos for an hour at night), Eric and Paul served as guest hosts for MTV for an afternoon in 1989. During the segment, you'll spot Paul introducing the Red Hot Chili Peppers' clip for 'Higher Ground' (which serves as a bit of foreshadowing of the alt-rock movement that would soon usurp hair metal), the two of them discussing the 'Hide Your Heart' clip (Eric recalls how strange it was to work with helicopters buzzing overhead), and the impending world premiere of Aerosmith's 'Janie's Got A Gun' video.

HARD 'N' HEAVY VOLUME 4 (Picture Music International, 1989)
featuring Gene Simmons

Gene was seemingly quite popular with the higher-ups at the *Hard 'N' Heavy* franchise, as he was asked to return for volume 4, accompanied by two young ladies dressed in S&M gear. This time, he takes part in a 'Trick Or Treat' segment, in which a renowned rocker picks artifacts relating to their history from a bag and discusses each one. Some of the themes covered include the *Alive!* album, KISS comic books, and a baby T-shirt printed with the words 'My Daddy' alongside Gene's face in makeup. (He says this is his son's, which makes sense, as Nicholas Simmons was born in 1989.) And then, at the end of the segment, a surprise guest briefly appears … Paul Stanley!

HARD 'N' HEAVY VOLUME 6 (Picture Music International, 1989)
featuring Paul Stanley

Paul is interviewed—in makeup—on the set of the 'Rise To It' video, and talks about how the band wanted to get back to their roots on *Hot In The Shade*, how 'you're a real wimp if you think that only wimps get involved in relationships, or only wimps show their feelings,' and how most love triangles have dangerous endings.

Clips from the actual 'Rise To It' video are shown, too, including the opening scene, in which Gene and Paul are applying their makeup … and, interestingly, it appears from this that Gene has on a full face of makeup *before* applying the white paint and trademark batwing design!

RAW FOOTAGE FROM MTV NEWS INTERVIEW (MTV, 1992)
featuring Paul Stanley and Eric Singer

During rehearsals for the *Revenge* tour, Paul and Eric speak to MTV for a music news segment, which includes talk of the upcoming tour and what to expect from the setlist, both members noting how excited they are, and the answer to the question, 'What draws kids in 1992 to come see this band?'

Paul's response: 'Some people come out of curiosity, some people have caught on to the band in the last couple of years, some of them come because they've been coming since the beginning, and other ones come to see if we live up to what we're supposed to be.'

Paul also talks about the current state of the KISS Army and how popular KISS fanzines are (adding that they're not a 'merchandising ploy'), how rock concerts have hit a recession business-wise, and whether any KISS members have ever been injured by an onstage mishap (Metallica's James Hetfield having recently injured himself in a pyro stunt gone wrong).

HEADBANGERS BALL (MTV, 1993)
featuring Gene Simmons and Paul Stanley

Gene and Paul appear on MTV's weekly all-metal show, hosted by Riki Rachtman, to promote *Alive III*, and are asked point blank if the original lineup will get back together. If that was to happen, Gene replies, 'Then what's the difference between us and a Vegas show?'

NEWS INTERVIEW (WWOR, 1993)
featuring Gene Simmons and Paul Stanley

WWOR is a local TV channel for the New York City area, broadcast from Secaucus, New Jersey, that is probably best known for airing New York Mets games for decades and giving Howard Stern his first regular TV show (*The Howard Stern Show*). And of course for the time in 1993 when news anchorwoman Heidi Kempf took a stroll around New York City with Paul and Gene, 'retracing KISS's roots.'

Truth be told, they really visit only *two* spots connected to KISStory: a street corner where Gene and Paul used to sing on back in their Wicked Lester days, and the loft where KISS used to rehearse on 23rd Street (which, at the time of this interview, looks to have become some sort of kitchen connected to a restaurant).

While the segment itself was a good idea, plenty more locations could have easily been visited—for example, the spot where the *Dressed To Kill* album cover was shot (the corner of 23rd Street and 8th Avenue), Electric Lady Recording Studios (where KISS's original demo and such albums as *Dressed To*

Kill, *Destroyer*, and *Asylum* were all recorded), Madison Square Garden (where KISS have headlined many times over the years), and so on.

THE ARSENIO HALL SHOW (syndicated, 1993)
featuring Gene Simmons, Paul Stanley, Bruce Kulick, and Eric Singer

While *The Arsenio Hall Show* was not exactly known for featuring a plethora of hard-rock performers, there were some notable exceptions, such as an episode aired on May 20, 1993, when KISS performed two classic tunes ('Detroit Rock City' and 'Deuce') and sat down for a chat with the host. To the best of my knowledge, this was one of the first times that Bruce was not only present for a TV Q&A with the band but actually spoke (and, in a classy move, made a point of also including new member Eric in the chat).

Other topics covered include why they took the makeup off in '83 (Gene's response being more honest this time than they had been during the ten years prior: 'I think we had to do it. By the beginning of the 80s, we had gone through every area that we could have gone to. The thing had just run its course. You just had to move on or become a caricature.'), the fact that KISS were supposedly going to be offered the keys to Los Angeles (something the city later rescinded), the time Gene's hair caught fire, and the passing of Eric Carr.

THE HOWARD STERN INTERVIEW (E!, 1993)
featuring Gene Simmons and Paul Stanley

Although best known as a radio personality, Howard Stern has hosted several different TV shows over the years, including *The Howard Stern Interview*, which aired from 1992 to 1993. Here, guests Gene and Paul discuss a variety of topics, the first order of business being to clear the air between Stern and the KISS duo.

The point of contention is a comment Stern made on his radio show about Eric Carr that Gene took the wrong way, resulting in Gene reportedly threatening Howard via his producer, Gary 'Baba Booey' Dell'Abate. (Here, Gene says he threatened to 'publicly thrash' Howard, but later in the interview says, 'I was going to beat the piss out of you.')

Once they move past that subject, we see a brief clip of people on the street singing their favorite KISS songs, followed by discussions about whether the members of KISS worship the devil, the money they've earned, Gene's relationship with Cher, and *Alive III*, plus the inspection of a few samples of vintage merchandise.

HEADBANGERS BALL (MTV, 1993)
featuring Gene Simmons, Paul Stanley, Bruce Kulick, and Eric Singer

This segment was shot on location at the Foundations Forum in Burbank, California, where KISS were performing to around a thousand people on September 11, 1993, with the promise that they were going to play tunes from the first four records only. (This proved not to be entirely true, as 'Makin' Love,' from studio album #5, was also included in the set.)

The live excerpts show how great KISS were sounding live at this stage. The show's host, Riki Rachtman, then interviews first Gene and Paul, followed by Bruce and Eric, in what seems to be a hotel room. Gene and Paul discuss bootlegs, why they chose to play the Foundations Forum, and the importance of soundchecking. Bruce and Eric talk about the forthcoming *Kiss My Ass* tribute record and what to expect from it—probably one of the first times the release was discussed on TV—before mentioning working on demos for the next KISS studio album, which would have been *Carnival Of Souls*.

RAW FOOTAGE FROM DICK CLARK'S NEW YEAR'S ROCKIN' EVE (ABC, 1993)
featuring Gene Simmons and Paul Stanley

KISS appeared on Dick Clark's annual show, performing the tune 'Makin' Love' to mark the year's end (not broadcast live but taped a few weeks before). But what makes this raw footage interesting is that it captures what appears to be an actual honest-to-goodness verbal confrontation between Gene and Paul.

After Paul scoffs at a few of Gene's comments, Gene tells the cameraman to 'cut this off for a second,' then proceeds to say, to Paul, 'Would you stop cutting me down in front of the camera? I don't go for that shit. It's like, whatever I say, all of a sudden, *Don't listen to this idiot*. Don't do that anymore.' Paul's response? Not even looking in Gene's direction, he simply tells the interviewer to 'go on.'

Also of note is that while many of Paul's interviews in the 80s seem to show him hamming it up in his 'rock star' persona, here he is extremely down-to-earth, especially when he says, 'You can always make up stories or tell things about women, and rock'n'roll, and partying, but I think the best thing and the biggest thing and best gift we've ever gotten is twenty years of doing what we do.'

RAW FOOTAGE FROM THE KISS CONVENTION IN TROY, MICHIGAN (1994)
featuring Gene Simmons and Paul Stanley

On July 17, 1994, a KISS Convention was being held in Troy, Michigan, when all of a sudden, two unexpected guests arrived … Gene and Paul! However, they weren't just there to pop in and say howdy to the fans—they arrived with police in tow, and promptly reclaimed costumes that they said had been stolen from then over the years.

A fan happened to be on site with a video camera, filming the items on display, when suddenly, Gene and Paul emerged and started gathering all the items. The fans started shouting questions at the surprise duo, who eventually give in and conduct a spur-of-the-moment Q&A, answering questions about how much of *Alive!* and *Alive II* were recorded live, how close Anton Fig came to joining KISS, and, 'What's your son's name?'

HARD COPY (syndicated, 1995)
featuring Gene Simmons, Paul Stanley, and Eric Singer

Hard Copy was a tabloid news show that ran from 1989 to 1999, and which on February 22, 1995, decided to run a piece on KISS, in a segment discussing, per the show's intro, 'Rock'n'roll groupies—what really goes on backstage.' However, despite promising to 'expose the real world of sex, drugs, and rock'n'roll,' all they do is show the women backstage at a show in Melbourne, Australia, who are trying out to appear onstage with the band during 'Take It Off.' And (gasp!) one of the dancers at one point stands next to Eric Singer, as he warms up on a practice drum pad before the show. Nothing shocking or scandalous here, I'm afraid.

GIMME MORE: MARTIN POPOFF ASSESSES KISS'S KOMPETITION

The author of such books as *The Top 500 Heavy Metal Albums Of All Time* and *The Top 500 Heavy Metal Songs Of All Time* discusses the notable hard-rock/heavy-metal releases issued during KISS's non-makeup era, showing how the competition stacked up, year-by-year ... and how much rock/metal changed over this thirteen-year period.

1983: Def Leppard—*Pyromania*, Quiet Riot—*Metal Health*, Mötley Crüe—*Shout At The Devil*

I think KISS's *Lick It Up* relates the most to the phenomenon of Mötley Crüe, and also, the meteoric rise of Quiet Riot. And I think *Lick It Up* is almost a cross between those two records—*Shout At The Devil* and *Metal Health*. But, really, Mötley Crüe are important because they are the second coming of KISS. They're like the new generation of KISS, in look and everything—a little bit of makeup and some leather.

It's this new kind of American party-metal, and this is the first year for it, after the big switchover from the New Wave Of British Heavy Metal to things really taking off in California. And *Lick It Up* is a very California-feeling record, even though they are a New York band. But there is a lot of the anthemic Mötley Crüe on it, there's a lot of the anthemic Quiet Riot on it, and Def Leppard's *Pyromania* is another anthemic album. There are a lot of songs about 'rocking' on all these records, and KISS were like that as well, at this time.

1984: Van Halen—*1984*, Twisted Sister—*Stay Hungry*, Scorpions—*Love At First Sting*

What we have in 1984 is hair metal *really* taking off, and then you have 'previous-generation' bands starting to do well—and KISS are one of those, as well as Van Halen, and another previous-generation band, Scorpions, who are even older than KISS. But what you have is a simplified, dumbing-down of a sound that Scorpions are doing. I always considered *Love At First Sting* to be 'Scorpions' first KISS album.'

And the Van Halen album ... I don't know if it's that directly relatable, other than it's almost like a metaphor for the fact that this isn't just a young person's game—even bands from a previous generation can do great. And Van Halen *are* doing great—they're almost having a second life, after three albums that were a little bit obscure and underground [1980's *Women And Children First*, 1981's *Fair Warning*, and 1982's *Diver Down*]. Now, all of a sudden, they're *meteoric*. They do bring keyboards in, but they bring them in in an obscure way—it's not the way we think of keyboards in later hair metal, for example, but it's still a very Led Zeppelin–esque, strange keyboard style.

And the Twisted Sister album is interesting, because you have another band—like Mötley Crüe—that are like the second coming of KISS. They're a makeup and garish clothes band—just like KISS. And they even have a little bit of that Alice Cooper element that KISS also have, and they also happen to be from New York. So you get the first hair-metal band from New York, essentially—you've got somebody to keep KISS company, I suppose. The Scorpions record and the Twisted Sister record are essentially KISS records … and KISS are making a KISS record at the same time.

1985: Mötley Crüe—*Theatre Of Pain*,
Ratt—*Invasion Of Your Privacy*, Dokken—*Under Lock And Key*

What you have in 1985 is almost an early 'mature' period for hair metal, and with that you get a little bit of a lull—a little bit of a malaise. I mean, Ratt's album is arguably as good as the first one [1984's *Out Of The Cellar*], but it is a little bit bloated compared to the first one. So they're already sounding and feeling a little bit mature.

Mötley Crüe put out their third record, and it definitely is feeling some bloat—some tiredness and malaise. Some maturity, but not *positive* maturity—it's more like *old age*, all of a sudden. And they're not making a great album.

Dokken are doing the same thing—Dokken came out with an exciting debut album [*Breaking The Chains*, first issued in Europe in 1981, then in the 1983 in the USA], they came out with almost the quintessential Dokken album with their second album, *Tooth and Nail*, and now they are showing some corporate bloat, as well. So the parallel there is, KISS, on *Asylum*, are also feeling a little bit of *bloat*.

1986: Metallica—*Master Of Puppets*, David Lee Roth—*Eat 'Em & Smile*, Bon Jovi—*Slippery When Wet*

In 1986, you have hair metal going great guns. Bon Jovi are ascending to the top *so* fast. You've already got the fracture of Van Halen, and basically, David Lee Roth starts a 'Van Halen on steroids' band—a solo band that sounds more or less like Van Halen … like super-fireworks-y Van Halen. His costumes now look as much like KISS's as anybody's. I mean, they're basically a cross between Twisted Sister and KISS costumes at this point. Musically, there's not a lot that relates to KISS, except KISS are trying to be flashy at times during this period.

With Bon Jovi, you get another East Coast band, which is kind of neat—so you've got Bon Jovi being big, Twisted Sister being big, KISS being relatively big. And what you also get is the first curls of dissatisfaction and annoyance with hair metal, in the rise of Metallica. So thrash is actually at a pretty mature stage itself, with the third Metallica album being great, and Anthrax doing well, and Exodus finally being out there. Some of the kids on the cutting edge are starting to stray and get excited about this new metal, thrash. And in many polls—polls for my books, even—*Master Of Puppets* wins the 'greatest heavy-metal album of all-time.' You've got a band taking over—not taking over the same way as a massive hair band would take over, but really taking over in the creative and excitement sweepstakes.

1987: Whitesnake—*Whitesnake*, Def Leppard—*Hysteria*, Guns N' Roses—*Appetite For Destruction*

In 1987, you get Guns N' Roses coming onto the scene, but they don't make a lot of waves in 1987—it's kind of a slowly gestating album. But you get the rise of what I often call 'dirty-hair metal.' That album is going to spawn a lot of dirty-hair metal to come, but in 1987, they're kind of the first, where people are saying, 'This is getting ridiculous. Bon Jovi looks ridiculous, KISS looks ridiculous. Poison, Cinderella … *whatever*. It's time to clean the slate, and come up with something dangerous again.' But Guns N' Roses aren't *that* dangerous—they're actually just a little to the left of hair metal. *Metallica* are dangerous at this time—not so much Guns N' Roses.

Whitesnake are another anomaly—it just proves that old Englishmen and journeymen can get together and cash in on the hair metal sweepstakes. So they're doing great. A lot of these old-guard bands are looking around, and seeing a lot of records go diamond—ten-million copies sold—and five, six, seven-times platinum by young bands or bands that are very improbable. Whitesnake are not a young band, but they're very improbable. And Def Leppard finally come up with this comically long-awaited follow-up to *Pyromania*. I hate the record—I think it's terrible. But it does amazingly well. And it has all these hits. It's very synthetic, and there are fake harmonies and fake drums, and a lot of layers to it.

There are various ways bands are taking off, and they're pursuing formulas that KISS are not pursuing. I've done books on Scorpions and Judas Priest, and I've definitely seen a lot of sort of second-guessing and complaining, like, *How come these young whippersnappers with no track record are doing amazing, and we're not?* But KISS are still in there, doing OK, and an interesting artist that is a parallel at this time is Alice Cooper. Alice Cooper is with the same kind of act, same kind of records—being pretty heavy—and is having a slight career renaissance … although I don't think he even went gold with his first two comeback albums, *Constrictor* (1986) and *Raise Your Fist And Yell* (1987).

1988: Iron Maiden—*Seventh Son Of A Seventh Son,* Queensrÿche—*Operation: Mindcrime,* Poison—*Open Up And Say … Ahh!*

In 1988, Iron Maiden are still around, although I don't know if *Seventh Son* is all that important an album in Iron Maiden's trajectory. It eventually goes gold, but Iron Maiden are another band that just feels stalled, and they feel like an anachronism at this time. They don't go hair metal, but they're watching all these hair-metal bands do great. Iron Maiden are actually on a decline, really, with *Somewhere In Time* (1986) and *Seventh Son*.

Seventh Son is a concept album, and, oddly enough, Bruce Dickinson compares it to Queensrÿche's concept album, *Operation: Mindcrime*. Queensrÿche got some kudos for a concept album at this time, but Queensrÿche are an anachronism as well—they're just kind of like a progressive, Iron Maiden–like band. They're from Seattle. Their time is past a little bit, but this album does quite well—it goes platinum.

Poison come along, and they're another one of these bands that are totally ripping off KISS. Because Poison are essentially *exactly* like KISS. There's really almost no band that is as similar to KISS—musically and lyrically—as Poison, really. And even the look essentially lines up with the KISS look at this time—they're just basically that slightly more colorful, trashy Aerosmith look, with a little bit of Twisted Sister.

Poison look exactly the way KISS look onstage—the production is kind of the same, you get the same sort of one-armed drumming on Poison albums and KISS albums. The songs are really simple, and they're all about the same thing—just partying and chicks. So, again, KISS are taking a little time off, but all of a sudden, they're watching this band go crazy with their second album. It's *massive*. So this is another example of another young band who didn't pay their dues, just galloping past the old guard.

1989: Alice Cooper—*Trash*, Skid Row—*Skid Row*, Faith No More—*The Real Thing*

In 1989, you get the second big dirty-hair-metal album, Skid Row's debut album. And it does great. They're another East Coast band, but they are essentially a slightly more complicated version of KISS. Nothing that creatively crazy about them. But now you get the rumblings that something else is happening on the West Coast.

Hair-metal people are getting impatient with hair metal, and you get this exciting, new, complicated, cross-genre, cool, heavy band—Faith No More. They've got an underground swell, but at this point they've got a new lead singer, Mike Patton, and they put an album out that goes platinum. You get this cool thing happening—it's sort of on the backs of the Red Hot Chili Peppers and Jane's Addiction that there's a new kind of heaviness happening. And that is also mirrored by what is happening in Seattle. Grunge is a good year and a half or two years old at this point, and it's about to take off, and hair metal is getting long in the tooth.

Alice Cooper's *Trash* has a lot of parallels with KISS. Basically, you've got a guy who is the predecessor to KISS on his first big album after the comeback, so it takes him three albums to get this big. He switches labels at this point, and he's basically writing KISS songs. And, like KISS, he's working with song doctors. And Alice gets a surprise hit with 'Poison,' and he later does well with *Hey Stoopid*, too.

255

1990: Judas Priest—*Painkiller*, AC/DC—*The Razor's Edge*, Anthrax—*Persistence Of Time*

At this time, hair metal is about to go under. Maybe we don't know that yet, but grunge is really starting to make some waves. Also at this time, you've got Anthrax entering a mature period—this is their fifth album at this point. They're doing great—they are one of the Big Four thrash bands. Thrash is an exciting thing—it's not selling huge, but Metallica, Megadeth, Anthrax, and Slayer are all doing well, so there's this scrappy kind of metal that is way cooler than what hair metal is doing. Much less what KISS are trying to do—which is essentially to slide in and be a hair-metal band, right?

AC/DC are having a nice renaissance, after three not well-received albums. AC/DC are another band who are looking around during the hair-metal era— just like KISS—saying, 'Why aren't we big?' But fortunately for them, they've already won the Super Bowl, because they already have a diamond album in *Back In Black*, and another massive album with *For Those About To Rock*. *Flick Of The Switch*, *Fly On The Wall*, and *Blow Up Your Video* are not that well received, and they don't sell very well. But all of a sudden, AC/DC have another couple of hits with this new record in 1990, and they get a second wind. So, they're having a great year, where KISS are having their usual kind of year: *Are we gold? Are we barely platinum? Applaud being platinum.* AC/DC go five times platinum with that record, so they're doing great. And they're an old-school band—just like KISS—and they've already had a massive period back in 1980 and 1981, and here they are doing it again, while KISS are still just stuck on this straight line.

Judas Priest are another one of these bands that we've discussed … K.K. Downing overtly complains that they just could not break through to that 'next level.' They tried a hair-metal album with *Turbo*, and that did well enough—they were semi-happy it went platinum. But then they had an album that was very overseen, 1988's *Ram It Down*, that just went gold. And now they come back with *Painkiller* in 1990, and they just say, 'You know what? We're just going to give up this hair-metal thing that we were trying for one record—KISS and other bands are still doing it—but we're going to try to take a little taste of that thrash thing.' And they put out their 'try harder' album, which is how I refer to these albums where bands go to Vancouver and try really, really hard to make a good record—à la Bon Jovi, Mötley Crüe, Aerosmith, Whitesnake, and Scorpions. It's this pilgrimage you make, when you *really* want to try hard … after a while of not trying that hard.

So, Judas Priest do their try-harder album. It isn't a 'go to Vancouver' album, but it has Chris Tsangarides, the production is amazing, it's heavy, the songs are still cheesy—but it's pretty heavy and thrashy. It's now considered one of the greatest Judas Priest albums, but at the time it struggled to go gold as well. It didn't do that great—it was considered too heavy … it was probably considered *too cheesy*, really. Because heavy music was maturing, and it was going to be quite mature when it came to the grunge era.

1991: Metallica—*Metallica*, Guns N' Roses—*Use Your Illusion I & II*, Nirvana—*Nevermind*

This is considered the year that hair metal basically goes off the cliff. It's signaled by a few things. There's a balls-out thrash success in a record that goes diamond, Metallica's self-titled 'Black Album.' It's not very thrashy—they've slowed down and gone mainstream to do so but, basically, all the hair-metal audience goes, *Yeah, thrash is actually cool. And Metallica is cool—we're going over here.*

You also get the rise of grunge, with Nirvana's *Nevermind*. So, essentially, this is a big, big year for grunge. Nirvana were already considered a really cool band with *Bleach*, but this is a more polished album. And it's an instant success, and Seattle *really* is the thing that says, 'Hair metal is over.' These bands, like KISS, Scorpions, Judas Priest … you can be a 70s band, you can be an 80s band, they're all looked at as ridiculous peacocks and materialistic and misogynistic and just basically stupid. So grunge really takes over, and Nirvana's is the album that signals that.

Around the same time, and on the same label, you get Guns N' Roses—the last heave of the last guard—and one of the reasons why grunge had to happen, as well. Because Guns N' Roses were drama queens and divas, and not showing up to gigs on time, and being drunk all the time, and feuding with each other and other bands.

Guns N' Roses are one of the big reasons people just said, *I've had it with this stuff.* Even though they claim they're not a hair-metal band, I think they're *totally* a hair-metal band. They're almost like the worst kind of hair-metal band—in many ways, they're worse than the cleaner, squeakier hair-metal bands. I mean, they're essentially Mötley Crüe all over again.

So here they are in 1991, they finally come out with this follow-up, after all this drama. Now, granted, it's two records worth or music, so it's not like they weren't doing anything. I mean, they didn't come back with a ten-song, thirty-eight-minute album—they came back with, like, *one hundred and fifty minutes of music*. So, it's pretty cool, and it does amazing. I think those things went pretty quickly upward to seven times platinum. They were an instant massive success. But it's funny that *Nevermind* comes out around the same time, on the same label, and you have these two competing scenes.

1992: Pantera—*Vulgar Display Of Power*, Megadeth—*Countdown To Extinction*, Alice In Chains—*Dirt*

In 1992, hair metal is considered more or less dead—even though there is some great hair metal around this time: Warrant's *Dog Eat Dog*, Mötley Crüe's self-titled album, Cinderella's *Still Climbing*, and so on. That's also testimony to hair metal changing and getting way better. But also, at the same time, you had the rise of Pantera, which were basically going to be the new, heavier version of Metallica, and were going to rule metal in the 90s. They come out with this exciting album, *Vulgar Display Of Power*—a totally revolutionary way of recording, a new vocal approach, a more extreme James Hetfield.

You also have Megadeth doing great—they come out with *Countdown To Extinction*, which is their version of 'The Black Album.' It's a more polished, more radio-friendly, beautifully produced thrash album. So you've got this new form of heavy metal, but it's still well done and professional—just like the hair metal of the previous generation. And people are excited about it—*Countdown* goes triple platinum and *Vulgar* goes double platinum.

And you've got grunge at its mature phase, with Alice In Chains' *Dirt*. Grunge is basically as big as hair metal was in '84, '85, '86—grunge in 1992 is *massive*. There's a Big Four of grunge—Soundgarden, Alice In Chains, Pearl Jam, and Nirvana. They're all platinum bands … or soon will be, anyways. You've got this great, new, exciting, dangerous form of heavy metal in Seattle, that everybody has sort of turned their attention to, and thrash is still doing pretty good at this point. And into this waved KISS, finally, with their try-harder album, *Revenge*.

1993: Aerosmith—*Get A Grip*, Tool—*Undertow*, Pearl Jam—*Vs.*

So, 1993 is an interesting year. Grunge is still doing great. Pearl Jam put out their second album, and it does fantastic. Everybody loves it—it's critically acclaimed, it sells like crazy. Tool come along, proving that grunge and doomy-ness and what is essentially alternative metal is going into an exciting, creative phase for hard music. Aerosmith come along, and it's interesting—Blue Öyster Cult were always jealous of Aerosmith, in the same way that we've been talking about all these 70s bands being jealous of these hair-metal bands. Blue Öyster Cult were always like, *Man, Aerosmith always does so great, and we can't really break through.*

So Aerosmith are up in this era, and KISS are probably … they're probably jealous, again. First they were jealous of the hair-metal bands, and now they're jealous of Aerosmith, who have this massive track record of three records in a row that do amazing—*Permanent Vacation* through to *Pump* through to *Get A Grip*. *Get A Grip* has a ton of hits on it. It goes seven times platinum—just hit after hit after hit. It's a little bloated—I'm not crazy about it. It's an album that did great commercially, but critically, I think people don't think of *Get A Grip* as a great album.

1994: Soundgarden—*Superunknown*, Nine Inch Nails—*The Downward Spiral*, Stone Temple Pilots—*Purple*

In 1994, grunge is still going good. Maybe it's spinning its wheels a little bit. Stone Temple Pilots were always put down as kind of an 'also-ran' grunge band when *Core* came out, and they really resented being called grunge—but they certainly were. But *Purple* was a little bit more critically acclaimed—it did great. They really are doing well. I mean, they are essentially the fifth—and you can put Smashing Pumpkins in there, too, at sixth—of the great grunge bands. But they're from California. *Purple* is a well-received album—'Interstate Love Song' is a huge hit off of that. So, alternative metal is doing great—but it really is still grunge at this point.

An even *more* alternative metal is the Nine Inch Nails album. It's going down the road of, *he's not from California, it's industrial, it's weird.* It's bringing in a little phase of industrial metal—which did well with White Zombie and whatnot. So there's all these alternative flavors of metal. But we're moving farther and farther away from any kind of *hair* metal. By this point, almost all of those pretty good hair-metal albums of 1992 are a distant history. They've dropped off by '93, and they're almost nonexistent by '94—I can't even think of any. There is basically *no* hair-metal scene by 1994.

Soundgarden are having their first massive hit album with *Superunknown*, and they're going to have another big one with *Down On The Upside*. And *Badmotorfinger* did well, as well. But *Superunknown* … this is the year of Soundgarden. I would say Soundgarden are the biggest band in the world at this point, in terms of excitement level for any kind of heavy band. It's a mature year for grunge, but it's actually a massive year for Soundgarden— they're having this great huge year, as are Stone Temple Pilots and Nine Inch Nails. And what you're starting to see in the CD stores is that the labels are moving from grunge or heavy metal into something called 'alternative metal.'

1995: Smashing Pumpkins—*Mellon Collie And The Infinite Sadness*, White Zombie—*Astro-Creep: 2000*, Foo Fighters—*Foo Fighters*

This is the nadir year for heavy metal. Heavy metal is a bad word … but there's all kinds of heavy music being made. But *actual* heavy metal is not selling. Everybody in heavy metal is complaining about their lot. Machine Head do a little bit, Pantera are the biggest 'new' exciting band, Metallica are just soldiering on and doing well. But this is a big year for *hard* alternative. Smashing Pumpkins put out a double album that goes diamond, and this is the biggest year ever for Smashing Pumpkins. This is their year, with this masterpiece of a double album.

The Foo Fighters come out of the gate—a feisty little band who have a continual rise based on the ambition and talent of Dave Grohl, who used to be a drummer and is now the front man, singer, guitarist, and main writer. They come out with this punky, heavy, fairly up-tempo version of Nirvana, essentially, and they do great.

And White Zombie are on to their second hit album, *Astro Creep*. It's kind of a bloated version of *La Sexorcisto*. But we're in that era where there is this little bit of excitement around what is known as industrial metal—a lot of electronic sounds and beats woven into heavy metal. White Zombie and Nine Inch Nails are the two biggest. So you've got this *mélange* of all sorts of alternative metal.

1996: Marilyn Manson—*Antichrist Superstar*, Rage Against The Machine—*Evil Empire*, Sepultura—*Roots*

In 1996, KISS are looking around, and it's still a bewildering, disorienting world for heavy bands: 80s bands, 70s bands, they're all out of vogue. Basically, all the heavy music being made is by brash young upstarts. You get a band out of Brazil, Sepultura, who are like the nastier, more aggressive, more belligerent, more violent version of Metallica or Pantera—with this really ragged sound. And also ushering in something even more virulent than thrash and death metal—showing that fans of hard music can even like stronger stuff still. And it will get even stronger with death metal and black metal and everything, as time goes on.

At the same time, you get another industrial band, Marilyn Manson, who are shock-rockers—the way KISS used to be shock-rockers. This is their second album, and they're an instant hit, because Marilyn Manson is very, very shocking. He's way more a shock-rocker than W.A.S.P. or Mötley Crüe—who are both KISS clones—and KISS before them, and then Alice Cooper before KISS. Basically, he's the new version of shock, and the level just went up.

And Rage Against The Machine—they're another creative flavor of alternative metal. They're combining rap with metal, which is something that is going to be *really* big for about ten years, starting soon. It's just the next sort of block phase of metal to come. But they come up with this crazy formula of rapping and politics—about as far from KISS as you can imagine. But still a very heavy sound. A lot of rhythm to it.

So into this, KISS realize their next cool career move—they come up with a full-blown makeup reunion. They looked around and said, *Nobody is making music like KISS in this environment*. So what can they do? They have to skip the early 90s, skip the 80s, go all the way back to the 70s—and try *nostalgia*.

CARNIVAL OF SOULS: THE FINAL SESSIONS

Released October 28, 1997. Produced by Toby Wright, Gene Simmons, and Paul Stanley. US #27. US certification: none.

SIDE ONE

Hate (Gene Simmons/Bruce Kulick/Scott Van Zen)

Rain (Paul Stanley/Kulick/Curtis Cuomo)

Master & Slave (Stanley/Kulick/Cuomo)

Childhood's End (Simmons/Kulick/Tommy Thayer)

I Will Be There (Stanley/Kulick/Cuomo)

Jungle (Stanley/Kulick/Cuomo)

SIDE TWO

In My Head (Simmons/Van Zen/Jaime St. James)

It Never Goes Away (Stanley/Kulick/Cuomo)

Seduction Of The Innocent (Simmons/Van Zen)

I Confess (Simmons/Ken Tamplin)

In The Mirror (Stanley/Kulick/Cuomo)

I Walk Alone (Simmons/Kulick)

SINGLE

Jungle (promo only)

As you have probably realized by this point in the book, according to the opinions of many of the interviewees (and your humble narrator), while there is no denying that KISS certainly offered their share of classics during the non-makeup era, a common complaint was that for some of that time, they were following trends rather than being true to themselves. With the arrival of *Revenge* in 1992, it seemed as though the quartet had finally recognized their folly and returned to the heavy KISS sound we all knew and loved in the first place. But by the time of their seventeenth studio album (and what would turn out to be the final studio album of the non-makeup era), *Carnival Of Souls*, the old habit of *following* rather than *leading* had reared its ugly head yet again—resulting in a sound best described as 'grunge KISS.'

A valid argument could be made that by the time that *Carnival Of Souls* was originally going to be released, sometime in '96, grunge's peak had already passed. After all, Nirvana were no more, following Kurt Cobain's suicide in '94; Alice In Chains were entering a dormant period due to Layne Staley's ongoing—and eventually fatal—drug addiction; Soundgarden were on the verge of collapse, and would split in '97; and Pearl Jam were battling Ticketmaster, which meant they were not touring consistently. All of which makes KISS decision to suddenly 'go grunge' at *this* point all the more baffling.

What made the move even harder to swallow was that the aforementioned Big Four of grunge were all *influenced* by KISS to some degree (especially the Pearl Jam precursor band Mother Love Bone, whose flamboyant singer, Andrew Wood, was a KISS fanatic). But then again, if you were to reach back a bit further into the 80s, you could make a similar case concerning how all the hair-metal bands were influenced by KISS, and that KISS didn't have to feel the need to ... well, you know what I'm going to say next.

Looking back at 1996, it was an incredibly difficult time to be a veteran heavy-metal/hard-rock act, as it seemed like MTV and radio were only interested in alt-rock, revival-punk, nu-metal, and rap-metal. Heck, even Metallica hit a rocky road around this time, causing them to significantly dial down the 'metal' part of their sonic equation, change their instantly recognizable logo, cut their hair, and pencil on eyeliner (just take a gander at the ridiculous photos of the band inside the *Load* CD booklet to catch my drift). So when it was announced that KISS were working on new material with Toby Wright—the producer of Alice In Chains' self-titled album, their *Unplugged* offering, and AIC guitarist Jerry Cantrell's solo debut, *Boggy Depot*—you didn't have to be Dick Tracy to figure out what their next album was going to sound like.

When you think of KISS's music, arena-rock anthems—and, to a lesser degree, power ballads—usually come to mind, with their go-to lyrical topics mostly being partying, romance, and relationships. In other words, 'angry,' 'depressed,' 'dark,' 'dreary,' and 'sludgy' are not terms you would associate with KISS. But that was exactly the sonic and lyrical path that KISS opted to travel down with *Carnival Of Souls*.

From the get-go, listeners will discover that there is nothing really organic nor natural-sounding about *COS*—in that sense, it is comparable to *Music From The Elder*. Not stylistically, but certainly in that it is the sound of KISS trying *too hard*, reaching too far outside their comfort zone—with results that sound extremely forced. Especially on the album opener, 'Hate,' where Gene tries to sound like he is filled with … hate. However, the most preposterous track, however, is 'Rain.' Never mind that it starts off with a guitar riff that sounds like it was a reject from Alice In Chains' *Dirt*—how about the fact that Paul actually lifts a direct line from the earlier AIC song 'Rain When I Die'? (Both songs utilize the word 'rain' in their titles, and they even share the same chorus line, '*I think it's gonna rain*.')

From there, things don't improve much, as it seems like the only time the KISS we all know and love break through all the cloudiness is on the chorus to 'Jungle' (a song that contains an opening bass sound and riff that sound very much like—you guessed it!—Alice In Chains). The shift in sound even affects one of the things you could seemingly always count on in the non-makeup era—Bruce Kulick's ability to deliver memorable and melodic guitar solos (especially when you take into account that the last album contained one of his all-time best solos, on 'Unholy'). Here, it sounds like he has been instructed to make his solos sound more in line with Jerry Cantrell's style … and he obeyed. But Kulick at least plays a prominent role in one of the album's more interesting tracks, the closing 'I Walk Alone,' which marks the first (and last) time he supplied lead vocals on a KISS album.

But all that said, you can't condemn KISS *too much* for *COS*, as it falls in the same category as other misfires from established rock acts, others of whom around this same time issued some of the most unfocused and unremarkable albums of their entire careers. (In case you've forgotten, I'm talkin' 'bout Van Halen's *Van Halen III*, Megadeth's *Risk*, and Metallica's *Load* and *Reload*—and, a few years down the road, you could certainly add their sonic stink bomb, *St. Anger*, to this best-forgotten list.)

In addition, due to the fact that a reunion of KISS's original lineup had been confirmed before *Carnival Of Souls* was completed, the album sat on the shelf for over a year, while Ace, Gene, Paul, and Peter rocked stadiums, festivals, and arenas the world over. As a result, *COS* was heavily bootlegged in fan trading circles before it was *finally* given an official release in 1997 (with perhaps the most *blah* album cover of all the KISS albums, the original cover image of a spooky-looking flaming head having been nixed in favor a shot of the band in the studio, to avoid any confusion as to which lineup played on the album).

Lastly, *Carnival Of Souls* holds the distinction of being the only KISS album from which not a single song has ever been performed in concert by the band.

KNOW THE SCORE: TOBY WRIGHT

The co-producer of *Carnival Of Souls* looks back on the making of the last studio album of the non-makeup era.

How did you get involved in producing *Carnival Of Souls*?

I was referred by Bob Ezrin to Gene, because of my work with some of the grunge bands—Alice In Chains, especially. They were looking to make that kind of a record. We had a nice meeting at A&M Studios, where they were trying to work at the time, and took over one of the rooms over there. We just went through, *What do you want? What do you need? What are you looking for?* I felt like I could really deliver the kind of record that they were looking for—for sure. The meeting was me, Gene, Paul, and I think Eric, if not Bruce.

The main criticism of KISS's non-makeup era albums seems to be that they were following trends that were popular at the time, such as Bon Jovi and

pop-metal in the mid-to-late 80s, and then Alice In Chains and grunge by the time of *Carnival Of Souls*.

They are always going to be doing that. Today, if Gene made a record, he would want to know who was at the top of the charts, and he would try to make a record like that. *I promise.* [*Laughs*] Because he and I got in an argument one time—it turned out to be about how he wanted to be like Billy Corgan. And I couldn't understand why a legend like Gene Simmons would want to be like somebody who was climbing the ladder. It went around and around, and finally, it came out—he said, 'I just want to sell records like him. That's it.' I was like, *Ohhh. After all this time, you just want to sell some records like that guy. OK—I gotcha.*

KISS's previous album, *Revenge*, was their heaviest in quite some time. Was there any mention of continuing in that direction on *Carnival Of Souls*?

No. When we had that little meeting/interview, after Bob had recommended me, it was clear that they were going for a grunge type of record. They wanted to follow that trend. And I kind of remember warning Gene against that, because I thought it would be a one-record trend. They'd hit it and quit it. And I was pretty right about that. I'm always of the opinion that you're an artist for yourself first, and for the rest of the world later. And once you satisfy yourself, then everything is good from there. I like artists' individuality. Personally, I don't like it when they follow trends, because they sometimes can't get their record out before the trend is even over. It's like, that thing comes and goes, and it's gone. Bye. And then … where's your record? *Oh, that was the one we made six months ago.* It turns out to be kind of useless at that point.

What was it like working with KISS in the studio?

It was awesome. All four members were there all the time. We had a good time—it was a lot of songs that they had written and co-written with people, so we had a lot of that going on. And then there was the picking of the songs. I think we ended up with thirty-two or thirty-three, when we went to pick out the ten or twelve for the record. I think it worked out pretty good, because we had some of the good, grungy stuff going on, and I thought it was pretty representative of what they needed to do at the time.

Bruce Kulick really made his presence felt on the album—co-writing many of the songs, and even singing lead on a track.

Bruce brought his incredible fingers and songwriting chops. He and I mostly constructed that record, after we picked the songs. It was mostly he and I that constructed it, put it together, and came up with the visions of how things should be, and then we went after those visions. And after the speakers would play back the songs, we'd ask each other, 'Well … what did you think of that?'

It was too hard to describe—at first—what we were trying to go for. *Oh, we're going to go for blankity-blankity-blank …* and then you'd just get blank stares. Then you'd be like, *We're just going to do it, and you let me know when you've got it, and if you like it or not.* That kind of a thing was happening in the studio, because sometimes, words can't really describe what your ears hear. That record never would have been made like that without Bruce. *Never.*

Let's go song by song, starting with 'Hate.'

That song is amazing. I really pushed Gene to sing hard on that song, because I wanted to *feel* the hate. 'Hate' is one of my favorite tracks, and it's probably one of the hardest tracks on the record. I think that was really brought about by Gene's vocal, and Bruce's real grinding-type guitar. He made some riffs out of it, and we were like, *It's hooky, it's almost dance-y … but it's got some snarl to it.* We really, really liked the snarl.

'Rain.'

[Songwriter] Curt Cuomo had that in his library for a while. I picked that one out. I *really* like it a lot. I think we revamped it to fit with what we were doing.

What struck me most about that song was the lyrical similarity to Alice In Chains' 'Rain When I Die.'

It was kind of similar, and I was kind of freaked out by the similarities. But, at the same time, we didn't cross any legal boundaries—so we were OK. [*Laughs*]

'Master & Slave.'

That one is one of my favorite grooves on the record. I wasn't real up on that one, but when we picked the songs, it was more a democratic vote than it was a dictatorship. So, when we picked all the songs, that one wasn't high on my list—but on everyone else's, it was.

'Childhood's End.'

That was an interesting song, because, again, it wasn't one of my favorites, but it was a Gene song, and we needed to get a couple of those on the record. As far as I can remember, that one was a lot of fun to record. I kind of let Gene do whatever he was thinking, vocally, on that one, because I didn't think it would be a big hit or anything. I came from the Ron Nevison school of production—of paying attention to the songs that were going to become hits, instead of spending all of your time on every single song. Sometimes, you just let them go.

'I Will Be There.'

That's a beautiful song. I actually wanted to put strings on that song, but that didn't come to fruition. I was told, 'That's not us. It's a little campy sounding.' So we didn't. Things that you try when you're in the production process are interesting, because you can do a ton of stuff to a song … but is it right for the song?

'Jungle.'

That's one of my faves. I actually played on that song as well. There should have been three or four singles off this record, but we only got the shot at one, and I think that was probably one of the best songs on the record. I thought it was very representative of what was going on at the time—*it's a jungle out there*. And I think we represented it quite nicely, musically speaking. I believe I played a lot of percussion—a lot of that groove under there is me with my djembes and stuff.

Which other tracks did you think would have made good singles?

The first two, for sure.

'In My Head.'

That's another one that I don't think I paid much attention to—except to dig out the tempos.

'It Never Goes Away.'

That was kind of a cool song. That one was aimed more at the grungy thing. It does have that grinding guitar—a pretty grungy sound. It doesn't have the glitz which some of the other singles might have had. The grunge thing was—as a whole—like, *Underplay it*. Like, *I'm not getting dressed up for you. I'm not putting on my nice shirt for you. I'm just going to put on my flannel and go as I am—because that's how I am right now.* It was all an attitude. So, I think that song kind of represented that attitude of, *Eh. It's good, it's whatever.*

'Seduction Of The Innocent.'

Awesome song. That one was a little scary. Some of the lyrical content, some of getting inside Gene's mind when he was writing that song, was just a little scary. It was fun, in a way, to turn it into that. I heard that song a lot more 'metal' than it turned out. We took it as far as we did—only because we didn't want to get further into the quote/unquote metal scene with it. And we could have. I think Bruce came up with some really crazy, fast guitar part, and I was like, 'Ooh, that's good metal!' And as soon as I said it, they were like, 'We don't want that!' Sometimes, words can make it all wrong.

'I Confess.'

That one's a pretty cool song. I do remember recording strings on that song—and that's about it. That one's kind of slipped my memory.

'In The Mirror.'

It's an awesome song. The lyrics are really good. And they deal with a number of different things. I think it was one of the more important songs on the record, intellectually speaking. That one kind of hit home for me—whether this was fake or not, I don't know, but it hit home, like, *We're getting a real glimpse into the real life of this artist, who I have been a fan of since I was ten years old.* It was kind of an eye-opening thing for me. Which was awesome, as a producer, because I just wanted more of that. That's always the conflict, so to speak.

'I Walk Alone.'

I really like that song, too. That was one of my higher picks. It's funny, because sometimes your favorite song winds up on the lower part of the record. But it's not always necessarily how they're thought of. It was for sequencing purposes that it ended up that far down. But I think it's one of the better songs on the record, for sure. And Bruce did a great job singing. He was very scared when he stepped into the vocal booth. It was just he and I, and I was like, 'Just lay down what you've got, brother. Be real easy, be real gentle, and do what you've got, and then we'll come back around and I'll give you some direction. We'll always have what we got, so don't worry about it.' So, we had a lot of that going on. [It was] rookie syndrome, basically, for Bruce at that moment in time. And I think he did a great job.

Do you recall hearing of any plans for the album after its release? I heard that a few tunes were possibly going to appear on soundtracks.
I remember hearing things like that. I think what broke my whole thing with that record was, when Gene left the studio, came back, and broke us the bad news, [which was] pretty much, 'Let's finish and then we'll just put it on the shelf'—because somebody had offered them an ungodly amount of money to put the makeup back on. And that broke everybody's spirit in the room—because he just came in and announced it, like, *Hey! I'm proud of this! Check this out!* Well, it's nice to be proud and everything … but be careful of what you're proud of. [*Laughs*]

Because we were almost to mixing, so then it became, 'What are we going to do? Are we finishing recording? Are you dropping the record now and we're not going to mix it? What's the deal?' They were like, 'Let's finish recording it, let's mix it, and we'll put it out.' And then it sat on somebody's shelf. But it was the biggest bootlegged record of whatever year we made it in. It definitely was *amazingly* bootlegged, unfortunately.

Did you see the reunion coming at all, or was it a complete and utter surprise?
Complete shock—to everybody in the room. And then weeks of depression followed that. Because it was a big blow—especially to Eric and Bruce. That was the last thing they wanted to hear. *No, don't do that!* But obviously they did, and it is what it is.

Do you remember anything about the original album cover image?

I loved that one. It was kind of patterned after the song 'In My Head.' I thought it was awesome. And then … we ended up with the worst cover in rock'n'roll! *Ever*. It's the worst cover ever made. Come on, it's *really* bad.

Interestingly, Alice In Chains would open several shows on the KISS reunion tour in 1996.

They were doing their thing, and KISS had always been a huge influence on them—especially Jerry [Cantrell], with a lot of his riffs and whatnot. He really loved KISS. I could see KISS taking bands like that out—just because they wanted to be identified as *masters of the genre*. You know how Gene likes to play. He was doing his Gene thing. If he can get a Soundgarden or an Alice In Chains out there, then he would look all that more legit.

How would you compare working with KISS to some of the other bands you worked with at the time, such as Alice In Chains and Slayer?

Alice In Chains never used outside songs—neither did Slayer, or most of the bands that I ever worked with. They all wrote their own material. There might have been a collaboration here and there, but never like that. Not that there's anything wrong with it—it's just the way it was. And is. Most of those bands still just write their own stuff.

As far as recording in the studio—not really. I try not to record using the same techniques each time, because I like for each band to sound different. I don't want Alice In Chains to sound like KISS to sound like Soundgarden, or anybody else. To me, that's what gives an artist their individuality—a sound of their record, a sound of their songs. That you, as a listener, are going to turn on your radio, hear it, and say, 'I know who that is,' right away.

If I did the same thing with every artist, you wouldn't know—you'd have to wait. You'd have to wait at least for the chorus, or if you can recognize their voice. But if they all sound the same, that's not really true music to me. [*Laughs*] It's just like … fabricated junk. And we don't need any more of that—we have plenty of that out there, we don't need any more.

What are your thoughts on the album now?

It's definitely one of KISS's most overlooked records. I think it has probably some of the best songs that KISS has ever done—I'll be bold and say that. I think that no matter what kind of a KISS fan you are, there is something on that record for you. You just have to listen and find it, and not be so judgmental. I talk to a lot of KISS fans, and they're like, 'Oh, I like *this* record.' 'But, I like *this* record.' '*This* is my favorite.' '*That one's* my favorite.' Why?

Some people can tell you why, but most people cannot. 'Because it was' is mostly what I get. 'Oh, OK, cool. Well, *Carnival Of Souls* is *my* favorite. You know why? *Because it is.*' They're like, 'It's because you made it.' I'm like, 'No. It's my favorite ... because it is.' But I'm the dude who likes the underdog, too. I'll go to Vegas, and I'll bet on the 25-to-1, because *you're the underdog, and I want to see you win—just because.* It's not because I want the big payday, it's because I want to see the underdog win.

Would you agree that *Carnival Of Souls* is KISS's darkest album?

Absolutely. And it's that way for a reason—because we went after that quote/unquote grunge-era type of music. And that wasn't very light or poppy. It was a very dark time in music, *period*. That whole genre was very dark. All the lyrics were pretty dark. Most everything was done in a minor key.

As dark as we could make it, we did—all across the board, with all the bands that I worked with, through that era. That was just what was happening at the time. It's the stuff that everybody was listening to and couldn't get enough of—so, keep making it. Today, if you played something like that, people would go, 'You're so dark. You're so metal. You're so *not* mainstream.' [*Laughs*]

KNOW THE SCORE: BRUCE KULICK

Bruce is back! This time, he discusses his final recordings as a member of KISS.

Do you agree that, along with *The Elder*, *Carnival Of Souls* is probably one of the biggest love/hate albums among KISS fans?

Yeah, I think it is. Well, I know *The Elder* has always been a very controversial record. But I still think this one is more polarizing, sadly.

Why do people seem to have such strong opinions about *Carnival Of Souls*?
I don't know. Well, it certainly was extremely different from anything prior. I'm actually very pleased with the love that a lot of fans have for it. I don't think there are fans that hate it, they're just like, *Well, I'm not into it.* The biggest issue with that album is that Paul has publicly admitted how much he doesn't like it. I'm not going to say that's going to make fans want to like it even more, but it is remarkable to see how many people make comments about their love for it.

I've heard people refer to it as KISS's grunge album. Is that a fair assessment?
Well, at the time we were recording it, grunge was big, and we were looking at doing a heavier, darker, uglier version of *Revenge*. So, if you want to call it grunge, you can call it grunge. But to me, I just know it had to be heavier, darker, and uglier. And, in many ways, it was.

Do you remember if Gene was listening to a lot of Alice In Chains at the time? That's the reason why Toby Wright was enlisted as the producer, right?
Yeah, but you've got to remember that Toby did have a KISS history, too [as the assistant engineer on *Crazy Nights*]. He knew the band very well. I do think that Gene was very open to a lot of the bands. He loved Beck. He thought the song 'Loser' was brilliant—things like that. Which is kind of weird, if you think about it, because Gene doesn't see himself as a loser. But I think he liked that there was a strong point of view by somebody, and it drew you in, and it made you connect to the artist. So Gene was more comfortable with it.

Paul wasn't so much, because even though Paul could write 'God Of Thunder,' he probably is more comfortable as a pop artist. I'm saying that as a compliment, not as a negative. Because in so much of my era, there was a balance [between] the two guys, but so many of the bigger songs were Paul's—'Tears Are Falling,' 'Who Wants To Be Lonely,' 'Forever,' et cetera.

***Carnival Of Souls* is the KISS album you were most involved with the creation of, as you co-wrote nine of the twelve songs.**
I was working really hard at trying to contribute. They didn't come to me for it, but they were happy that I was coming up with riffs.

What are some of your favorite tracks on the album?

Considering that Paul wasn't that comfortable in that kind of grunge era, certainly 'Master & Slave'—he came up with that riff, and it's a very catchy riff. 'Rain,' which was mostly music I provided—I thought he really sang great. His ballad was beautiful, which was written for [his son] Evan—'I Will Be There.' A lot of my favorites are actually Paul's on that album. I did like 'Hate'—I thought Gene had a great point of view and riff there. 'Childhood's End' was a kind of sentimental thing for Gene.

I didn't love the mixes of a lot of things, but that was because, by the time we were mixing, they announced to the band—and soon to the world—that they were going to do the makeup reunion tour. So their focus was a little whacky—how could it not be? It was a very uncertain thing, because ... *How is this going to work?* But I think there were enough strong highlights on the record to be proud of it from my point of view. 'Jungle' was a highlight, too—I really liked that track. And I think Paul really sang it with a lot of passion.

And, of course, the album closes with a song you sang, 'I Walk Alone.'

I forgot about that! I never intended to sing it. I sang it on the demo, because Gene and I worked on it for such a long period of time. Toby was the one that insisted I sing it. I guess they knew it would be kind of a prophetic lyric, when you think about it. It was a surprise to me, actually. It's intimidating, singing when you're in a band with Gene and Paul. I had nowhere near the ability of say, Eric Carr, Eric Singer, or Tommy Thayer. So it was hard for me. But I did the best I could, and I think the song fits my vocal style, so I was definitely proud of it.

Do you recall if the album's title was taken from the 1962 horror film of the same name?

Gene had that title, and I actually thought he might have had that title even for a song, but I'm a little fuzzy on that. It's definitely a Gene title. And then *The Final Sessions* was tagged on when the record company insisted on putting it out—and, of course, they *would* put it out, because they paid for that album!

Where did the band photo that was ultimately used for the cover come from?
It came from the magazine *Metal Edge*. Gerri Miller was there to cover it, and we didn't have a lot to choose from, so they found that photo—and there it is.

Eddie Trunk has said that *Carnival Of Souls* would have been a tough sell even if it came out when it should have originally. Do you agree?
Well, when you say *should have come out*, it would have only been about a year or so earlier. I don't know what it would have or wouldn't have done. But he could be right. It's hard to go back in time, in my mind, to know what was going on then, with the music business.

GIMME MORE: THE REUNION THAT WASN'T

Instead of touring in support of *Carnival Of Souls*, KISS opted to embark on their tremendously successful Reunion Tour, featuring the Stanley/Simmons/Frehley/Criss lineup. But rumors have circulated over the years that, supposedly, a possible return to makeup was being considered for a reunion tour circa 1989–90. There was only one catch—it was to feature the 1980–82 lineup, Stanley/Simmons/Frehley/Carr. Here, several KISS experts discuss whether they believe this rumor was built upon fact … or mere fiction.

MITCH LAFON From what I understand and what I remember from those days, they had hatched a plan—a good eight years before the KISS Reunion Tour of '96—to bring back Ace. I think the dialogue with Peter had been tense, but I think they were planning on bringing back Ace. And for whatever reason it didn't work out. Possibly because, at that time, Ace wasn't sober and probably wasn't reliable, and some of the Frehley's Comet stuff didn't go super-smooth.

What we hear in fan circles, and what we discuss behind the scenes, sometimes it's more fantasy than reality. But yeah, I certainly heard that rumor, and I think there might have been a plan in place. It would have made absolute sense, because had they managed to bring Ace back at the time, with Eric Carr—because Ace and Eric loved each other—it would have been fantastic. But then Eric got sick. I'm not sure on the timing, but that might have affected these plans. Plus, Ace was not at the level that Paul and

Gene would have liked. Again, speculation—not hard fact. But it would have been great, had it happened. Of course, they wound up doing the 'Rise To It' video from *Hot In The Shade* wearing the makeup, and that was gangbusters, because all the news media—MuchMusic, MTV, *RIP Magazine*, *Hit Parader*, and *Circus*—were like, *KISS put the makeup back on!* So they could sense the potential of [it], if they had been able to do it.

Music was changing in the late 80s. We were moving away from the hair bands into more Guns N' Roses/Metallica—more serious, more hardcore music. I don't think it was the right place at the right time. I think it would have done *OK*. They probably would have done one arena run—I don't think it would have been sustained throughout the world, like the Reunion Tour was.

I don't think they would done South America, necessarily. I think it would have probably done OK in Japan. I doubt they would have done the Australian market. Not sure Europe would have been on board like they were for the Reunion Tour—because it wouldn't have been 'the original four,' it would have been 'three plus one.' Regardless of how much people love Eric, it still would have been three plus one. Musically, it would have been great, but ... *three plus one.*

CHARLIE BENANTE I definitely would have been into that. I mean, I saw that lineup at the Palladium—Eric's first show [on July 25, 1980]. I thought they were great.

EDDIE TRUNK I know that Ace and Eric had a friendship—obviously, they were in the band together for a brief time. And I know that Ace and Eric were close. I know that when Ace was auditioning guitar players for his solo band around that time, Eric played drums during the auditions for him, because his drummer wasn't available. Ace and Eric remained close even through those years. And I do know for a fact that Eric Carr wanted to join Ace's band and play on the side from KISS. Like, when KISS wasn't working, to be able to go out and play clubs and theaters with Ace, for fun. And, obviously, Gene and Paul were not going to let that happen—and didn't. Eric was kind of upset about it, because it was something he really wanted to do. But when Ace was rehearsing at SIR in New York, Eric would go down there, hang out, and jam with Ace.

So there was that going on around that time. But I don't remember any real rumors about Ace coming back at that time. If it had happened, I think it would have done well, but I think waiting those extra years made it better. At that time, they were still very much a sign of the times. They were still about what was happening—the whole MTV thing, the hair, the spandex, the outfits. I mean, if you look at KISS's history through the 80s, there are moments—the *Asylum* tour, the *Crazy Nights* tour—where they look *utterly ridiculous*. But that was the sign of the times—that's what I'm talking about when I say everybody was trying to keep pace with what was happening at the time. It was *them* trying to chase what was happening at the time. It really wasn't them, it didn't look right for them—but that's what they were going for then.

So, around the time of *Hot In The Shade*, although they had found a much better balance, they were still in that mode. That was still the era of MTV and videos, and before Nirvana and before grunge wiped everything out. What they were doing at that point was building and made sense and was good. Most people genuinely liked Bruce. Bruce had a perfect disposition for the band—he fit the band, he knew not to overstep those guys, he knew his place, he handled all the material really well, he brought his own stuff to the table at that point. As a KISS fan, I wouldn't have wanted it to happen at that point, because I thought what they did around that time, and on the *Hot In The Shade* tour, was great. I was happy with the band, and Ace was doing good things at that time, too—which I was a part of.

I think, across the board, it was a good time, and I think when they ended up doing the reunion, it was a good time, too, because things had run their course, and they had to do something again to mix it up. The things that they were representing and doing and standing for in the 80s, with *Hot In The Shade*, that was no longer cool. That was now on the out. So they had no other card to play. They had to do something different. It started to wind down. Because, like I said, as much as they made a recovery in the 80s and did well, they still needed a lot of help.

They were never Bon Jovi, they were never Mötley Crüe. You know, Bon Jovi played *Giants Stadium*. They were looked at as the older guys that kind of got cool again—by doing what they were doing. Then, all of a sudden, the 90s roll around, and everything changes again, and the old stuff is looked at as, *Well, that was the cool stuff.* So I think that was the right time to go back to that. And I know, having listened to *Carnival Of Souls*, and having heard that before it ever was officially released, I knew that was going to be a tough sell at that time. So I was not surprised—having been at *MTV Unplugged*, the writing was on the wall. The time was right for that all to happen.

JULIAN GILL I think it would have been the wrong time. I don't think it would have done as well as the reunion did. As KISS fans, we had a couple of down periods. We had a decline in the mid-80s, from *Animalize* through *Crazy Nights*. *Hot In The Shade* was a little bit of a blip; the fans love *Revenge*, but it was a dog on the road. I think we had to suffer a bit longer in order to get to the point where a lot of fans had grown up—a lot of *music* fans had grown up—to the point where the original KISS era became more of a legend. And then it was the perfect time. Early 1990s? It would have gotten smothered by Nirvana and grunge. It would have been terrible timing, in terms of the other music scene that was going on.

BRUCE KULICK I just know that, at the time you're talking about, that somehow they were in touch with Ace more than [in] other years. So I used to hear little rumors that something could happen. But I don't really think it was as real as those rumors [suggest]. And then again … how would I know? [*Laughs*] Those are things you'd rather *not* know.

GIMME MORE: ACE, GENE, PAUL, AND PETER

It seemed like ever since the original KISS lineup split up, in the early 80s, rumors would circulate about the possibility of a reunion—which eventually took place in 1996, with a blockbuster tour. In this excerpt from another one of my earlier books, *Survival Of The Fittest: Heavy Metal In The 1990s*, former KISS members and renowned admirers discuss the moment that KISS closed the door on the non-makeup era.

GILBY CLARKE [guitarist, Guns N' Roses, 1991–94] I remember Eric Singer was telling me they were starting their [*Revenge*] tour in San Francisco, and they were going to play the Stone—which is a small, three hundred, four hundred–seat club. And they weren't wearing makeup or anything. I actually rode my bike up to check it out. Shooting Gallery was opening—which had Andy McCoy [of Hanoi Rocks] and Jo Dog from Dogs D'Amour in the band, who I was friends with. And to this day, that's *the best* rock concert I've ever seen in my life!

BRUCE KULICK We did a promotional tour, and it was a good way to get a lot of hype. I thought Larry Mazer—the manager at the time—had a good concept there. He knew we were a very tight band and didn't have to have lasers, bombs, and a giant stage to be powerful. So doing these events in clubs, which would be ridiculously oversold and could work with the radio stations—we'd have a dinner afterward, with special winners. We were doing a lot of good groundwork to set up the album. We played the Ritz in Manhattan, and there was probably a club in Baltimore [Hammerjack's] we did and Philly [Trocadero Theatre] and Arizona [After The Goldrush]. It was like a little mini-tour of these places. Yeah, those were great shows. We did the Troubadour, I can really remember that. In fact, someone found it recently on YouTube, and I couldn't believe it. That's really cool that Gilby remembered that one. The funniest thing is how a band like KISS ... now that I've played every kind of venue possible all around the world, it's mostly arenas, occasionally it's a theater kind of thing. But it's never a club. So here we are in these regular clubs and I'm going, *OK... this is backstage?* We would already be dressed in our rock'n'roll clothes, pull up in a van, and get the heck out of there right after that. There was no room for us.

GILBY CLARKE I've got to tell you, I was a big KISS fan as a kid—I knew all the songs. And without the makeup, without the theatrics, to me, the songs were just speaking to me. The band could play great. Once again, it was kind of like with GnR—Eric is a better drummer, Bruce is a better guitar player. It was just really, really strong and powerful. And it really, really hit me. Like I said, to this day, it's the best show I've ever seen.

BRUCE KULICK I'm really glad that I wasn't aware that so much behind-the-scenes negotiations would happen [around the time of the *MTV Unplugged* taping in 1995], because it would have been distracting and nerve-wracking.

Playing on MTV back then, on a show that was going to be filmed in that quality, that was a big deal for us. So that was enough pressure. I wouldn't want the pressure and then to think that was my last gig—which it kind of was, my real last gig with the band. It was a natural progression from the convention performances [of 1995], and it was Alex Coletti, who was the brilliant leader of the *Unplugged* brand for MTV, who was a big KISS fan and wanted us to do it as pure as possible.

And I think he sold them very heavy, with Gene and Paul ... you've got to remember that Eric mentioned, 'Why don't you have Peter come down?' So that broke the ice ... anyone who thinks that Eric Singer caused the reunion or started the reunion, they're dreaming, but clearly that was Eric being a fan of the old KISS, too, and never thinking that MTV would push the issue once they asked us to do it. They weren't that interested in us doing it. Some people just didn't take that version of the band that seriously. But every network that has a hit show wants to score a coup like that, where you can get a reunion happening right on your television to bring in your living room. And then they own part of the record, part of the DVD. They made it happen. And then the next thing you know, they're reaching out to Ace and Peter. Ace and Peter looked at it like, *WE WANT TO BE BACK IN THE BAND!* And here you have a very functioning group, with Eric Singer and myself. Granted, do I think the reunion would have happened right there, had *Revenge* gone double or triple platinum? Probably not. But it was a *gold* record, and music was changing. It seemed like maybe we did run our course.

I like to say sometimes that in the same way there was a time for grunge to happen in the 90s, each generation wants its different thing. There are also cycles about popular music. And enough years [had] gone by since the heyday of that version of KISS, to put it back on and for it to be hugely successful. I think Ace and Peter's position was, *Yeah, we'll do this, but we want to do a reunion*. I know Ace, during some of my years in the band, would reach out to Paul and those guys. Because [Ace and Peter] were just doing like, club gigs, and we're still doing arenas. I mean, not that we were selling out all the time, but we could go to South America and do multiple dates, and Monsters Of Rock. And even the *Revenge* tour, as much as it wasn't huge, it was still very respectable, and we were out there for quite a while, and we played the arenas and did great shows.

ACE FREHLEY I'm not sure who exactly reached out first. It may have been KISS to me and Peter, because I think they had just finished a string of KISS Conventions, and I think they realized there was a lot of money in a reunion tour. And subsequently we started planning it, and the *Unplugged* sessions happened, and it just kind of broke everything wide open.

BRUCE KULICK So the negotiating started to happen, and there was even drama on the day of the dress rehearsal for *Unplugged*, that they didn't come, but they did rehearse at SIR. And I think that had to do—and I can't be 100 percent sure, because I wasn't privy to contracts and stuff like that—that those guys were looking to make the commitment, but I think they were just wrangling over things like that. And the next thing you know, they did the performance. It was a big moment for everybody—including myself, even though it was the thing that would end my reign in the band. But I went out on a high note. It was a great performance, and I'm very proud of *Unplugged*. *I photographed very beautifully that day.* [*Laughs*]

ACE FREHLEY I knew the fans were going to react in a big way, but I didn't expect what happened. I mean, the place … it was *pandemonium*.

BRUCE KULICK So I have good memories of that, although that was the reason that Gene and Paul were willing to entertain the reunion tour. But they were smart. Even though they were hesitating starting *Carnival Of Souls*, which is like, come on, you can't have anything more opposite: go back and do *Alive II* with these guys, or forge forward and do a new record. But we had to do the new record, because we were already committed to the record—they took money from the record company to do the record. And, well, what if Ace and Peter freaked out and didn't play ball? Your best move in business is you've got to keep a few eggs in the basket, you've got to always hold on to the sure thing. Well, the sure thing was Eric Singer and I doing the right thing. And we did. So we finished the record. It didn't come out for a few years—Paul promised me it would come out, and he was true to his word. Even though it came out like an afterthought, we had a little hit with that song 'Jungle,' which was my riff, and I was very proud of that.

EDDIE TRUNK The KISS reunion [is] another thing that people don't quite understand. People a lot of times will be like, *KISS did great in the 80s and early 90s. They were doing great business, 'Tears are Falling' was all over MTV, and Lick It Up was a success.* To some degree, yeah, KISS did better than they did in the early 80s, that's for sure. And they did get some support from MTV, and that certainly helped. But it's an enormous fallacy for people who think that KISS was huge in the 80s. It was very, very misleading. They were still not a sure thing at all selling out arenas. They were still going out on two/three-band bills, and still struggling in some places to sell tickets. And that's what led to the reunion. It wouldn't have mattered what was going on, that reunion *needed* to happen, because, quite frankly, they were struggling. And they went to a whole other level by having that reunion happen.

I remember going to the press conference [announcing the reunion tour, on April 16, 1996], which was on the *Intrepid*. I got a ride to it with Sebastian Bach, who was a huge KISS fan, and geeked up out of his mind. I remember driving there with him, and I kept having to tell him, 'You realize you're not going to a concert, right?' Because he was in concert mode, he was so excited about it. I was like, 'We're just going to hear them *talk*,' and he's like, 'Yeah, I know! I know!' But there was just so much excitement about it, and rightfully so—the initial touring turned out to be great for it. And I think what was cool about it also beyond that was it showed that there was still an interest, and kind of put the spotlight back on performance and theatrical aspects of a stage show and dressing up and being *rock stars* again. What was so important about the KISS reunion—beyond the fact that, if you were a KISS fan, it was a chance to see the original band and show again—was that it put the spotlight back on the fact that it's cool to dress up, it's cool to be rock stars, it's cool to put on a show. Instead of just putting on a flannel shirt. I think that was a really big point. And then going forward, of course, some of the same issues that plagued KISS and the chemistry with those guys showed up.

ACE FREHLEY We were basically just doing what we did in the 70s, right? I always thought KISS were in their own category—theatrical hard-rock group, with also catchy songs … and a big spectacle. I always thought we were kind of in our own category. It wasn't that difficult at all for me, and oddly enough, when I was onstage I even had feelings of déjà vu. Because, with the makeup on, we look a lot younger. [*Laughs*]

BRUCE KULICK People embraced KISS in '96 in makeup, because that was unique. It's a throwback, in fact, as close as possible to like a '75 kind of thing. And they were nervous about it—they didn't know if it was going to do great or not. And then you sell out Tiger Stadium, you knew, *Oh, this is a good idea!* Because maybe people did want to be entertained, by '96.

RIKI RACHTMAN [host of MTV's *Headbangers Ball*] Obviously, everybody knows they didn't do it for the credibility, and they didn't do it to 'give the fans what they wanted.' They did it like I think they do everything—pretty much for money. And I'm not putting them down for that, that's their thing. There's episodes of *Headbangers Ball* where I ask KISS, 'Why don't you guys get together, one show, and play it in makeup?' And they said, 'No.' Just like I asked Glenn Danzig, 'Why don't you get together for one show and do the Misfits?' And he said no. People got so offended when I said that. *Oh, it's a step backward.* Well, funny that when it didn't work as well as they planned [with their careers], they *all* made that step backward! But I think KISS going back and going to the old style with the makeup and the explosions is fucking great. Thank God they did. I don't think people would see them if they didn't.

CHARLIE BENANTE I couldn't wait for it, and, of course, I saw it a bunch of times. I saw it at the Garden every night. I happened to have a night off in Boston, and I went to see them, and I went up the front of the stage to watch most of the show, and Paul cracked the guitar and handed it to me. That was one of the greatest moments *ever*. [*Laughs*]

REX BROWN [bassist, Pantera] We were starting to play with all of our idols at this point. We were selling tickets. So they wanted us to help sell tickets. When you get the opportunity to play with your idols, be it KISS or Black Sabbath, you just don't turn down that opportunity. They sold out Detroit in four minutes [at Tigers Stadium]. When you write songs like 'Parasite,' if that's not as metal as it gets, I don't know what is. And then going back out onstage and playing some of those great riffs that they had created in the 70s, and then putting the paint back on and doing it in a really big way … you have to look at the nostalgia of it. That was a pretty big move. It was very cool, I thought.

GILBY CLARKE I did see that tour and it just … I thought Ace was doing fine. Peter just wasn't killing it, for me. It didn't look like he was hitting [the drums] or even moving. And from seeing Eric do it, it was just like, *Wow*. So that was not my favorite KISS tour.

ACE FREHLEY I don't think the shows were as spontaneous [as they were in the 70s]. Some nights I felt like I was going through the motions. I remember looking at a video from when we played Vegas, and it just seemed like—in some parts—we were in slow motion. I'll be the first to admit it, I don't jump around like I did in my twenties. So I think it was a special tour and everybody enjoyed it, but I don't think we recaptured what we had in the 70s. That will never be duplicated or recreated.

BRUCE KULICK Of course I went—when it was in LA. I remember a friend of mine, she was working me out in the gym—she was my trainer, but also a really good singer—she kind of propped me up, because I was like, *Oh, God*. I knew it would be hard for me emotionally. I think it was at the Forum, and they sold out. Meanwhile, all the fans were just thrilled to see me. They were saying things like, 'We'll see you next year,' because they really believed it would only be for a year anyway, and then we'd go back to *Revenge* and *Carnival Of Souls* kind of KISS. Did I think they were good? I did. I enjoyed it. I know they worked their ass off to get it together. Peter had a coach—a drummer friend of mine that I know [Sandy Gennaro]. And we all know that Tommy Thayer coached Ace. I think they were really hard on Ace and Peter to get their act together, to pull this off. But they did. *And it was huge.*

AFTERWORD
BY ANDREAS CARLSSON

My first encounter with Bruce Kulick was a rather confusing one. With posters of Super KISS from 1980 on the walls of my teenage bedroom, I was expecting something else than the band standing onstage at Olympen located in Lund, Sweden, on the 25th of October, 1984.

First, Olympen was a small venue, holding less than 2,500 persons. It was so small that half the KISS logo was covered up by the stacks of Marshall speaker cabinets and Eric Carr's drum kit, and no pyro could be used due to the low ceiling. It was a club gig with KISS standards. The small stage used was the old *Unmasked* stage from years earlier, newly modified with animal print to work with the theme of the brand new album, *Animalize*. Gene was wearing a wig due to his previous filming of the Hollywood movie, *Runaway*—he did not look like himself at all.

A bigger surprise, however, was the tall guy on the right side of the stage. He seemed a bit shy, and his outfit seemed to have been thrown together last minute. He was playing a gold-plated Charvel, mostly facing the floor. Who was he? It was not Mark St. John, who was on the cover of the tour program that I just had bought. But in all fairness, at this time it was hard to know who the guitar player was in KISS. I just became used to the idea of Vinnie Vincent being the new guy. Remember, this was a time of no social media, and very little news about KISS would be in the press or on TV, at least in Sweden. You had to read the international rock press to know what was going on.

Nevertheless, it didn't take long to realize that the tall guy onstage with the same 'KISS hairdo' as the other guys (minus Gene) was not just an excellent player but the perfect fit to my favorite band. He had a unique tone and could make the guitar sing! Bruce's solos had melody—something both Vinnie and Mark had lacked—and even for us fans who did not know him, he seemed to have a great personality. He was really good, and OK with letting Gene and Paul take the front seat and stir KISS to new success. Super KISS or not, that night kick-started a lifelong love affair with the band KISS for me, and Bruce played a big part in that.

It was not the makeup KISS wore that was the basis of my band; my KISS was the 80s version of the band with Bruce Kulick on guitar. From that moment on, KISS became part of my everyday life—part of my growth as an aspiring musician, and a part of my growth as human being.

Bruce's first album as a member of KISS, *Asylum*, is a musical milestone in my life. It was so highly anticipated that once it landed on my vinyl player, I played it for weeks straight. The solos in 'Tears Are Falling' and 'King Of The Mountain' were nothing less than epic.

Bruce gave KISS a needed stability so they could focus on making great music again. The records that followed, with Bruce on guitar and as a writer, contain some of the strongest material ever released by the band: 'Reason To Live,' 'Crazy Crazy Nights,' 'Hide Your Heart,' and the masterpiece 'God Gave Rock And Roll To You II' from *Revenge*. Besides Bruce's incredible musicianship and his innovative style of playing, it's his personality that has made [him] one of the most beloved members of KISS. As the band applied the makeup again and Bruce went on to form the band Union, he always seemed sincerely happy for the success of the band and remained family.

Nearly twenty-four years to the day of that night at Olympen, I finally was able to sit down and talk with Bruce during the KISS Kruise [in November 2018]. Apart from being the same brilliant player as he has always been, he was just as I always thought—a real, terrific guy.

In 2019, the KISS brand has grown stronger than ever, uniting generations of fans across the globe. All with their favorite era of the band. Some like the later years with Tommy Thayer and Eric Singer, some like the classic lineup with Ace Frehley and Peter Criss, and some of us discovered KISS during the non-makeup years with Eric Carr and Bruce Kulick. It's not really important anymore, but what has become clear is that KISS is so much more than a band today. It's family, it's an institution, it's a way of life that will be around for a long time coming.

ANDREAS CARLSSON, PRODUCER/COMPOSER/SONGWRITER, JANUARY 22, 2019

EDDIE TRUNK'S TOP 20 KISS SONGS OF THE NON-MAKEUP ERA
IN NO PARTICULAR ORDER...

1. 'A Million To One'
2. 'Exciter'
3. 'Who Wants To Be Lonely'
4. 'Tears Are Falling'
5. 'Jungle'
6. 'Hide Your Heart'
7. 'I'll Fight Hell To Hold You'
8. 'Reason To Live'
9. 'I've Had Enough (Into The Fire)'
10. 'Thrills In The Night'
11. 'Under The Gun'
12. 'Trial By Fire'
13. 'Secretly Cruel'
14. 'Unholy'
15. 'Not For The Innocent'
16. 'Young And Wasted'
17. 'Rain'
18. 'Rise To It'
19. 'Little Caesar'
20. 'King Of The Mountain'

PICTURE CREDITS

OTHER BOOKS
BY GREG PRATO

MUSIC

SPORTS